ATONEMENT
AND PSYCHOTHERAPY

ATONEMENT
AND
PSYCHOTHERAPY

by

DON S. BROWNING

THE WESTMINSTER PRESS

Philadelphia

Grateful acknowledgment is made to the following:

Houghton Mifflin Company (1951), for quotations from *Client-centered Therapy,* by Carl Rogers.

McGraw-Hill Book Company, Inc. (1959), for quotations from *Psychology: A Study of a Science,* Vol. III, edited by Sigmund Koch.

The University of Chicago Press (1954), for quotations from *Psychotherapy and Personality Change,* by Carl Rogers and Rosalind F. Dymond.

LIBRARY OF CONGRESS CATALOG CARD No. 66-13506

Published by The Westminster Press ®
Philadelphia, Pennsylvania

PRINTED IN THE UNITED STATES OF AMERICA

75,094

To my wife and daughter,
Carol and Beth

CONTENTS

PREFACE

This book was written to stimulate thinking and research into the possibility of using psychological analogies for the purpose of theological construction. Charles Hartshorne, Schubert Ogden, Daniel Day Williams, and John Cobb on the American scene and Dorothy Emmet in England have suggested and used an analogical approach to theological thinking. In line with these programs, I want to suggest that we look to psychotherapeutic psychology as a source for theological analogies. As will be demonstrated in Chapter VI, I am not advocating a new kind of natural theology. My use of analogies is placed within a context of a theology of revelation. Revelation provides the broad outlines of truth and affirmation that form the theologian's mind. But within this confessional framework, there is still a need for empirically discernible analogies that will both clarify and confirm the Biblical witness to the saving event of Jesus Christ.

This book is addressed to all those who are interested in the task of constructing a clear, meaningful, and commanding Christian theology — one relevant to the modern mind, yet anchored in the basic substrata of religious intuition and revelation that has formed the Western world. Since it turns to psychotherapy for the analogies that it employs, it may be of interest to teachers, seminary students, and ministers who have come to find psychology and the area of pastoral counseling relevant to their vocational tasks. Professional psychologists and psychiatrists may find this book of interest to them, although it fails to address many of the issues discussed in these fields. It at least will remind them of the fact that the data and constructs which they use engender an ideology whether they intend this or not. From one perspective, this book is an effort to adjust the ideology surrounding much present-day psychotherapy with the cluster of values and affirmations surrounding the Christian faith.

This book grew out of research for a dissertation written for the Divinity School of the University of Chicago in the field of religion and personality. Many professors contributed to my thinking and helped guide my research. Dr. Seward Hiltner and Dr. Perry LeFevre were important influences on my personal and academic development early in my studies. Later, Dr. LeRoy Aden, Dr. Charles Stinnette, and Dr. Bernard Loomer were immeasurably helpful in the criticism and guidance of my work. Considerable revision of certain parts of this study has taken place since it left their hands, and the final responsibility for the content of these pages is entirely my own. Others have given of their time and energy. Dr. Robert Simpson, my former colleague on the faculty of Phillips University, freely shared his competent grasp of the history of Christian thought and possibly helped me make fewer errors in this difficult field than otherwise would have been the case. Finally, Dr. Tom Oden, professor of Christian ethics of the Graduate Seminary of Phillips University, must be thanked for reading large portions of the manuscript and making several penetrating criticisms, some of which have deeply influenced my thinking.

Miss Wilma Mosley, Miss Bonnie Holt, Mrs. Ann Cox, and Mrs. Linda Mosley diligently and competently typed the text. And finally, my wife gave freely of her time in proofreading the manuscript and, by virtue of her sensitive and enlivening spirit, provided a context of inspiration and support that serves to call forth the best in everyone around her.

D. S. B.

The Divinity School
University of Chicago
Chicago, Illinois

KEY TO SYMBOLS

CDH Anselm, St., *Cur Deus Homo,* in *St. Anselm — Basic Writings,* tr. by S. N. Deane. The Open Court Publishing Company, 1962.

FL Bushnell, Horace, *Forgiveness and Law.* Scribner's, Armstrong and Co., 1874.

GIC Bushnell, Horace, *God in Christ.* Charles Scribner's Sons, 1903.

NS Bushnell, Horace, *Nature and the Supernatural.* Charles Scribner's & Co., 1867.

VS, I Bushnell, Horace, *The Vicarious Sacrifice,* Vol. I. Charles Scribner's Sons, 1903.

AH Irenaeus, St., "Against Heresies," *Writings of the Ante-Nicene Fathers,* Vol. I. Edited by Alexander Roberts and James Donaldson. William B. Eerdmans Publishing Co.; reprinted 1951.

CCT Rogers, Carl, *Client-centered Therapy.* Houghton Mifflin Company, 1951.

PASS Rogers, Carl, "A Theory of Therapy, Personality, and Interpersonal Relationships," in Sigmund Koch, ed., *Psychology: A Study of a Science,* Vol. III. McGraw-Hill Book Company, Inc., 1959.

I

THE ATONEMENT AND
PSYCHOTHERAPEUTIC ILLUMINATION

The motive behind this study is a simple empirical observation. The observation is this: in certain quarters of the
present-day theological world, theological thinking seems to
be substantively informed by insights derived from study of
psychotherapeutic psychology. When I say "substantively
informed," I mean that judgments seem to be made about
the relative adequacy of certain historic doctrinal options
on the basis of an understanding of the psychotherapeutic
process. The psychotherapeutic sciences are not indigenously
theological sciences. Theological questions and assumptions
were not basic to their historical development as sciences.
Yet when theological thinkers have brought certain theological assumptions to the data and constructs of psychotherapy, they have often returned to their theological enter-
prise feeling that their own constructive thought has been
illuminated.

The purpose of this book is to test the possibility of making positive theological statements on the basis of insights
derived from psychotherapy. This process should be tested
because such statements are in fact being made. In certain
quarters, the importance of psychotherapeutically derived
insights for present-day theological thinking is only dimly
acknowledged even by those so informed. In other quar-

ters, it is self-consciously done but on the basis of very uncertain methodological principles. Since it *is being done,* I think it behooves us to ask whether it *can be done* and if so, on what basis.

We are not particularly surprised by the present-day tendency to illuminate certain anthropological issues with insights from psychology. But we are more surprised and sometimes concerned when Christological issues or issues relevant to the doctrine of God are addressed upon the basis of psychotherapeutic constructs. Not only are anthropological issues like sin, guilt, and creation addressed in this way, but occasionally issues relevant to God's grace, love, forgiveness, judgment, and the atoning work in Jesus Christ are addressed from this perspective. Actually, the possibility of addressing anthropological issues probably assumes the same methodology and presuppositions as does the possibility of addressing specifically Christological and theological issues. Yet we are more permissive and less prone to attacks of anxiety when confronted by examples of the former than when confronted by examples of the latter.

It is precisely at the level of this latter order of theological issue that we intend to address this work. For instance, there are examples today of statements made from the standpoint of psychotherapeutic insights about the doctrine of the atonement. Any statement about the atonement based on psychotherapy is quite likely also to be a judgment. This is true because of the multiplicity of constructive options that the Bible and the history of Christian thought offer with regard to this doctrine. To say anything at all about the meaning of Christ's death is, at the same moment, to say something that most likely will contradict some other historically prominent view of its significance. On a directly conceptual basis, these different theories are difficult to reconcile. And if this positive statement is based upon a psychotherapeutic insight, we soon find ourselves using psychotherapy to judge or adjudicate between historic options on this issue. Let us turn to a brief examination of examples in which men who identify themselves primarily as theologians have involved themselves in judgments of this kind.

An example can be found in Reuel Howe's small but widely read book entitled *Man's Need and God's Action*. In his book Howe makes several statements about the cross and resurrection which are highly informed by his understanding of the psychotherapeutic process. The insight he uses is the well-known concept of " acceptance." Although he never clearly identifies its clinical meaning, the critical reader can sense that his use of the word is rooted in clinical and dynamic understandings. In direct reference to the word " acceptance " he writes, " At first it seemed wholly psychological, but now it seems religious and theological." [1] Howe characterizes acceptance as a relationship of such security that we can expose our most unlovable selves without fear of rejection. In the context of such a relationship, Howe believes that we are able to face facts about ourselves we would otherwise be unable to admit into consciousness. Facing these despised and rejected parts of ourselves helps us to integrate them and move toward becoming whole persons.[2]

How does Howe interpret the cross and the resurrection of Jesus Christ in the light of this concept? First, by positing the principle that complete and perfect acceptance seems to be a need of mankind, and then by making the observation that no finite and sinful person can ever completely love and accept another person; he looks beyond the possibilities of the human community to a perfect and transcendent source of love and acceptance. He believes this transcendent source of acceptance was expressed in the cross. Let us quote Howe at some length:

The only place we can see love that has the power to love the unlovable in his moment of greatest unlovableness is the love that we see on the Cross. And what do we see there? We see love suffering. It is more than just the suffering of a dying man; pure love is suffering the awful burden and pain of the unlovable. It is loving to the uttermost, and for a moment following the suffering, the agony of loving the unlovable brings extinction — death. Love dies in the process of swallowing up, absorbing, taking unto itself that which is its opposite — unlovableness. This is the kind of demand that unlovableness makes of love. . . . Just as trust must contend against mistrust, so love must contend against hate. The final struggle between them took place on the Cross. The Resurrection is the victory of the love of Christ on the other side of his struggle with the hate of men.[3]

Later in the book, Howe gives the meaning of the resurrection when he writes: " He is Lord because He is God. But I know Him as my Lord because He let me Kill Him, and then He came back." [4]

Although Howe sees the cross and the resurrection as perfect, unqualified, and unambiguous expressions of love, his interpretation of these key Christian symbols is strongly influenced by the clinical meaning of acceptance. A cardinal principle of much psychotherapy is the acceptance of negative as well as positive feelings. When a therapist's acceptance is real, he can affirm his client in spite of his client's angry and hostile attempts to reject the therapist. This analogy is implicit in Howe's entire discussion of the meaning of the atonement.

In understanding the atonement in this way, Howe is excluding certain prominent historic options and confirming others. But it is easier to discern what he is excluding than it is to specify what he is confirming. It is clear that he is excluding all substitutionary and satisfaction theories of the atonement. Certainly he is not saying that Christ's suffering is a result of God's wrath poured out on him instead of us, as the penal substitutionary theory would assert. Certainly he is not saying that Christ's suffering is an obedience even unto death which is of such infinite value as to satisfy God's injured honor and thereby removing the guilt of our disobedience. Even though Howe referred to this love as a " struggle " and a " victory," are we to assume from this that he is suggesting a *Christus Victor* view of the atonement? If so, where is mention of the devil, or what takes his place, as the one against whom the Lord contends? Or does Howe's interpretation of the atonement, informed by psychotherapeutic concepts as it is, suggest something on the order of an exemplar or moral influence understanding? We are not sure, except to say that we are definitely clear that he is excluding the first two options.

Hence, Howe's small book is an illustration of the phenomenon about which I am speaking. Unfortunately, his treatment of the subject as well as the methodological procedures underlying it are so briefly and sketchily drawn that we cannot be certain that his analogy can bear the weight of a mature theological discussion with the historic options which it seems to exclude as well as with those it may confirm. Howe cannot be criticized for not attempting a full-scale dialogue with the historic positions on atonement; in fact, he should be commended for suggesting the possibility of such a discussion. But now that the possibility has been suggested, it should be tested.

A study that moves toward the kind of mature discussion we are suggesting was attempted by Daniel Day Williams in his recent book entitled *The Minister and the Care of Souls*. Here Williams attempts to interpret explicitly the atonement according to the concept of acceptance as it is understood and practiced in the clinical setting. In addition, in a brief, inexhaustive but nonetheless concise and suggestive way, he attempts to set this interpretation in the context of Gustav Aulén's threefold grouping of theories of the atonement into Classic, Latin, and Modern or Moral. Williams does not claim that a " new " doctrine of the atonement can be derived from the concept of acceptance, but he does have some dissatisfaction with the traditional theories and feels that we should turn to the " experience of forgiveness in human relations " for a " clarifying analogy." [5] Acceptance, for Williams, describes a clinical mode of relationship in which the therapist communicates his willingness and capacity to be " with " the client in spite of the " cost " and " suffering " this " withness " may bring to the therapist.[6] It is an acceptance that accepts into relationship the total self of the client — the real self, the ideal self, and the empirical self. This total acceptance seems to communicate a sense of justification to the client that frees him to assimilate his real self.

Williams then turns to the task of applying this so-called " clarifying analogy " to the central symbols of the atonement. He interprets the meaning of the cross in the light of the aspect of empathic " withness " which he believes to be an element in acceptance. The cross means that in Jesus Christ, " God stands by us, in spite of our estrangement from him, that he remains with us in our need, at cost to himself." [7] He writes:

This is the heart of the New Testament assertion of redemption, and surely this is directly related to the experience of acceptance. We are given to know that nothing in our brokenness destroys the possibility of being understood by another who cares.[8]

Williams compares Christ's suffering as a consequence of our sin to the therapist's suffering of the defensive hostility of the client. He asserts that the suffering of Christ judges and convicts us, but also removes guilt by regenerating and reconstructing our personality through the mode of real personal forgiveness. The " suffering of Jesus is the human expression of God's own suffering for us." Further, " his suffering expresses the will of God to stand by the guilty one." [9] This capacity of God to " stand by " in spite of great suffering and cost to himself transforms us because " it gives assurance of a meaningful life no matter what evil or tragedy we face." [10]

Williams does not claim that he is developing a complete doctrine of the atonement just on the basis of the analogy from psychotherapy. For instance, psychotherapy does not claim that " Christ's suffering " is " a disclosure of the spirit of God." But once we accept this Christian assertion " we find analogies in experience which become luminous in the life of faith." [11] But he does use this " clarifying " analogy to make judgments about the relative adequacy of other historic interpretations of the meaning of Christ's death. He supports the " ransom " theory of the atonement in its affirmation that God fights for us against sin and death, but criticizes its tendency to picture this battle as a matter largely between God and the devil, thereby overlooking the importance of man's personal decision. He supports the Anselmian satisfaction theory in its tendency to take guilt seriously, but criticizes it for its subpersonal understanding of the meaning of Christ's death as a removal of man's guilt through the satisfaction of God's honor. He believes that the Abelardian view of the atonement does more justice to the importance of personal forgiveness, but it fails to take guilt seriously enough and relies too heavily on the efficacy of persuasion and moral influence. Hence, on the basis of an analogy drawn from a source external to the Bible and the historic tradition of the Christian faith, Williams attempts to make judgments about the adequacy of theories and analogies internal to the Bible and Christian history. He uses psychotherapy for constructive theological purposes.

But once again, we wonder whether Williams' " clarifying analogy " can really bear the weight of a mature discussion with the historic options about which it ventures to make judgments. Williams' discussion bears the marks of competence, but it is a brief and in no way exhaustive handling of the issues. In addition, some of the interpretations to which he is led open up and suggest new problems which he makes no effort to answer. For instance, when on the one hand he asserts that the suffering of Jesus expresses " God's own suffering for us " and on the other hand asserts that " nothing . . . destroys the possibility of being understood by " God, he is asserting on the one hand that God is subject to certain *contingencies* which cause him to suffer and on the other hand that God is an *absolute* God and that nothing can cause him to fail to understand us. Both of these assertions — i.e., that God suffers and that God is absolute in that he cannot fail to understand us — seem to be generalizations that he gleans from his understanding of the clinical meaning of acceptance. But can this concept be generalized to this extent? Can it bear the weight of such an application? Only in a very few instances has a Christian doctrine of the atonement ever explicitly included the idea of God's suffering in its exposition of the meaning of Christ's death. In addition, it has been the overwhelming opinion of the history of Christian thought that the idea of " suffering " and the idea of " absoluteness " were incompatible concepts. Yet Williams' use of the clinically derived concept of acceptance to clarify the meaning of the atonement has led him just to this kind of defiance of the overwhelming weight of Christian thought.

The task of this study can be stated on the basis of these observations and can be expressed as follows: What is the potency of the psychotherapeutic disciplines to generate a "clarifying analogy" with which to interpret the doctrine of the atonement that will be sufficiently mature to bear the weight of serious theological discussion with other prominent constructive alternatives inherited from the history of Christian thought? And secondly, On what basis, if any, can such an analogy be used to make judgments about the relative adequacy of these historically prominent theories and analogies?

Let us now turn to a discussion of the way this study will be programmed in an effort to answer these questions.

THE PROGRAM FOR THIS STUDY

The possibility of psychotherapy's being used for theological purposes in this way will be tested by taking the possibility seriously and pushing it to its limits. Yet this study should still be taken as a tentative and heuristic effort. Only in this way can its presumptuous character be excused. The focus of our study will be narrow enough, i.e., the meaning of Christ's death. But this doctrine will be approached by paying full attention to the entire range of theological issues relevant to it. Only by doing this can the adequacy of an analogy drawn from psychotherapeutic sources be sufficiently tested.

I understand the doctrine of the atonement to deal with the meaning and place of Christ's death in the economy of salvation. It is a doctrine of crucial importance to Christian theology. But theology can be understood in at least two ways. *Confessional* theology attempts to declare and give some explication to Biblical affirmations, but primarily in terms of the dramatic and mythological images character-istic of the Biblical witness. This must be distinguished from theology as *inquiry*. The latter attempts to state the sys-tematic interrelation of Biblical affirmations with sufficient rational specificity as to make intelligible discourse a pos-sibility both among the faithful and between the faithful and the unfaithful or skeptical. At the level of confessional theol-ogy, the meaning of Christ's death can be expressed in terms of metaphors of the battlefield, the altar, or the law court. As J. S. Whale has pointed out, the Biblical witness has spoken of Christ in his death as a " victor," as a " victim," and as a " criminal." [12] Aulén suggests that the metaphor of the " victor " and the " battlefield " were elaborated into the ransom or *Christus Victor* theory of the atonement.[13] But the elaboration of this metaphor, mostly attempted by the earlier church fathers, hardly moved beyond a confessional articu-lation even though, upon occasion, it was done in the context of apologetic and rational concerns. The " altar " and " vic-tim " metaphors received elaboration that transcended con-fessional articulation in Anselm's reasoned and cautious work on the atonement in *Cur Deus Homo*. The " criminal " and " court " metaphors have received further systematic elaboration in the thought of Calvin and our contemporary Emil Brunner. The point is that at the level of systematic elaboration the tension which may have existed between the Biblical metaphors has been amplified to the extent of sys-tematic contradiction. These important systematic differ-ences that now exist between various historically prominent theories of the atonement have been well illustrated in Gus-tav Aulén's *Christus Victor*.

What is psychotherapy that it can lead some people to

think that positive theological judgments are possible on the basis of its findings? Psychotherapy is a branch of psychology that attempts to specify those elements in interpersonal interactions which tend to be therapeutically efficacious for people with broken, unhappy, and distorted lives. It is a perspective on healing. It studies individual and group pathology with a view toward *cure*. Because its investigation is guided by this intent toward cure, it has tended to focus upon pathology with reference to those modes of interpersonal interaction which tend to overcome pathology.

It will be beneficial, just for the sake of clarifying the purpose of this book, to indicate briefly the possible basis upon which psychotherapy as a perspective upon healing may be a resource for Christian theology. A full articulation of these premises must wait for a more appropriate occasion later in the study. It can be said that theology is also a perspective on healing. It would claim to be the *ultimate* perspective upon healing. Its task is to declare and specify the meaning and manner of God's ultimate attempt to overcome man's sin, which, it would contend, is the fundamental element in all expressions of human brokenness. In addition, Christian theology will always center upon the event of Jesus Christ as either the *clue to* or the *occasion for* God's ultimate healing or salvatory activity or act. Since both theology and psychotherapy are perspectives upon the phenomenon of healing — the former reflecting upon what God does to heal man and the latter reflecting upon what men do to heal each other — upon what basis can psychotherapy provide clarifying analogies for theology?

The premises upon which this possibility becomes credible must necessarily be theological in nature. There must be some principle indigenous to theology that will permit this possibility. It seems, both on the basis of theoretical considerations and on the basis of observing what thinkers like Howe and Williams are attempting, that the premise has something to do with the monotheistic principle that is foundational to all Christian theological thinking. The monotheistic principle is the basis upon which Christian theology can assert that the God who creates the world and the God who saves the world is *one and the same* God. This is held to mean that the world in all its *essential* respects is basically *one world*. It follows from this that every limited and preliminary healing-producing activity is fundamentally grounded in, participates in, and finally, is derivative of God's ultimate healing activity. Insofar as it is grounded in God's ultimate healing activity, it must show some proportionality to the structure and form of the ultimate source of all healing.

Correlative to the principle of the fundamental oneness of all healing activity is the principle of the fundamental oneness of all forms of human brokenness. On strictly formal grounds, this means that, fundamental to all forms of pathology which the psychotherapist may attempt to investigate, is the ultimate structure of brokenness which Christian theology has called sin. This does not mean that there is an unequivocal identity between all forms of human brokenness and the ultimate structure of brokenness called sin. It simply means that there must be some proportionality of structure, i.e., some similarity of essential form. Later in this study, I will attempt to set forth both a Biblical and a theological rationale of more detail and precision for this premise. But at present, we must be content with the assertion of this premise as containing both the grounds upon which this study will proceed and the grounds that other similar attempts have appeared to assume. It does follow, though, if this principle is true, that psychotherapy might have something important to say to theology in its attempt to give precise, systematic articulation to the nature of God's healing and saving activity. The reverse possibility of theology's speaking to psychotherapy would also seem credible. Both could illuminate and inform the other as long as the distinctions between ultimate and preliminary, infinite and finite, holiness and sinfulness were adequately preserved.

Our procedure will be simple: (1) Three theories of the atonement will be set forth. They will be representative of certain broad, but diverse, tendencies in the history of the development of this doctrine. Variations of these three themes will be briefly mentioned. (2) Certain broad issues that every mature theory of the atonement feels compelled to address or answer will be isolated. These principles will be used to judge whether a clarifying analogy from psychotherapy can possess sufficient maturity to speak to what nearly every historic option has in some way felt it necessary to address. (3) The nature of the psychotherapeutic process will be discussed and certain key elements relevant to the doctrine of the atonement will be elaborated. (4) In Chapter VII these elements of psychotherapy will be generalized into a doctrine of the atonement. The crucial symbols of the atonement, the cross and the resurrection, will be interpreted in the light of this analogy. (5) The formal adequacy of this clarifying analogy will be judged by determining its capacity to account for issues that every mature theory of the atonement has felt compelled to address. (6) A general discussion will be attempted between the clarifying analogy and the three representative theories in an effort to determine (*a*) at what point there are congruences between this analogy and the three historic options, (*b*) wherein the clarifying analogy would disagree and, hence, judge the historic options, and (*c*) to what extent these judgments are valid and of some lasting importance.

The three representative theories used in this study were selected along the lines of Gustav Aulén's grouping of atonement theories into Classic, Latin, and Moral or Modern. This typology has been used because it is a roughly valid guide to the most prominent constructive alternatives that the history of Christian thought has to offer. The Classic view — so named because Aulén feels that it is most typical of the New Testament and the early fathers — is characterized by its understanding of the atonement as a continuous work of God from beginning to end, a struggle between God (through Christ) with the devil, and a struggle from which God in Christ emerges as the victor (*Christus Victor*) but at the expense of a great price or cost, a cost or price that was both a ransom and a sacrifice. The Latin view of the atonement is characterized by an understanding of Christ's death as a payment by man which restores God's honor. The most fundamental idea of the Moral Influence theory is that Christ's death is chiefly an example of how man is to live. In his death, Christ shows forth the love of God which is to be the law of man and arouses in us a similar kind of sacrificial love. The emphasis upon the dynamic change in man effected by this sacrificial love has often led this position to be referred to as the " subjective " view of the atonement. The other two are often called " objective " views because they seem to be based upon an objective change either in the metaphysical situation in general (as is the case in the Classic view where God defeats the forces of evil) or in God's attitude toward man (as is the case in the Latin view where Christ's sacrifice compensates God's honor so that forgiveness can become possible).

Many scholars do not find Aulén's categories trustworthy for the specific purposes of historical research. In this study, they are used as convenient and roughly valid ways to group the various positions on the atonement. The interpretation given to the figures selected for study will be my own.

Since this study is more of an exercise than an exhaustive study, certain limitations are necessary. We will discuss three theories at some depth; other theories will be mentioned but given less exhaustive discussion. We hope that this approach will give us the advantages of a depth discussion with a few theories as well as a broader dialogue with many.

The three thinkers who will be addressed are Irenaeus, Anselm, and Horace Bushnell. Their theories are commonly referred to as examples respectively of the Classic, Latin, and Moral view of the atonement. Aulén himself makes judgments that place Irenaeus and Anselm as preeminent representatives of the Classic and Latin views. The judgment upon which I was originally depending in selecting Bushnell as a representative of the Moral Influence view came from Robert S. Paul in his respected book entitled *The Atonement and the Sacraments*. Paul substantiates his judgment with this observation concerning the exemplar character of Bushnell's understanding of Christ's death when he writes, " Obedience unto death is the law of his followers just as it is for Christ." [14] Although there is enough validity in this judgment to establish Bushnell as holding a Moral Influence theory of the atonement at least in some sense, our own interpretation of Bushnell will place some qualifications on it. He is sufficiently an illustration of this approach to be used for the purposes of this study.

I have come to agree with Aulén in his judgments about the *importance of the doctrine of God as a central issue for any theory of the atonement*. The doctrine of the atonement is not just a Christological doctrine. In all cases that I know about, and specifically in the cases to be studied in this investigation, the significance and meaning of Christ's death is crucially determined by certain presuppositions or controlling ideas about what is *appropriate and consistent with the nature of God*. The meaning of Christ's death in the examples we shall study will be shaped by certain ideas about the *perfection of God*. These ideas about the perfection of God may or may not be derived from the Christ event itself. Certainly, ideas about the nature of God's perfection are not the only determinative elements in a thinker's understanding of the meaning of Christ's death. The concept of sin a thinker uses is also of crucial importance. But given a certain idea of the perfection of God and a certain idea about the nature of sin, a thinker's understanding of the work of Christ may follow from them.

Each of the three theories of the atonement will be examined with the following aspects in mind: We will search for the thinker's understanding of (1) the nature of God, (2) the nature of human brokenness, (3) the nature of the person of Jesus Christ, and (4) the essential dynamics of the work that Jesus accomplished. Each of these aspects will be discussed from the standpoint of its implications for the nature of God. Although the major concern of this study is to test the possibility of informing atonement theory by a clarifying analogy derived from psychotherapy, it will be a secondary but still quite important concern to ask the following question: *What is an adequate doctrine of God upon which a theory of the atonement can be based?*

II

IRENAEUS: ATONEMENT AS DEFEAT
OF THE DEVIL

Irenaeus was a second-century bishop of Lyons. The major part of his energy was directed toward a defense of the faith against the heretical teachings of the Gnostics. Much of what he wrote about the atonement was elaborated in the context of his attack against Gnosticism.

THE TWO HANDS OF GOD

What Irenaeus had to say about the nature of God must be understood within the context of the dualistic presuppositions of the Gnostic heresies he was attacking. The problem of the Gnostic was how to get together that which was essentially separated. The problem for Irenaeus was how to reunite, or reconcile, that which was essentially related or in communion.

Many Gnostics taught that the world was created by some superhuman being other than God. They asserted that God was either ignorant of the creation of the world by another being,[1] or limited by this other being, which constituted a second and autonomous creative principle uncontained and uncontrollable by the Supreme Being.[2] Irenaeus argued that if either is the case, then the Supreme God is less than supreme, for he is neither truly omniscient nor omnipotent;

or — and this is worse — he is simply careless and less than supremely good.[3]

In response to these Gnostic qualifications placed on God's sovereignty, Irenaeus reasserts and defends the principle that God must be the source of all life — his own and that of all other beings — and the source of his own ends. This is what it means to be God. If God in any way derives a portion of his life or part of his ends from something external to himself, then he becomes less than God. Hence, God is *a se.* Nothing external to God contributes to or limits his creative capacities whether it be another god or whether it be some kind of preexistent matter.[4] There is, in fact, only one God and one creator and they are one and the same. All references to a creator in either the Old or New Testament, by whatever name these references are made, refer to the same God who is Lord of all.[5]

Irenaeus expresses his understanding of God's intimate and immediate involvement in the processes of creation through his doctrine of the " two hands of God." This doctrine sets the stage for understanding the work of the Word and Spirit in both creation and salvation. It points to the strong relationship between creation and grace and suggests that creation should, in Irenaeus, be placed under the rubric of grace.

In refutation of the Gnostic view of the world's creation by an angel or a demiurge, Irenaeus asserts that " God did not stand in need of these things . . . as if He did not possess His own hands." [6] God's hands have been present with him always and are " the Word and Wisdom, the Son and the Spirit, by whom and in whom, freely and spontaneously, He made all things." [7] Irenaeus' concept of the two hands of God — the Word and the Spirit — is a way of emphasizing that God alone is the author of creation. But as John Lawson insists, it " is much more than a corollary of the doctrine of creation. It is itself the expression of the doctrine of an immediately present and active God." [8]

Not only is God immediately involved in the process of creation, but the immediacy of his creative activity also contains a self-revelatory element. Both the relationship of God as creative sustainer and the self-revelatory element it entails must be seen within the framework of fellowship. This fellowship and communion with the world constitutes a "light" which provides man with a knowledge of God.[9] In addition, God's self-revelation has always "co-existed" with man since the beginning of creation.[10] To assume that, before the advent of Jesus, God made no provision for his self-disclosure would make him appear careless and would indicate that in revealing himself in Jesus he had changed. Believing this would undermine one's faith in God.[11] It is God's basic propensity to reveal himself. In contrast to the teachings of the Gnostic Valentinius, Irenaeus believed "that it is the express will of the Father, that God should be known." [12]

If the doctrine of the "two hands of God" serves to provide Irenaeus with a way of talking about God's unmediated involvement in creation and revelation, what is the meaning of Logos in his thought? Why did he need the concept of the Logos that generally served, for its more philosophical exponents, as a way to mediate between the world and a remote and impassible God? Harnack, Lawson, and Wingren seem to agree on the unphilosophical character of Irenaeus' use of the concept Logos.[13] It is not so much a hypostatized Divine Reason of the Godhead as representative of the entire Godhead seen from the perspective of its primordial and preexistent propensity for and concrete activity toward creation and self-disclosure. The Logos of the Word is not a substance that is identical to but yet separate from God the Father. At the same time, it should not be thought that Irenaeus holds an economic or modalistic understanding of the Trinity. The Word and the Spirit are preexistent. God has been Creator, Nourisher, and Redeemer from all eternity. These are not contingent and accidental elements in the Godhead. These attributes flow from the character of God as God. This is what Irenaeus means when he says:

But if Christ did then [only] begin to have existence when He came [into the world] as man, and [if] the Father did remember [only] in the times of Tiberius Caesar to provide for [the wants of] men, and His word was shown to have not always coexisted with His creatures, . . . the reasons for so great carelessness and neglect on His part should be made the subject of investigation. For it is fitting that no such question should arise, and gather such strength, that it would indeed both change God, and destroy our faith in that Creator who supports us by means of His creation.[14]

If God's activities as Creator, Nourisher, and Redeemer were anything less than a part of his preexistent character, then God would be less than a completely trustworthy God.

To some extent, God needs man to fulfill his character. But God, according to Irenaeus, is the *a se* (self-derived) creator. As Irenaeus writes, "In the beginning, therefore, did God form Adam, not as if He stood in need of man, but that He might have [some one] upon whom to confer His benefits."[15] God must have a creation upon whom to fulfill his self-derived end as the conferrer of benefits. God's end is self-derived, but nonetheless his end is external to himself. God creates to benefit others and not himself. He demands obedience not for his sake but for the sake of those who receive life by being faithful to the source of life.[16] Nor can man do anything to add or detract from the glory and honor of God. Irenaeus writes, "They did not glorify Him when they followed Him; but that, in following the Son of God, they were glorified by Him." [17] God's honor and glory reside in this; he is dependent upon nothing external to himself to derive or implement his end as a God for the benefit of others.

THE BONDAGE OF MAN

Irenaeus believed that man in his original state had a natural knowledge of God, the decalogue being " written on the hearts of men." [18] In the beginning man was created upright, i.e., he was created in fellowship with God with the propensity for voluntarily remaining in contact with God's creative fellowship as both the source and goal of his life.[19] This is what it means to say that man was created in the *image* and *similitude* of God. It does not mean that in the beginning man was created perfect. Rather, it means that in the beginning man was created a creature, a child who was neither imperfect nor perfect but incomplete. Birth is the beginning of creation, not its end. The creative process occurs all through life.[20] But the capacity for growth is a derivative of God's relationship with man and is not anything that man owns or possesses himself.

God seems to be both the beginning and the end of a process, the efficient and final cause of the pilgrimage of life. He is the efficient cause of growth, because growth is a derivative of God's original creative fellowship with man. God is the final cause of growth, because the *end* toward which the original relationship is directed is a mature and adult conformation of man with the character of God.

Sin is man's attempt to find both the source of life and the justification of life in something other than his relationship to God. Sin is basically alienation from God as the source of physical life and moral rectitude. " But communion with God is life and light. . . . But on as many as, according to their own choice, depart from God, He inflicts separation from Himself which they have chosen of their own accord. But separation from God is death." [21] Sin as a loss of righteousness is noted by Irenaeus when he writes, " They, men . . . going about to establish their own righteousness, have not submitted themselves to the righteousness of God." [22] Sin as alienation from God as the source of life and righteousness is organic in nature and affects his total being.

Several factors coalesce to bring about the fall of man. First, the devil held out a temptation to man — the temptation to anticipate the end and fruits of " being like God " without remaining in patient reliance on God's processes of growth. [23] Secondly, this temptation played upon the moral inexperience of an infant. " But the man was a little one, and his discretion still undeveloped, wherefore also he was easily misled by the deceiver." [24] Thirdly, man's responsibility is a factor. Man's alienation from God has put men in " darkness which they have chosen for themselves." [25]

Irenaeus attempts very little speculation about why the devil fell. Even though the devil stands as opposed to God, he derives his strength from the power of God, is not himself a creator, and is subject to the Lordship of God even though in mortal conflict with him. [26] In addition, although man is partially responsible for succumbing to the temptations of the devil, once he does, he is totally in bondage to him. "He that committeth sin is the slave of sin." [27] And again, " He holds who binds, but *he is* held who is bound." [28] The one who holds is the devil, and the one who is held is man. Being bound to the devil is a perceptual, moral, and physicalistic bondage. Being bound to the devil, we are blind, cannot see the light, and are in darkness. Being blind to the light, we are blind and unreceptive to the life of the light and are in death. Being blind and unreceptive to the light and life, we are cut off from the source of righteousness and hence are unjustified. Blindness, death, and unrighteousness — these are the consequences of bondage.

This bondage cannot be considered as direct punishment of man by God for man's rebellion. God lets those who turn from him "become the cause to themselves that they are destitute of light, and inhabit darkness." [29] Of course, Irenaeus upholds the sovereignty of God even here, which means, in this case, that although God does not cause man's alienation, insofar as he permits it, it can be said that he provides a habitation "worthy of their flight." [30] To this extent, the consequences of alienation constitute the "just judgment of God." [31]

The thrust of Irenaeus' thoughts about God's relationship to man in his situation of fallenness is to demonstrate the faithfulness of God and his dedication to the fulfillment of his original intentions for creation. God cannot be made to let go of man simply because of man's initial defeat by the devil. "Nor does the light fail because of those who have blinded themselves." [32] In accordance with this thinking, Irenaeus insists that it was necessary for God to save Adam as well as the offspring of Adam. Adam must be saved in order that God, as Irenaeus writes:

might not be conquered, nor His wisdom lessened, (in the estimation of His creatures). For if man, who had been created by God that he might live, after losing life, through being injured by the serpent that had corrupted him, should not any more return to life, but should be utterly (and for ever) abandoned to death, God would (in that case) have been conquered, and the wickedness of the serpent would have prevailed over the will of God. But inasmuch as God is invincible and long-suffering, He did indeed show Himself to be long-suffering in the matter of the correction of man and the probation of all.[33]

Gustav Wingren makes this point about Irenaeus' under-standing of the constancy of God's relationship to creation even after the fall when he writes:

From the Creation onwards the Spirit and the Son are the hands of God through whom the world was created and they cannot be made to discontinue their activity simply because man has fallen into sin.[34]

What is perceived as God's creative activity when viewed from the perspective of man's situation of original justifica-tion is perceived as God's grace and redeeming activity when viewed from the perspective of man's situation of fallen-ness.[35]

We must attempt a brief discussion of law and grace in Irenaeus' thought. Irenaeus does make a distinction between law as the natural precepts elemental to God's original cre-ative fellowship with man [36] and the Mosaic law which ap-peared and disappeared at certain points in history and which served as a way to order and discipline fallen man by heter-onomous means.[37] But in reality, they are the same law and come from the same God. In order to maintain his govern-ment of the world, God imposes his law from without dur-ing man's fallenness.

Christ is the fulfillment of the law in both of its senses. Irenaeus points out that the great commandment, the " love of God and neighbor," is the demand of both the law and the gospel.[38] In addition he points out that Christ is the be-ginning of the law as well as its end.[39] It is true that Christ frees us from the bondage of the law. But this does not mean that Christ is antithetical to the law. In freeing us from the law, he reconstitutes our relationship to it so that its heteron-omous character is removed. It is also clear that redemption from the law is not predicated on legalistic satisfaction of it.

God will confer more on the sinner than he deserves as long as this is consistent with God's ultimate aim to redeem the sinner.[40]

THE PERSON OF HIM WHO SAVES US

For Irenaeus, the event of Jesus of Nazareth, his life, death, and resurrection, is the supreme event upon which our salvation rests. Since we are indeed saved by this man, it must be that he is God, since only God can save us.[41] Yet Christ does not save man simply by imbuing man's corruptible nature with his incorruptible, divine substance.[42] Christ's divinity is the precondition of his work and is not efficacious in and of itself.

But not only is Jesus Christ God. He is also man, i.e., he is natural man in mature and unambiguous conformation with the image of God in man. As Adam was an " infant," a beginner in the earlier stages of a creative process designed to bring him to an adultlike conformation to God's creative relationship, Jesus Christ is man matured to a perfect conformation to the image of God. From the perspective of who it is that conforms to this image, Jesus Christ can be called man. From the perspective of that to which he does conform, Jesus Christ is God. But the full meaning of the incarnation and what it signifies for both God and man must be seen in the light of Irenaeus' concept of " recapitulation." But we must delay our discussion of this aspect of his thought to the last section of this chapter.

The uniqueness of Jesus Christ is not found in the difference that in Jesus, Christ is " present " whereas in the Old Testament and covenantal history he was only promised, as Lawson contends.[43] The novelty of Jesus Christ is that of completeness — a completeness that is categorically different from that which is incomplete, unfulfilled, and partial. As

Irenaeus says, "For by His advent He Himself fulfilled all things." [44] Had it not been for the Fall, the appearance of Christ as the fulfillment of creation might have been gradual and evolutionary. But because of the Fall, this fulfillment required a unique and novel act on the part of God. In addition, as Gustav Wingren reminds us (and in contrast to the contention of Lawson), God's objective and unique act in Jesus Christ *is not* a " redemption-supernaturalism " or a divine " interposition." [45] As Wingren writes, " The gift which Christ bestows surpasses the undeveloped and immature, or as man is stronger than a child." [46] Sin and death, for Irenaeus, are unnatural, and the fulfillment of creation in Christ is natural.

If what God did in Christ is continuous with what he intended in his primordial nature, if its uniqueness consists only in its quantitative completeness, then we can agree with the following generalization expressed by L. S. Thornton when he writes:

First, the incarnation was in essence an accommodation of God's infinite perfection and majesty to our finite limitations; and secondly, the method of the incarnation was the method which characterizes the whole of God's dealings with man.[47]

It is the meaning of the incarnation both in its ontological and soteriological sense which finally gives the key to the primordial structure of God and the character of his dealings with man in all times and at all places.

The Work of Him Who Saves Us

To understand Irenaeus' concept of the atoning work of Jesus Christ, we must approach it through his understanding of the cross and his concept of " recapitulation."

When Irenaeus describes Jesus Christ, his person and

work, as a recapitulation, he means that Christ " summed up all things." [48] The phrase " going over the same ground " seems to best capture the meaning of the term.[49] It is man that Jesus Christ recapitulates or sums up; but this recapitulation operates in two directions. First, Jesus Christ repeats, or sums up in himself, Adam's original integrity, i.e., his original conformation to the image of God, but at an adult-like level of maturity.[50] Secondly, Jesus recapitulates or " goes over the same ground " of Adam's fall, but with the opposite results.[51]

In communicating the meaning of Jesus' recapitulation of Adam's fall, Irenaeus used several dramatic images that must be interpreted in the light of one another. Irenaeus refers to it as a matter of " stooping low," [52] a matter of being made " the very same thing " that man is,[53] a process of becoming " flesh," of putting " upon Himself the burden of man's sin," of putting " Himself in our position " [54] and of taking upon himself " our infirmities " and " our ills." [55]

Let us call the aspect of recapitulation in which Christ identifies himself with man's fallen situation the " dynamic element." At times Irenaeus refers to this process of taking man's " position " as God's attempt to accommodate his work to the peculiarities of man's unique needs. In one place, Irenaeus says that God became man in order to present Himself as " milk-nourishment "; he " passed through the state of infancy " so that man, in his infantile and immature condition, could confront God, not as he is, but as man is " capable of beholding Him." [56] Let us call this aspect of the recapitulation doctrine the " noetic element."

Jesus Christ participated in the conditions and consequences of Adam's sin, but this does not mean that he sinned. Irenaeus sees the New Testament temptation narrative as an example of Jesus' confrontation of the original conditions that caused Adam to fall. The devil's temptation takes the same line it did in the Garden of Eden,[57] i.e., he tempts Jesus to justify himself ("if thou be the Son of God, cast thyself down") and to seek the means and power of life elsewhere than from God ("command that these stones be made bread" and "all these things will I give thee").[58]

Jesus submits himself not only to the original conditions but also to the consequences of Adam's fall. Death and hostility toward God's love are consequences of man's fall. Irenaeus tells us that the devil, out of envy and malice, took it "in hand to render this [workmanship] at enmity with God."[59] Jesus' task is to reconcile man, who "had formerly been in enmity."[60] To perform this reconciliation, "the Lord summed up in Himself this enmity."[61] In one place Irenaeus writes that God in the form of the Word became man so that He might be "capable of being tempted, dishonored, crucified, and of suffering death."[62]

To *become* man is to *suffer* the distortions of man's existence. The strong relation between the "incarnation" and "suffering," between *incarnatus* and *passus,* is observable in several places in Irenaeus. "Learn then, ye foolish men, that Jesus who *suffered* for us, and who dwelt among us, is Himself the Word of God."[63] Irenaeus explicitly denies that only the man Jesus suffered, while Christ was impassible to suffering.[64] He who "underwent suffering, and shed His blood for us, was both Christ and the Son of God."[65] Nor does he say that the Son of God suffered in any way as to belittle or disparage him. Irenaeus makes an explicit value judgment and tends to see suffering love as the highest value. If man suffers, but Christ did not, "we shall be even above the Master, because we suffer and sustain what our Master never bore or endured."[66]

The cross is the supreme culmination of Christ Jesus' suffering the conditions and consequences of Adam's fall. But his whole life and ministry are of the same character and meaning as is the cross. Irenaeus proposes the surprising theory that Jesus lived to be an old man. The logic of his recapitulation concept demanded it. For if Christ Jesus summed up the predicament of mankind, he must also sum up the situation of every stage of life, from infancy to old age.[67]

The cross has efficacy because in Jesus Christ both God and man *endure*. What is God's *actuality* becomes man's *possibility* once again. It is God, using the man Jesus as his instrument, who enters into battle with the devil, who submits himself to the devil's attacks, and who wins the day by enduring with obedience. "For He fought and conquered; for He was man contending for the Father and through obedience doing away with disobedience completely."[68]

But we must ask, what did Irenaeus understand to be the content of obedience? In order to get a picture of the content of obedience, we must back up several lines preceding the quotation to which we have just referred:

And from this fact, that He exclaimed upon the cross, "Father, forgive them for they know not what they do," the long-suffering, patience, compassion, and goodness of Christ are exhibited, since He both suffered and did Himself exculpate those who had maltreated Him. For the Word of God, who said to us, "Love your enemies, and pray for those that hate you," Himself did this very thing upon the cross; loving the human race to such a degree, that He even prayed for those putting Him to death. If, however, anyone, going upon the supposition that there are two [Christs], forms a judgment with regard to them, that [Christ] shall be found much the better one, and more patient, and the truly good one, who, in the midst of His own wounds and stripes, and the other [cruelties] inflicted upon Him, was beneficent, and unmindful of the wrongs perpetrated upon Him, than he who flew away and sustained neither injury nor insults. . . . But as our Lord is alone truly Master, so the Son of God is truly good and patient, the Word of God the Father having been made the Son of man. For he fought and conquered; for He was man contending for the fathers, and through obedience doing away with disobedience completely; for He bound the strong man, and set free the weak, and endowed His own handiwork with salvation, by destroying sin. For He is a most holy and merciful Lord, and loves the human race.[69]

What, then, appears to be the content of " obedience " according to the above quotation? It seems to be found in Christ Jesus' capacity to " forgive," to " pray for those putting Him to death," to have beneficence for those inflicting upon him " wounds " and " stripes " and " other cruelties," and finally to " love " his enemies. It is a matter of " patience " and " long-suffering." In brief, obedience seems to consist of the capacity to wish for and work for the life and benefit of the " other " in spite of the other's resistance to it and attempt to reject it. This is man's obligation because it is God's character. In Jesus Christ this becomes a reality because in him God became man. And by becoming man, God unambiguously expresses love and offers life even though he completely participates in man's attempt to reject it. But it must be remembered that man rejects this life and love because of the promptings of the devil. This is precisely how the devil is defeated. In Jesus Christ, because God endures, it becomes clear that there is nothing the devil can do to make God give up man. The obedience of Christ does not represent only the moral obedience of the Second Adam; it represents the soteriological faithfulness of God himself revealing the fact that God cannot be made to " reject " man or give man up to annihilation:

It was necessary . . . that the Lord . . . should save that very man who had been created after His image and likeness, that is, Adam. . . . This was necessary, too, inasmuch as the whole economy of salvation regarding man came to pass according to the good pleasure of the Father, in order that God might not be conquered, nor His wisdom lessened. . . . For if man, who had been created by God that he might live, after losing life through being injured by the serpent that had corrupted him, should not any more return to life, but should be utterly [and for ever] abandoned to death, God would [in that case] have been conquered, and the wickedness of the serpent would have prevailed over the will of God. But inasmuch as God is invincible and long-suffering, He did indeed show Himself to be long-suffering in the matter of the correction of man and the probation of all.[70]

The concepts of "long-suffering" and "patience" bear the meaning of forgiveness and the cross. This is also the meaning of the resurrection from the standpoint of what this event says for the nature of God.[71] God's endurance and long-suffering is the actuality that constitutes the basis for the obedience of the man Jesus Christ. It is the obedience of the man Jesus and the faithful endurance of the God that was in him that worked the victory over the devil, that broke the hold that the devil had upon mankind, and that restored creation to its original relation of submission and dependence upon God's creative fellowship. The resurrection testifies to the endurance of God's original *a se* character as Creator, the consequence of which is the victory of creation over the bondage of sin and death.

In several places Irenaeus directly declares that the passion of Jesus Christ reveals the very nature of God. The meaning of this passion is that God forgives. The meaning of his forgiveness is that God endures in his relation of creative fellowship in spite of the devil's attempt to break this relation for all time. " Therefore, by remitting sins, He did indeed heal man while He also manifested Himself who He was." [72] In another place, Irenaeus says that in the obedience of Christ Jesus on the cross, " He clearly shows Himself." [73]

Such passages remind us of the close connection pointed to at the outset of this chapter between the " two hands of God " and God himself. Irenaeus' relentless insistence that Christ and not just the human Jesus suffered on the cross must also mean that God himself suffered in the passion of Christ Jesus. Since the entire object of Irenaeus' concept of the " two hands of God " is to deny any possibility of subordinationism as well as any hint of the idea that a being other than God himself is the one directly involved in the processes of creation and redemption, we can gather from this that God himself is the one who was " buffeted " and " suffered." It is true that there is probably a split in Irenaeus' thought at this point. There are passages in his writings that would seem to indicate that Irenaeus believed in the absolute aseity of God in all respects. " He is a simple, uncompounded Being, without divers members, and altogether like, and equal to Himself." [74] In another place he writes, "God alone, who is Lord of all, is without beginning and without end, being truly and forever the same and always remaining the same unchangeable Being." [75] But we cannot conclude, as does J. K. Mozley, that these passages mean that Irenaeus held a thoroughgoing conception of the impassivity of God, although we can conclude that he was somewhat ambiguous on the point.[76] But we have already seen what the immutable and unchangeable character of God means for Irenaeus. On one hand, it means that God is always faithful to the purposes of his creation and from the beginning was attempting to win man back into his creative fellowship. God's immutability serves to assert God's absolute soteriological faithfulness.[77] It was not just in the time of Tiberius Caesar that God began to provide for the salvation of man. Such a belief would make God "careless" and "neglectful" and "both change God, and destroy our faith in that Creator who supports us by means of His creation." [78] It seems clear that the function of Irenaeus' stress on the immutability of God is to establish the self-identity of God as both Creator and Redeemer and to suggest that God's character as Redeemer necessarily follows from his character as Creator and is in no way a secondary or contingent factor in his essence.

It is in this sense that God in Christ is a "ransom" for our sins. The price that he pays is not an offering given from man's side to satisfy the honor of God; nor is it a ransom paid to the devil because the devil had just rights over man. It is a ransom in the sense of a great cost that God himself, in Christ Jesus, expends in confronting the devil in battle, even though God endures to victory.

Biblical Sources of Christus Victor

The understanding of Christ's ministry as a battle and victory over demons, principalities, and powers can be found abundantly in the Gospels. Often Jesus' healing miracles were accomplished through the expulsion of demons. The epileptic boy (Matt. 17:14-21), the Canaanite woman's daughter (Matt. 15:21-28 and Mark 7:24-30), the dumb demoniac (Matt. 9:32-34 and ch. 12:22-24), and the Gerasenes wild man who identified himself as "Legion" (Mark 5:1-13 and Luke 8:26-33) were all healed by an act which liberated them from the demon which possessed them. Jesus' power over demons was so spectacular that his opponents tried to accuse him of healing with the power of Beelzebul, the prince of demons (Matt. 12:22-32).

Jesus' missionary concerns also were related closely to the

idea of battle and defeat over the devil. When the Seventy returned from their evangelistic labors, they summed up their efforts with the words, "Lord, even the demons are subject to us in your name." Jesus responded to this by proclaiming his victory ("I saw Satan fall like lightning from heaven"), and announcing that he had given his disciples authority "over all the power of the enemy" (Luke 10:17-20). A mixture of *Christus Victor* motifs with sacrificial and servanthood motifs may be evident in the words attributed to Jesus: "Even as the Son of man came not to be served but to serve, and to give his life as a ransom for many" (Matt. 20:28). The Son of Man becomes reinterpreted in the light of the Suffering Servant concept. The forces of evil are defeated by the sacrificial self-giving of the Servant Messiah (Mark 8:31).

Gustav Aulén argues that the demons of the Synoptic accounts are present in the Pauline epistles in the form of a close association between the "principalities and powers" *and* the law.[19] The law becomes a hostile power when man attempts to rely on it for his justification. In fact, though, anything in the created order (the world of flesh, or *sarx*) that man uses to gain his justification can become a principality and power binding man to sin and condemning him to death. Although Aulén can find some Pauline passages that depict Christ's work as a dethronement of His enemies (I Cor. 15:25) and their capacity to separate man from the love of God in Christ (Rom. 8:35), he actually points to only one passage in Col. 2:15 (of doubtful Pauline authorship) which specifically associates the death of Jesus on the cross and the defeat of the forces of evil: "Having put off from himself the principalities and the powers he made a show of them openly, triumphing over them in it [the cross]." Yet it is Aulén's contention that all Pauline passages that imply the idea of salvation through vicarious sacrifice, such as the phrases " for our sake," " in our stead," or " our Passover sacrificed for us " (I Cor. 5:7), must be interpreted within the *Christus Victor* motif of seeing God in Jesus Christ contending in our behalf against the devil, even at great cost to himself.

One of the most remarkable expressions of the *Christus Victor* concept can be found in Heb. 2:14-15, where Jesus is depicted as assuming the same flesh as man so that " through death he might destroy him who has the power of death, that is, the devil, and deliver all those who through fear of death were subject to lifelong bondage." Other passages suggesting this theme can be found in I John 3:8: " The reason the Son of God appeared was to destroy the works of the devil." Some passages, such as Eph. 1:7 and I Peter 1:18, indicate that Jesus' blood constituted a " redemption " of man from sin.

The meaning of Christian discipleship is determined by the meaning of the cross. We have already seen how early acts of healing and evangelism received *Christus Victor* interpretations in the Gospels. That the doctrine of the ministry should find the heart of its self-understanding from the meaning of Christ's atoning work can be seen in what may have been the words of Paul when he wrote, " I complete what is lacking in Christ's afflictions for the sake of his body, that is, the church " (Col. 1:24). The healing ministry, down through the history of the church, continued to be articulated in images of conflict and battle. The practice of anointing the sick involved the ritual of making the sign of the cross with holy oil on the impaired parts of the body and over the senses and orifices; it was thought to drive out demons and give protection against their return. As the practice of anointing, or unction, became more specifically associated with the last rites of a dying person (thereby becoming extreme unction), it still involved the idea of making the sign of the cross as a defense against and victory over the forces of evil.[80]

The exorcism connected with Jesus' acts of healing later became associated with the practice of baptism. The candidate received the sign of the cross on his head and the devil was commanded to submit to the judgment of God.[81] This practice has continued into modern times in some churches. In the Roman Catholic Church the order of exorcist, as one of the four major orders of the church, was gradually absorbed into the priesthood. In our own time, interest in the meaning of exorcism has revived. A recent book by Harvey Cox entitled *The Secular City* has suggested it as the major guiding image for a proper understanding of the mission of the church, integrating and setting into the correct context its threefold responsibility in kerygma (proclamation), diakonia (service), and koinonia (demonstrating the character of the new society).[82]

The purpose of this study is not to embark on an extended discussion of pastoral practices. Instead, we mean to show the essentially parallel meaning of the atonement theory with certain functions of the ministry. We will argue in the process of this essay that the essential structure of the psychotherapeutic relationship will show great affinities with the *Christus Victor* concept of the atonement. In turn, this will suggest that pastoral practices, insofar as they gain their essential meaning from the atonement theory, should be substantially informed by this image. This will entail a generalization of the meaning of exorcism beyond the functions it has touched, like healing and unction, to other practices it has less significantly influenced, namely, the meaning of repentance, confession, and forgiveness.

III

ANSELM: ATONEMENT AS THE
SATISFACTION OF GOD'S HONOR

The title of Anselm's famous treatise on the doctrine of the atonement is *Cur Deus Homo*. The question it asks is one that both infidels and Christians ponder in their hearts, the infidel out of ridicule and the believer in an effort to understand. The question is simply this: "For what cause or necessity, in sooth, God became man, and by his own death . . . restored life to the world."[1]

Anselm is not simply interested in demonstrating the meaning of Christ's passion and death; he wants to show that salvation can come in no other way. In this respect, among others, he differs from Irenaeus, who attempts to demonstrate the meaning of Christ's death but does not attempt to show that it could have been done in no other way.

THE CHARACTER OF GOD FROM WHICH HIS
SOTERIOLOGICAL ACTIVITY ISSUES

Cur Deus Homo is written in the form of a dialogue. Boso, who is a believer, for the sake of argument, takes the role of skeptic in order to increase his understanding of "what we believe." Boso puts the subject of the dialogue in the following manner: "For what necessity and cause, God, who is omnipotent, should have assumed the littleness and weakness of human nature for the sake of its renewal? "[2] Boso's belief in the omnipotence of God is the assumption that prompts the question. By the " littleness and weakness of human nature " he is largely referring to the suffering of Jesus on the cross. He will be satisfied with no argument based upon poetic fittingness (*conveniens*). Instead, he wants Anselm's argument to be based upon necessary reason (*necessarium*).[3]

It quickly emerges that Boso and Anselm — as well as the infidel skeptics — share a common presupposition about the nature of God, i.e., that it would indeed be unfitting for God to " stoop to things so lowly " as to suffer as did Jesus on the cross. Was there no other way for God to save man? Could not God have saved man by fiat,[4] or created a new Adam and started afresh?[5] To suggest that the " Most High " should " do a thing with such toil " as to suffer seems to question either God's omnipotence or wisdom.[6]

Anselm's answer to this line of questioning is to reject the assumption that God participated in Jesus' agony. He writes:

For we affirm that the Divine nature is beyond doubt impassible, and that God cannot at all be brought down from his exaltation, nor *toil* in anything which he wishes to effect. But we say that the Lord Jesus Christ is very God and very man, one person in two natures, and two natures in one person. When, therefore, we speak of God as enduring any humiliation or infirmity, we do not refer to the majesty of that nature, which cannot suffer; but to the feebleness of the human constitution which he assumed. And so there remains no ground of objection against our faith. For in this way we intend no debasement of the Divine nature. . . . In the incarnation of God there is no lowering of the Deity; but the nature of man we believe to be exalted.[7]

The major question that started the dialogue has now been disposed of. It would indeed be unfitting for God to suffer because he is impassible and immutable. Now the discussion turns to a new question. Why would a just God allow his Son to suffer and be treated in such a manner?

The answer to this question also involves the issue of God's immutability. What is meant by the immutability of God as Anselm understands it? It serves as the basis for Anselm's understanding of the " honor " of God — a concept so crucial for the development of the rest of his argument. To gain a complete understanding of the concept of immutability, we must refer to sources in Anselm's writings outside of *Cur Deus Homo.*

Anselm has much to say about the immutability of God in both his *Proslogium* and *Monologium.* In general, this concept conveys the idea that God is and does depend entirely upon his own character. There is no external necessity that determines the nature of God. " Whatever thou art, thou art through nothing else than thyself." [8] In one place he writes:

No necessity or impossibility exists before his choice or refusal, so neither do they interfere with his acting or not acting, though it be true that his choice and action are immutable.[9]

To assert the immutability of God is to assert the self-identity and the unchangeableness of his essence by contingent events or accidents.[10] Since God is subject to no accidents, he is not subject to time, " is true eternity, is not distributed among past, present, and future," and is absolutely simple, not subject to a " multiplicity of parts." [11]

There is a sense in which the word " necessity " applies to God; but it is a necessity that follows from his own character.[12] This statement gives us an understanding of the relationship between God's " immutability " and his " honor." God's honor, for Anselm, is God's immutable and " unwavering disposition " to maintain the order of things (*rerum ordo*) in the created world. God's immutable disposition to maintain the order of things is the basis for the totality of Anselm's soteriological structure and is determinative for a whole series of concepts that bear the weight of his soteriological thinking.

THE SIN AND GUILT FROM WHICH MAN MUST BE SAVED

Why must this just man suffer and die for our salvation? Before Anselm can answer this fully, he must demonstrate what man was originally intended to be and what man's fall means in the light of this.

In the beginning, God created man *rational, holy,* and *immortal.* This is to say that man had the rational capacity to discern the good (the *summum bonum,* the will of God) [13] and the inclination to choose it. For this reason man was holy. And finally, man was created immortal, originally destined to " enjoy eternal blessedness." [14]

It is interesting to note that there is no developmental understanding of man's *justitia originalis* in Anselm as there is in Irenaeus. In Irenaeus, man had the original propensity to trust in God as the source of his life and righteousness, but he saw this as something that should develop as man increased. Although Anselm seems to understand this *justitia originalis* more in terms of ethical discernment rather than personal trust as in Irenaeus, it is still the case that for Anselm, man seems to be fully developed with regard to these powers, even from the beginning.

Before defining the nature of sin, Anselm adds one more dimension to his concept of the upright will. Being subject to the will of God means rendering " unto God his due." [15]

Not rendering God his due is an offense to his honor; it "robs God of his own and dishonors him." [16]

Anselm believed that although the devil tempted man, man himself is personally responsible and blameworthy for sin. He believed that death is the consequence of sin and something God directly wills.[17] In addition, all men are born contaminated by the sin of Adam and Eve.[18] It is this element in the nature of sin that will later set the necessity for the principle that the one who saves man must be a member of Adam's race.

Anselm's understanding of God's reaction to sin is determined at all points by his concept of God's honor. The concept of God's honor dictates both the *shape,* or *form,* of salvation and the *necessity* of salvation. It determines both *how* salvation must come about and *why* salvation must come about. The same concept of God's perfection, immutability, and aseity that makes him unqualifiable and above suffering is also the defining characteristic of all the attributes of God. God's honor is also immutable and therefore cannot actually be lessened and qualified.[19] Anselm's assertion that sin dishonors God is based upon a distinction between the honor of God considered in-and-of-itself and the honor of God considered as a subjective response by his creatures. From the standpoint of the creature's subjective orientation of his life around God's will, God can be dishonored. But from the standpoint of the objective " isness " of this will and order, God's honor, which is his will and the order of things, cannot be injured.

Certainly this is a difficult concept for us to understand and it has proved to be so for the history of Christian thought. On the one hand, it led Harnack to criticize his doctrine of sin as simply a personal insult to God considered as a " mighty private man " conceived in the spirit of medieval feudalism.[20] At the other extreme, John McIntyre understands Anselm to mean that sin " is an intensely personal thing." He says that Anselm's concept makes sin both an infraction and a personal insult and, as a consequence, gives him a very personal view of the nature of sin.[21] Regardless of which interpretation is more adequate, it is true that Anselm believes that sin does not constitute an actual infringement on God's immutable honor itself.

It is necessary for God to save man in such a way as to maintain the integrity and immutability of his honor. For this reason, God cannot save man by simply forgiving him of his sin and disobedience. Simply to show compassion and forgive man of his sin would mean that God was forgoing the necessity of maintaining the moral order and management of his universe. God's compassion cannot be defined in such a way as to jeopardize God's honor. To maintain his honor before the fact of sin, God must either punish the sin or obtain satisfaction for it.

First, let us examine how God maintains his honor by reacting to sin with *punishment*. Anselm insists that all things must be subject to an immutable system of rewards and punishments according to the strict measure of law.[22] Forgiveness is an obligation for man, whereas vengeance not only " belongs to none but Him who is Lord of all " but also is a necessity stemming from his attribute of justice.[23] Anselm does not wish to eliminate the idea of God's compassion, but claims that there must be no incompatibility between his compassion and his justice. The supreme Nature is not a composite of goods but is one good with many names. But all attributes must be defined in such a way as not to jeopardize God's managerial perfection and immutability. God's managerial perfection seems to be the controlling attribute around which the others are defined. In view of this, there can be no place for God's free forgiveness.

How does God's punishment assert the immutability of God's managerial law and keep man in subjection to his will? God accomplishes this subjection by taking from man what belongs to man, i.e., his happiness.[24] Therefore, it is " impossible for God to lose his honor; for either the sinner pays his debt of his own accord, or, if he refuses, God takes it from him." [25] We should note that even then punishment does not obtain from man his obedience. It only deprives him of his blessedness and immortality.

It must be some such realization on the part of Anselm that makes him push on to discuss a second way in which God can maintain his honor. This is the way of *satisfaction*. Whereas punishment supposedly takes from man that which he owes God, satisfaction amounts to man's repaying this debt himself. But the seriousness of sin makes this impossible.

Anselm opens his discussion of the nature of satisfaction by developing a theory about God's original intention to replace the number of fallen angels from the race of man.[26] But in view of man's fall, to restore man in such an " unwashed " state would mean that God " could not accomplish what he designed, or else that he had repented his good intent." [27] The first would be a limitation on his omnipotence and the second would be a limitation on his wisdom. Therefore it is necessary that God demand satisfaction.

But the seriousness of sin makes the payment of satisfaction impossible. Sin is such a serious matter before God that not even the slightest glance contrary to his will is worth doing, even if it were to save the entire universe. The dilemma of the sinner is this: he owes everything to God to begin with. Therefore, he has nothing left over to pay to God for past sins.[28] Since sin is so gravely serious, and since we owe everything to God to begin with, it would be impossible to repay even the smallest sin. On the one hand, man *ought* to make payment for the guilt of his sin, but on the other hand, he *cannot* make payment. The fact that he cannot make payment is no excuse, for man is responsible and blameworthy for both *needing* to pay and being *unable* to pay.[29]

Anselm has moved to that ultimate point in his discussion at which it becomes necessary to introduce Christ. Man, who ought to pay his debt but who is unable to pay it, cannot save himself. Not only must Christ be introduced from the standpoint of man's *need,* but he must also be introduced from the standpoint of God's necessity, i.e., the necessary character of God. We have already seen how God's honor as administrator of justice determines the *form* of Christ's work. But it is God's honor as creator that determines the *necessity* of Christ's work.

God's immutable honor as creator and designer makes it *necessary* that man will ultimately be saved. Anselm writes, " It is necessary for him to perfect in human nature what he has begun." God was not forced by external necessity to create man, but upon " freely " choosing to do so, " God as it were bound himself to complete the good which he had begun." [30]

The Person of Him Who Saves Us

The honor of God as administrator of justice determines that salvation must come by satisfaction. How must this satisfaction work? First, sin is so serious that " the price paid to God " must be greater than everything in the universe besides God. [31] Hence, it follows that none but God can make this satisfaction. Second, none but man ought to make this satisfaction, since it was man who sinned. Hence, he who makes the satisfaction must be the God-man.[32] The one who makes the payment must be man, since only man *ought* to make the payment. The one who pays the debt must be God, since only God is *able* to make the payment. " For he cannot and ought not to do it, unless he be very God and very man." [33]

This expresses the soteriological significance of the traditional formula of two natures in one person. Anselm clearly asserts this principle, although he does not believe that the divine nature participates in the " injuries " and " scorn " of the human [34] or that the human is devoid of the omniscience characteristic of divine intelligence.[35]

Anselm takes great care in establishing Christ's solidarity with the human race. It is necessary that the God-man be of the same race as Adam, since it was through Adam that sin was introduced into human history. The thrust of these efforts to establish Christ's identification with man is simply this: *the act that finally restores man to his original status must be an act by man.* The man-upward-to-God movement is clearly seen in the following passage and serves as the basis for the kind of judgment that Aulén makes about the *discontinuous* line of God's act in Anselm's soteriology:

Moreover, as Adam and his whole race, had he not sinned, would have stood firm without the support of any other being, so after the fall, the same race must rise and be exalted by means of itself.[36]

It is important to note the distinction between Irenaeus and Anselm in the way that they conceive the role of the Son between the creation and the incarnation. Because of the developmental scheme in which Irenaeus puts man, the Son is present with man working through the processes of growth even after the Fall and before the incarnation, as is the case (we will see later) with Bushnell. There is no developmental scheme in Anselm. Man in the beginning is full-grown in his powers of rationality and holiness. Hence, after creation, what man does he is supposed to do on his own. Had Adam and Eve not sinned, they "would have stood firm without the support of any other being." And "any other being" must be thought to include the Son or Word. Also what occurs, for Anselm, in the incarnation *is not* of a piece with what is characteristic of God's total dealings with mankind. In the incarnation, man is given a "more" to pay back to God — a "more" that he does not possess at any time before the incarnation. Hence, it appears that the Son's work between the creation and the incarnation is discontinuous with what actually occurs in the incarnation. For Irenaeus, what is done in the incarnation in no way can be considered a contingent event, for it is continuous with what God began in creation, continued to do in the general process of growth, and then finally completely and unambiguously accomplished in the figure of Jesus Christ. For Anselm, although in one sense what was done in the incarnation is a necessity if God is to remain consistent with his immutable honor as creator and lawful administrator, in another sense it is a contingent event in that it is not of a piece with what he does for man between the creation and the incarnation. In fact, the tension between his character as immutable and perfect creator and immutable and perfect administrator of justice finally forces this contingent event: this giving of man a "more" which permits him to repay what he owes to God. In Irenaeus, forgiveness is much closer to a necessary element in the structure of God than in Anselm, where it appears as a contingent event. In Anselm, God's foremost necessity is to maintain the law. Emil Brunner's *The Mediator* discusses the contingent character of forgiveness from the standpoint of a modern employment of the Anselmian framework.[37]

The Work of Him Who Saves Us

In the last pages of *Cur Deus Homo*, Anselm discusses how Christ's satisfaction makes our salvation possible. He elaborates even further the requirements that determine the form this satisfaction must take, and then demonstrates how Christ's obedience "even unto death" meets these requirements. The requirements seem to be twofold: (1) in order to be a *perfect* satisfaction, Christ must be sinless, and (2) in order to be an *effective* satisfaction, he must submit to death voluntarily. Both at the point of his sinlessness and at his voluntary death, the problem becomes that of reconciling freedom and necessity in such a way as to show how Christ had the power to be sinless and meet death without being determined by a prior necessity.

Anselm shows the voluntary *sinlessness* of Jesus by pointing to the relationship between God's aseity and Christ's freedom. God cannot sin, because he chooses not to sin, and there is nothing that can compel or constrain him from fulfilling his decision.[38] God's "infinite unchangeableness" is the basis of the fact that Christ has the power to sin but the desire not to and the capacity to resist any force that would sway him from his intentions.[39]

Anselm explains the voluntary *death* of Christ in much the same way. The aseity of God is also the aseity of Jesus; therefore nothing external to himself could cause him to die. And since Jesus was sinless, death was not required of him as it was of Adam's race because of sin.[40] But at this point, Anselm resorts to an additional argument. He asserts that it is more appropriate to think that God the Son, rather than God the Father, was incarnated in the God-man. Since the honor of the Godhead applies equally to each of its persons, it can be said that the Son offered himself for his own honor as well as that of the Father and the Holy Spirit.[41] Hence, Christ's death was voluntary, caused by no external necessity and endured for the honor of God the Son without being specifically required by God the Father.

In being obedient unto death, Christ demonstrates an obedience that goes beyond that which was required of him. In addition, his obedience was an act of infinite worth because it is the offering of God himself. Since his life was of infinite worth and since it was freely given, even though not required, it serves as a sufficient offering to pay back to God the honor that man's sin took from God. The sacrifice of Christ's death serves to pay back to God that which man owes God but is unable to pay.

Such an offering saves man in that it behooves a just God to reward such a worthy offering.[42] The necessity of the reward is predicated once again upon the immutability of God's administrative justice; if he did not reward Christ's offering, God would be either unjust or weak.[43] But it is equally impossible to think that Christ needs a reward, for he neither owes anything nor lacks anything.[44] Therefore, it is fitting that the reward go to man, whom the Son came into the world to save.[45]

Anselm concludes the dialogue by pointing out how it becomes possible to understand God's compassion. Nothing could be more compassionate than for God to find a way for man to pay the debt that his sin justly incurs. As Anselm writes:

For what compassion can excel these words of the Father, addressed to the sinner doomed to eternal torments and having no way of escape: " Take my only begotten Son and make him an offering for yourself." [46]

In the end, it can be said that God is truly compassionate but only, once again, within the confines of what is compatible with the immutability of God's administrative justice.

Forgiveness seems to be a contingent aspect of the character of God. It is in no way continuous with God's general relation to his creatures. This is different from the case in Irenaeus and, as will be seen later, with Bushnell. In Jesus Christ, for both of these thinkers, God makes his forgiveness *manifest*. In Jesus Christ, God's forgiveness is *effectively* manifested. What God does in Christ, for both of these men, is of a piece with what God does at all times and in all places. In this sense, forgiveness follows from the most fundamental aspect of the character of God.

The Latin View and the Bible

Proponents of the Anselmian doctrine and its many variations rely strongly on Old and New Testament cultic, priestly, and sacrificial traditions. In the New Testament, the epistle to the Hebrews, in its application of the priestly tradition to the ministry and death of Jesus, has been of crucial importance to the support of this view. The idea that Jesus is the perfect priest (Heb. 7:28), making the perfect sacrificial offering (Heb. 9:14), which is expressed through a perfectly obedient life (Heb. 10:5-7), provided the rudimentary outline of the Anselmian structure. Scriptures such as I Cor. 5:7, "For Christ, our paschal lamb, has been sacrificed," references to Jesus as the "Lamb of God" (John 1:29, 36), or passages such as Eph. 5:2, "Christ loved us and gave himself up for us, a fragrant offering and sacrifice to God," have also been important sources for this view.

More immediate historical antecedents to the Anselmian view of the atonement may be, as William Wolfe has pointed out, the "institution of penance in the Latin Church." [47] The problem of postbaptismal forgiveness of sins led to a systematizing of rabbinic practices into the three elements of repentance (*metanoia*), confession (*exomologēsis*), and satisfaction (*satisfactio operis*). According to Wolfe, atonement began to be associated with the act of satisfaction which was interpreted by Tertullian as a compensation a man must make before restoration could be granted. Tertullian introduced the idea of supererogatory merit as a deed done beyond what God requires, and Cyprian later added the idea that such merit could be transferred from one person to another. The structure of this penitential system was amplified by Gregory the Great into a theory of the atonement which anticipated much of the Anselmian argument.

The structure and dynamics of the therapeutic relation will demonstrate, we believe, the fundamental error of identifying atonement with the idea of a compensatory satisfaction. It will also suggest, we believe, that the priestly act of receiving confession and announcing forgiveness should be revived by Protestant churches but should be reinterpreted in the light of *Christus Victor* meanings.

Two Variations on the Priestly Theory

Let us first review the work of the Genevan Reformer John Calvin. Calvin's theory of the atonement is frequently referred to as a penal-substitutionary theory of the atonement. But clearly it is a priestly view, strongly relying on Old and New Testament sacrificial images that receive, under Calvin's interpretation, a distinctively penal-substitutionary meaning.

The ground and necessity of the atonement is the sovereign love of God for man. But against the background of sin, this love becomes highly selective and discriminating. Sin provokes God's wrath. God hates sin and must be considered the enemy of man insofar as man is a sinner. Looking at Rom. 5:10 and Gal. 3:10, 13, Calvin concludes that God's response to sin is to put the curse of death upon man; this is the appropriate penal consequence that God's justice demands.[48] Man's guilt is something that God cannot accept. It appears that for Calvin, God's penal justice is an absolute and immutable part of God's perfection, something very similar to what was found in Anselm. One major difference is that for Anselm, salvation is God's alternative to punishment; for Calvin, salvation is accomplished through the punishment of an innocent substitute. In addition, what Anselm discussed under the rubric of God's honor has now been anthropomorphized by Calvin into God's wrath.

Christ, for Calvin, is not so much a perfect penitential offering capable of paying to God what man owes but is unable to pay, as was the case for Anselm; he is more like a perfectly pure sacrificial victim, in line with the Mosaic sacrifices of the Old Testament, who constitutes a propitiation of God's wrath by becoming a substitute, bearing the burden of the curse of the divine law.[49] Calvin quotes Isa. 53:6, "The Lord hath laid upon him the iniquity of us all," and states that God imputed to Christ the punishment that sinful man deserved, thereby saving man from the penalty of eternal death which God's justice rightly demands. Calvin writes, "Christ has redeemed us from the curse of the law, being made a curse for us: for it is written, 'Cursed is every one that hangeth on a tree: that the blessing of Abraham might come on the Gentiles through Jesus Christ.'"[50] In the resurrection, the power of the cross, in defeating death and removing the curse of the law, is shown forth.

The penal-substitutionary theory has been important for

the history of Christian thought and is felt with particular strength in much present-day evangelical and fundamentalist preaching. It can be safely said that in the United States, those who preach the atonement with any noticeable vigor, proclaim some variation of Calvin's doctrine. From the standpoint of the therapeutic analogy to be developed later, we will ask these questions: (1) Does this view of the meaning of Christ's death contain a constructive understanding of punishment, and (2) Does it understand Christ's participation in the penal consequences of sin in a truly dynamic way?

The work of McCleod Campbell is the second variation on the priestly theme I want to mention. Strictly speaking, Campbell's theory of the atonement is probably more often considered a Moral Influence view than a position that might have continuity with Latin and priestly themes. This is true. His theory is certainly not Latin. The legal and juridical dimensions are nearly absent. But it does develop certain priestly and sacrificial themes which have had exceptional influence on British theology (especially the work of Robert C. Moberly in his *Atonement and Personality*). Campbell's work also appears to be consistent with some of the best present-day Biblical scholarship on this doctrine — notably that of Vincent Taylor in *The Atonement in New Testament Teaching*.[51]

Campbell was a nineteenth-century Presbyterian minister in Scotland. His book entitled *The Nature of the Atonement* was one of the earliest and most daring repudiations of Calvinistic theology on the meaning of the cross. Its association with Moral Influence theories is due partly to its strong emphasis on the organic relationship between God and man, a relationship that sees God as the "Father of man's spirit" and that sees man as enjoying a sonship with God, given in

creation. The initiative for the atonement springs from God's
"heart" as the Father of man.[52] This spontaneous fountain
of fellowship between God's Fatherly spirit and the spirit of
man is absolute and fundamental. The law, on the other
hand, is subordinate to the gospel, as our relation to God as
our righteous Lord is subordinate to our relation to him as
the Father of our spirits — "the original and root-relation, in
the light of which alone all God's dealings with us can be
understood."[53] This does not mean to depreciate that which
is subordinated, but simply to put into the right perspective
the center of man's life and his salvation.

Campbell looks at the work of Christ from two points of
view — from the perspective of what Christ does in behalf
of God toward man and what Christ does in behalf of man
toward God. With regard to the first vantage point, Christ
shows forth to man the perfect trustworthiness of the Fatherliness of God; he demonstrates the trustworthiness of
God by trusting him with his own faith and obedience.

For our purposes we will dwell longer on what Christ did
in behalf of man toward God. It is in this that the priestly
dimensions of his theory reveal themselves. Jesus Christ, as
God's obedient Son, is in perfect sympathy both with the
righteousness of God and the sin of man. Jesus Christ experienced a "perfected personal experience of the enmity of
the carnal mind to God."[54] Christ carried and bore upon
himself sin's hate of the light of God. Being in perfect sympathy with God's righteousness, he also rightly reflected
God's judgment of this sin. Perfectly reflecting the mind of
God, Christ knows sin for what it is. From this position of
vicarious identification with the carnal mind of man, Christ
turns toward God and makes a perfect confession of the sin
of mankind.[55] This is what is meant and accomplished when
Christ utters on the cross, "Father, forgive them; for they

know not what they do." Christ, on the cross, makes a confession, on man's behalf, of the sins that man, because of his
fallenness, cannot make for himself. Campbell acknowledges
contingent elements of wrath in the mind of God. But the
ground of the atonement is not fear engendered by this
wrath but a trust in the Fatherliness of God — a trust which
gave the confidence to Christ that God wanted, worked for,
and would kindly accept this confession.

But there is even a deeper kind of confession that Christ
performs in behalf of man. Not only does Christ confess the
sins of men, he confesses who men are — sons of God the
Father. This deeper confession quickens in man the consciousness of his own created status before God.[56] The adequacy of this view of the priestly dimension of the atonement of Jesus Christ will later be discussed in dialogue with
our development of an analogy drawn from psychotherapy.

IV

HORACE BUSHNELL: A MORAL INFLUENCE THEORY

Horace Bushnell is widely recognized as an important nine-teenth-century American preacher who significantly contrib-uted to a modern approach to religious education through his book entitled *Christian Nurture*. That he was also an im-portant theologian in his own right is something less often acknowledged. Several recent Bushnell studies seem to indi-cate that we may be standing at the threshold of a new era of heightened appreciation for this nearly forgotten Ameri-can thinker, writer, and pulpiteer.[1] Although Bushnell's thought is often associated with liberalism, antitrinitarian-ism, and optimistic philosophies of man, we will find his thought infinitely richer than these labels would seem to convey.

THE RELATIONAL GOD

The " given " upon which Bushnell based his analysis of God is the efficacy of suffering — namely, Christ's suffering upon the cross and other lesser examples. This is vastly dif-ferent from Anselm, who deduces his understanding of God's perfection from the premises of the ontological argu-ment. This " given," or starting point, in the suffering of Christ carries with it a presupposition that is clearly central to his entire thought about the nature of God — that suffer-

ing must go right to the heart of the redemptive process itself, and that whatever ultimate redemptive structure exists,
it must likewise be characterized by an element of suffering.

Bushnell makes a distinction between the law of God and
the will of God and asserts that there is a law of God to
which God himself is subject, prior to the specific *will* he
may have for any particular creature. The law to which he is
subject is the law of his nature, and it is from this law of his
nature that every particular willing of his must issue. Bushnell writes, " God's own nature was in law, or crystallizing
in eternal obligation, before he became a law-giver." [2] This
law is not external to his nature, as anything that constrains
or compels him, but something that constitutes a definite
structure of his own character. At the same time, this crystalline structure of law basic to God's own nature is also the
bedrock law " common to all moral natures," man included.[3]
Both God and man are undergirded by a common moral
law that constitutes the crystalline essence of both. Bushnell's
position of putting God's obligation prior to God's will must
be contrasted with certain Calvinist points of view that made
God's will more fundamental than his obligation. Bushnell
felt that this tended to make God arbitrary, voluntaristic,
and capricious. A note of voluntarism seemed to be present
in Anselm, since the ground for the salvation of man rests
on the necessity that God remain consistent with his own intentions (will) and restore man to his original status.

Bushnell's understanding of the moral law as the essence
of God's own character sets the framework for his concept of
God's aseity. Bushnell agrees with traditional theology in
its dictum that God is the source of his own life and ends,
and in this way is distinguishable from his creatures who are
dependent upon him for all that they have and can become.
But Bushnell is quite forthright in giving this concept an-

other twist, especially in contrast to his immediate Calvinistic predecessors. Even though it is completely true that God is the source of his own ends, it is precisely his end to act for the benefit of others. Nothing *ab extra* to himself determines this end, not even the created others whom his end or aim intends to benefit.[4] Since the created others were "perceived eternally in God's thought as possibilities in himself," they were as truly his ends before they began to exist externally "as they were after their created actuality."[5] Something similar to this point was found in Irenaeus when he said that it is the self-derived end of God to "confer benefits."[6] Yet, in Bushnell, the implication of this understanding of the aseity of God's end is worked out with a clarity that serves to make the contrast between him and Anselm distinct in outline.

This self-derived end of God as a being who lives for the benefit and fulfillment of others constitutes the law of God's nature. This is the law *of* his nature, *in* his nature prior to his will. In this respect the law of his nature is absolute and without exception or qualification; and in this absoluteness rests the divine perfection. Yet, the absoluteness of this end gives his law a peculiarly *relational* character. The eternal law of God's nature is the law of *right* and is the basis of his righteousness; but because of its peculiarly relational character, it can best be conceived as the law of love. Bushnell writes, "Indeed the necessary and absolute law of right, thus accepted, is very nearly answered by the relational law of love."[7] Bushnell's tendency to make a verbal distinction between the absolute law of right and the relational law of love should not be absolutized. The fact that he makes the latter the measure of the former gives the direction of his thought, i.e., that God's perfection must be thought to deal primarily with an articulation of his relational adequacy. He makes the point that although man, for defensive and sinful reasons, may attempt to dissociate righteousness and love, "this will not be the manner of God." [8]

Bushnell further specifies the nature of God's perfection by associating the relational law of love with the principle of vicarious sacrifice:

Love to him is Right and Right to him is Love. And as certainly as he is in this law of love, he will suffer the pains of love . . . put himself in a way to receive the wrongs and bear the violence even of personal enemies, if he can hope to do them good with no counter-balancing injury. In a word, he will so insert himself into the miseries and even the guilt of their state, as to have them as a burden on his feeling, contriving, by whatever method, at whatever expense, to bring them relief. All this is eternal obligation. [9]

Love leads God into sympathetic relation with the object of love in spite of the object's hostility and enmity. Love leads God to bear any cost in an effort to fulfill the object of love.

In vast contrast to the position held by Anselm, Bushnell understands forgiveness to spring from the eternal necessity of the law of God's nature. It is not a contingent or secondary phenomenon. It is fundamental to the structure of God in its most primordial sense. Bushnell believes that God's forgiving dispositions are "dateless, and are cast in eternal mold," that the "cross" is in God before the Son arrives, and that the "Lamb was slain from the foundation of the world." [10] As we will see more fully later, although it may well be that the death of Christ reveals that God is a suffering and forgiving God, Christ is not the *occasion* or the cause of God's forgiveness. The cross of Jesus Christ is the manifestation of what Bushnell calls the "everlasting predispositions of his nature."

What are the implications of this position for the question of the immutability and aseity of God? For Bushnell, finite creatures can invoke feelings of sympathy and suffering in the Godhead itself. Bushnell writes:

We can not have a God in fit sensibility unless the antemundane touch of it is in him. He can not be forgiving God if he is yet to begin the making cost for an enemy. A God therefore whose eternity has been impassible, untouched by suffering experience, will never be at all relational to my experience. He is wood, he is granite, or no better. What can he do for me, when he can not feel me: and what can I offer him, when he can not feel what I offer. . . . Just consider at this gate, as it opens what a living God must suffer and be suffering always in his good sensibility.[11]

In what sense, then, can it be said that God is immutable and impassible? God is absolutely immutable in his ability to be sensitive to the feelings of finite creatures and he is absolutely immutable in his capacity to always endure, i.e., remain sensitive, in spite of the pain that this sensibility costs him. Bushnell speaks of the manner in which God's immutable perfection and greatness should be conceived in the following passage:

The principle suffering of any really great being and especially of God is because of his moral sensibility, nay because of his moral perfection. He would not be perfect, if he did not feel appropriately to what is bad, base, wrong, destructive, cruel, and to everything opposite the perfection. . . . Is he not a "long-suffering" God, and is there no suffering in long-suffering? Is he not a patient God, and what is patience but a regulated suffering?[12]

Hence, the source of God's passivity and impassivity, his mutability and immutability is the same structural element in his nature, i.e., the absolute perfection of the appropriateness of his feeling to the circumstances of created individuals.

What does this understanding of God's immutable sensitivity mean for the doctrine of the providence of God? It means that Bushnell understands God as a "divine sensorium" who perfectly adapts himself, due to the flexibility of the fixed law of his nature, to the various needs and wants in his creatures.[13]

God's providential relation to the world legislates against conceiving God as the completely simple and self-identical being. Being the divine sensorium of the needs and wants of every finite creature, he will have "parts, forms, colors, utterances, motions, activities, assigned him." [14] He submits himself to the great law of "action and reaction." [15] He is the "One in the manifold; and the Absolute in the conditional; Spirit in form; the Motionless in motion; the Infinite in the finite." [16] In contrast, Anselm's God can be subject to no accidents or contingent events. But, for Bushnell, God's unity is found in his character as the One whose infinite and unqualified love makes him the final object of every finite event.

THE SIN AND ALIENATION FROM WHICH MAN MUST BE SAVED

As was the case with Irenaeus and Anselm, Bushnell's understanding of the fallenness of man is simply the reverse of the original conditions of creation. Bushnell is much more in the spirit of Irenaeus than Anselm. In the beginning, man was created with childlike trust, open and receptive to the inflow of God's Spirit.

It is not so much that man *was* made righteous but that he was *being made righteous*. Even though righteousness is fundamental to man's created essence, it is never something he owns. As did Irenaeus, Bushnell believed in an unstatic, developmental, and processive understanding of man's righteousness. Man is righteous in the sense " that he is always to be so derivatively from the righteousness of God." [17] Man's sense for the right, his righteousness, should be conceived as a " flowing in of God's righteousness upon the believing soul, thus and forever to flow." [18] Sin is the breakdown of man's trust in and openness to the inflow of God's righteousness.

Even though man's original righteousness was based on his openness to God's righteous powers, Bushnell teaches that man is nevertheless a free creature. In developing this point, he makes a distinction between " things " and " powers." Man is a " power " who stands above the closed system of cause and effect characteristic of the world of nature and " things." Powers are determined predominately by causal factors internal to themselves, and are considered free agents and moral beings. [19]

This distinction between things and powers marks the distinction between nature and the supernatural and points to the twofold system of the single economy of God's world. [20] God created men as powers. Man is supernatural in that he is above nature. Man, in a real sense, is a first cause, just as is God. Hence, God can make man righteous only if man consents. God's omnipotence must not be held to mean" absolute force " and thought to imply that God should be able to force man to be righteous. [21] Instead it means that God has all the force to do what force can do. In reality, God does not force the inflow of his righteousness, but instead conveys it by means of persuasion. [22] Persuasion and consent operate in the realm of the supernatural.

Being a power, man can violate his nearest proximate harmony — God's power to make righteous and man's predisposition to receive it. [23] Man can sin, and by following his " weakest motive," attempt to compensate for a sense of a "condition privative," a situation of moral inexperience that does not allow him to anticipate the consequences of his experimentation.[24] Although Bushnell speaks about his condition privative in somewhat cognitive terms, we are struck with the similarity between it and Adler's sense of "inferiority," Goldstein's concept of "imperfection," and Maslow's concept of "deficit motivation," all of which in different ways seem to suggest that human brokenness comes out of a prior sense of deficiency.[25] In addition, like Irenaeus and the late Teilhard de Chardin,[26] the import of this concept is to place man's fall in the context of a developmental scheme. Man's fall comes at the beginning of a nurturing process that breaks down partially because of the misuse of his freedom and partially because of the unsturdiness of his development.

Bushnell has a concept of the devil, but it differs from that of Irenaeus in that man's fall precedes the rise of the devil. Although God conceptualizes the possibility of the devil, the actuality of the devil represents the corporate and organic character of evil that emerges from man's misuse of freedom and hovers over man from generation to generation, constituting the context of evil into which each infant is born.[27] In actuality, Bushnell's fallen man is in a situation very similar to that which Irenaeus envisioned. He is in a state of captivity to the devil, withdrawn into self, estranged from the influx of God's righteousing and life-giving relationship, and "*imprisoned in darkness,* unbelief, idolatry." [28]

What is God's reaction to sin? To answer this, we must explain a series of distinctions between instituted government and law, nature and the supernatural, instituted government and commandment, justice and righteousness, and wrath and grace. The first terms in each of these sets of distinctions correspond in some way with one another just as do the second terms.

God's will or instituted government is his specific prescription to guide, control, and govern man in his fallenness.[29] It includes such things as the Ten Commandments, the civil law, the censure of community mores, and the constraints and natural bodily consequences of sinful living. It is through this realm of instituted government that God expresses his wrath against sin; but this wrath is measured, disciplined, and not an end in itself.[30] Through the working of the natural order, God " allows " that sin has consequences.[31] This is God's justice. But it is not vindictive, retributive, or directly equivalent to the weight and magnitude of man's sin. It is his *opus alienum* — a strategy, a means-end instrument designed to maintain God's administrative authority, control the order of society, and discipline, humble, and open the sinner to the workings of God's supernatural grace.[32] The wrath principle in God is nothing " original and absolute in God." [33] As Bushnell writes, justice " requires to be done, only because, and just so far as, it is means to ends in a way of maintaining government; not because God's nature contains a wrath-principle absolute, that must be exactly satisfied." [34]

Bushnell makes a distinction between God's justice and his righteousness. God's righteousness is absolute and is equivalent to the relational law of love. God's justice is his *strange work,* " variable and conditional," and mediated by the impersonal forces of the natural.[35] On the other hand, God's grace is God's *proper* work — supernatural and personal. Righteousness and grace are more central in God's character, but both are necessary — justice to work against hardened and self-contented souls and grace without which justice leaves man convicted, guilt-ridden, and hopeless.[36]

The Person of Him Who Saves Us

In discussing Bushnell's understanding of the person of Jesus Christ, we will approach it from the standpoint of three crucial areas: the meaning of " manifestation," the relation of the divine and human in Christ, and the relation of the incarnation and suffering.

Jesus Christ is the manifestation of God's grace. But this must be reconciled with Bushnell's contention that God is always living his forgiveness into the world through the work of the Holy Spirit.[37] While the Spirit works inwardly, the epistemology of salvation necessitates that Christ manifest himself externally in the realm of sense because it is the very nature of sin to be in bondage to the carnal and material.[38] Although Bushnell's understanding of " sense " is limited partially by Neoplatonic distinctions between carnal and spiritual with a consequent devaluation of nature, sense, and materiality, it is probably also true that Bushnell's use of the word " sense " and " carnality " are not completely devoid of Pauline meanings. For Paul, the word *sarx*, which can be translated to mean " sense," " flesh," " world," or " carnality," refers more to an orientation of one's life toward (and a subsequent living out of) the resources of the created world rather than referring to a direct depreciation of the world of sense and materiality.[39] The spirit of Bushnell's writing sometimes implies the Pauline meaning of the word, but there is also strong evidence for the other depreciatory dichotomy. Nevertheless, there is, to coin a phrase, an *epistemosoteriological* necessity for God to manifest himself in a tangible, observable form, since sin has blinded man to his own, inward spiritual depths. Hence, Jesus Christ is a dynamic manifestation, not of something " new " but of something dateless and eternal.

Of course, the very possibility of God's manifestation of himself in the realm of finite objects necessitates a passible God, a God who can allow a conditioned element within his life without ceasing to be God.[40]

We must move to our second consideration — the relation of human and divine in Jesus Christ. Here we find that, although Bushnell believes that God is manifest in all creatures, in Jesus Christ this manifestation is not obscured by sin.[41] Jesus Christ is so completely God for Bushnell that he rejects the two-nature formula for its tendency to make a distinction between the human and divine in Jesus at the point of his sufferings.[42] Whatever can be said about Jesus can also be said of God. The human qualities of Jesus are limited and finite expressions of elements of God's perfection.[43] Bushnell does not attempt to deny the human element in Jesus Christ. Instead, he simply denies that it is, in *any sense,* a distinct nature from the divine.

The third area of meaning we must investigate is Bushnell's teaching on the relation of the incarnation to suffering. Bushnell holds the incarnation and suffering so closely together that they are almost identical. As incarnation means being manifest in some finite medium in human form and under the laws of action and reaction, it also means entering into, submitting, and enduring the distortions of sin to which finitude is subject.[44] In God's incarnation, he takes our " curse " upon himself. But whereas he allows the consequences of sin to flow upon him, he does not allow them to erode him, distort his greatness, or cause him to sin in return.

THE WORK OF HIM WHO SAVES US:
THE DYNAMIC OF FORGIVENESS

In Bushnell's first theory, expressed in *God Was in Christ* and the first volume of *Vicarious Sacrifice,* Christ's life and death announce and demonstrate the fact and dynamics of God's timeless activity in reconciling man to himself.[45] The essence of this reconciling activity is captured in the concept of forgiveness, and forgiveness finds its meaning in the events of the cross and suffering of Christ.

Forgiveness entails more than a simple " letting go " of sin.[46] Forgiveness must also entail a communication of regenerative power — a communication of God's original righteousing power so that we will be transformed and removed from our captivity.[47] Bushnell calls it the power of " moral " persuasion.[48] As a moral power, it is not to be considered a " moral example." We need something to go before the example that will predispose us to copy the example.[49] By God's moral power, Bushnell means the power of " all God's moral perfections."

What is the transforming dynamic of God's moral power and forgiveness mediated through Christ? Bushnell identifies this moral power clearly with the peculiarly active character of Christ's passive virtues. By Christ's passive virtues, Bushnell means the comprehensiveness of Christ's capacity to be " afflicted " by our sins.[50] Christ's affliction for our sins can best be understood under the rubric of " sympathy," a " feeling of what we feel " and a suffering because of it.[51] Bushnell writes that this sympathy " needs to be such as amounts to virtual identification, where there is a contriving how to feel the man all through, and read him as by inward appreciation." [52]

The dynamics of forgiveness are seen in the fact that Christ's moral power and sympathy " is able to rise, at one, the sense of guilt and attract the confidence of the guilty." [53] But sin's reaction is to rise up against this divine sympathy in a torrent of hostile reaction, " bursting forth in a storm of deadly violence." [54] Bushnell describes how the divine sympathy works through this initial burst of guilt and hostility to a final resolution of trust:

But loaded as he is with insult, and dragged out to die, he bears the concentrated venom of his crucifiers with a lamb's patience. We see him, in fact, descending below our malignity, that it may break itself across his Divine Patience. He outreaches, by his love, the measure of our animosities — the wrong will in us, all the malignities of our devilish passions feel themselves outdone. Evil falls back from its apparent victory, spent, exhausted, conscious, as it never was before, of its impotence.[55]

It is clear what Bushnell considers to be the meaning of the cross. The cross of Christ represents a truth about God. It represents the eternal suffering in God consequent to his sympathy. The resurrection represents the perpetual endurance of God's love in spite of this suffering.[56] It represents God's absolute adherence to the law of his nature, an adherence that he accomplishes even at great cost. In this endurance and this obedience, the law of God's nature is fulfilled. The relational law of love that man has trampled and insulted in the Fall, God has upheld.[57] Such a supreme and inexhaustible love would lead ultimately to such a great suffering as was his death.[58]

At times, Bushnell conceives the passive elements in Christ's suffering and the active elements present in God's durability in the framework of a battle and victory. The

Christus Victor concept is not entirely inappropriate. Bushnell writes:

> If his streams ran all one way he would be too simply placid to be great, but he lives in everlasting countertides of struggle and victory — victory both over enemies without and violate good in himself.[59]

It is also interesting to note that Bushnell has some appreciation for the " ransom " image and interprets it to mean a payment made neither to God nor to the devil. Rather, the redemption that Christ " bought " refers to the great " cost " of his suffering given in our behalf.[60] The Suffering Servant passages of Isaiah are seen to have vicarious sacrificial meaning rather than penal substitutionary meanings.[61] And he interprets the sacrificial blood of the Old Testament to represent the very " life " of God given to restore the righteousness of man, rather than an expiation or propitiation.[62]

Bushnell's second theory is different from his first in that it represents an effort to incorporate some of the truths he feels might be resident in penal substitutionary and satisfaction theories of the atonement.

In *Forgiveness and Law,* Bushnell begins to feel that there is a place for understanding Christ's death as both God's reconciliation of man and God's reconciliation of himself.[63] Certainly, Bushnell asserts, God has moral disgust with man's sin. And certainly, this moral disgust must be removed if he is to forgive man freely. Along this line, Bushnell sees Christ's suffering as representing most of the elements he wrote about in his earlier works; but, in addition, he sees it as representing an internal compensatory act within God himself designed to move aside his offended feelings.[64] In coming to this position, Bushnell takes the human analogy of forgiveness even more seriously than before. God is offended by sin. Before he can reconcile the other, he must reconcile his own offended sensitivity. He does this by an internal compensation that moves aside his hurt feelings. In giving more foundation to God's offended moral sensitivity, he still does not hold these feelings as ultimate and determinative in God. They are still secondary and contingent. But nonetheless, they must be reconciled and removed before forgiveness can be granted. Nothing that Christ does *qua* man reconciles these feelings. Rather, Christ's obedience expresses how God is compensating eternally his hurt moral sensitivity within the Godhead itself. At a later time, we shall ask whether, from the standpoint of psychotherapeutic insights, Bushnell's second theory can be considered a genuine improvement over his first.

Moral Influence Theories and the Exemplar Motif

Bushnell is a good representative of so-called Moral Influence theories of the atonement in that he concentrates on man's subjective change, Christ's persuasive (although, in this case, quite dynamic) approach to man, and tends to subsume God and man under the same moral law. There is one element missing — his failure to present an exemplar understanding of the man Jesus. Many thinkers associated with the Moral Influence typology present Jesus as an example, pattern, or ideal archetype of what man is supposed to be and make this the crucial element in their interpretation of ·the meaning of his life and death. This view often strongly emphasizes Christ's role as a teacher and rabbi. His death on a cross was an act of instruction, revealing and demonstrating the extent of divine love and setting out the way of love his disciples are to imitate.

Vincent Taylor believes that, although the idea that Christ

came to reveal God's love seems to undergird much of the New Testament witness, it is only seldom stated as in Rom. 5:8 — " But God *shows* his love for us in that while we were yet sinners Christ died for us." Even here the emphasis is upon the " while we were yet sinners " rather than upon the " God shows his love " in the first part of the sentence.[65]

The first systematic presentation of the exemplar approach came from Peter Abelard, a younger contemporary of Anselm. Rejecting both ransom and satisfaction theories as crude, Abelard saw the efficacy of Christ's death in its function as a perfect pattern of the genuine love of Christ for man. This perfect example arouses within us a similar response of love, and it is through this transformation that our salvation is effected.[66] Modern commentators are prone to criticize such a view, saying that it condemns man by presenting him with a standard of perfection without providing him with the power to emulate it.[67] That this is not altogether true can be seen in the fact that Abelard connected Christ's work as a perfect example with the " world soul " of Greek philosophy which he in turn interpreted as the Holy Spirit. The work of Christ gives a clear example of the power of the second and third Persons of the Trinity to effect moral change in man, even among the pagans and those who lived before Christ.[68] From the perspective of our future argument, Abelard's mistake was his failure to understand the relation between Jesus' function as ideal man and God's act in Christ that frees man, through struggle and victory, from the powers that hold him captive. Psychotherapy will indicate that grace, conflict, and victory precede man's attempt to identify with an ideal archetype.

Other prominent instances in which the idea of Christ as exemplar is found can be seen in the thought of Friedrich Schleiermacher and, on the British scene, Hastings Rashdall.

The criticism prevails that these men, by emphasizing man's subjective response to the perfect pattern of Jesus' love, fail to demonstrate what God does objectively to free man so that he can imitate and identify with the form of this pattern. Often such criticisms are superficial and overlook, for instance, such relationships as can be found in Schleiermacher between Christ as *Vorbild* (perfect example) and Christ as *Urbildlichkeit,* which, according to Richard R. Niebuhr, must be interpreted to mean an " ideality " that " expresses the special presence of the creative power of God in him " — a divine power which is communicated to historical man by virtue of the *Vorbild* of Jesus' human perfection.[69] To some extent, for both Abelard and Schleiermacher, power and grace seem to precede, or at least accompany, the efficaciousness of Jesus as example — a point that is often overlooked by those who criticize the use of exemplar themes. Analysis of the efficacy of the psychotherapeutic relation will show, though, that insofar as exemplar views emphasize the pedagogical, instructional, and noetic function of the cross at the expense of dynamic and transactional elements, they indeed must be considered deficient.

A Brief Comparison

Let us consider these thinkers in reverse order. We have learned that Bushnell understood God to be *a se* in some respects but not in all, that Anselm understood God to be *a se* in all respects, and that, although Irenaeus was unclear, there is good evidence that he understood God to be *a se* in some but not all respects.

It is also interesting to note that Bushnell, as does Irenaeus, applies the principle of aseity to God's honor. For both, God's honor seems to be dependent upon what God does, and not so much on what man does. In this, they differ considerably from Anselm. For Anselm, God's honor seems to rest on his capacity to keep man in subjection to his law, whereas for Irenaeus and Bushnell, God's honor seems more to rest on God's capacity to provide man with the means of life and to remain faithful to his own divine end as the " conferrer of benefits."

When we come to Anselm, we confront a conception of God in which he is understood to be *a se* and immutable in all respects. God can be qualified by no contingent events and subject to no accidents. For this reason, God does not experience directly our suffering or sin. Nor can it be said that he has compassion. As Anselm puts it, God is compassionate in our experience, but from the standpoint " of his own being. . . . He does not experience the feeling of compassion," nor is he " affected by . . . sympathy for wretchedness." [70] Nothing like the concept of " sympathy," as we find in Bushnell, or " recapitulation," as we find in Irenaeus, is possible for Anselm's understanding of God.

On the Christological issue, in spite of different terminology, we have an amazing similarity between Irenaeus and Bushnell on the question of the relation of the incarnation and the work of Christ. Both see a strong identification between the incarnation and suffering. Both tend to see God's work in Jesus Christ as of a piece with his general work with mankind. For God to stand in history is for him to stand in the stream of the distortions that beset man and the consequences that flow from man's sin. Certainly, Irenaeus makes much more of God's role as man and his recapitulation of the first Adam. But Irenaeus also makes a great deal of God's work *through* man in recapitulating into his own life the circumstances and the consequences of man's fallen condition. For Irenaeus, the recapitulation of Christ is a recapit-

ulation by the perfect man, but it is nonetheless a recapitulation by the condescending God. In this respect, Aulén is correct in insisting that, for Irenaeus, the work of Christ is,
through and through, the work of God.[71] Even though Bushnell may make too little of the human element in Jesus
Christ, with these differences between Irenaeus and Bushnell
aside, there is marked similarity between Irenaeus' concept
of Christ's recapitulation and Bushnell's understanding of
Christ's sympathetic suffering and the way, I believe, both
of them (Bushnell explicitly, and Irenaeus implicitly) apply
these to God.

In both cases, the redemptive figure possesses a *passive* and
receptive element that permits Irenaeus' Christ to recapitu-
late and sum up the sins of the world into himself and that
allows Bushnell's Christ to be affected by the sins and sor-
rows of the world in sympathetic suffering. In both instances,
this summing up and balancing process is considered under
the metaphor of the " battleground " — what Bushnell calls
a " struggle and victory " and what Irenaeus means when he
says that " He fought and conquered." There is a sense in
which this act of balancing, this " struggle and victory " is
conceived by Bushnell in personalistic terms and by Irenaeus
in mythological and cosmological terms. This is due to the
difference in their concept of the devil, a difference that we
shall discuss at greater length later in our study. Taking the
lead of Robert S. Franks, let us suggest that Bushnell's Moral
Influence theory is nothing more than an internal and less
mythological view of the same truth that ransom theories of
the atonement have spoken of in externalistic, objectified,
and highly mythological terms.[72]

Hence, in neither Bushnell nor Irenaeus does Christ's advent represent any objective change in God. Because of Irenaeus' strong doctrine of the devil, God's work in Christ

does seem to effect a decisive victory over the devil, and, in this sense, there is an *objective* change in man's situation. The devil has now lost the major battle and although he is not annihilated completely, his effectiveness is on the wane. But in Irenaeus the devil can in no sense be associated so closely with God's wrath as to make it possible to say that the devil's defeat also constitutes a reconciliation of God himself. Because Bushnell does not have such a strong understanding of the devil, because man's subjective change in the acceptance of forgiveness precedes and hence effects the defeat of the devil, it can be said that there is *no change in the objective situation in his theory.* It is true that in his later theory, he does envision a continuous internal reconciliation, a perpetual process of God pushing aside his contingent sentiments of moral disgust. But this is nothing that is attached specifically to the advent of Jesus Christ; it is not a *subjective* view of the atonement if the meaning of *objective* is that " God does something." In Bushnell, God always is *doing something.* God always is summing up the sins of the world, taking them into himself and yet affirming his undistorted love for the world in spite of this sin and its distortions. Such an " activity " is represented best by the symbol of " cost " and is what is behind the ransom theory of the atonement. To this extent, there is an objective process preceding man's subjective change, although there is no specific change that Christ's advent effects.

FORMAL CRITERIA FOR A DOCTRINE OF THE ATONEMENT

Let us indicate briefly certain formal criteria for a doctrine of the atonement. Such formal principles must be native to each of the theories of the atonement that we have been discussing. Formal criteria for this doctrine would be those issues which each theory, regardless of its divergences, felt obliged to address and make provision for in the development of its view of the atonement. The specification of these formal criteria is itself a judgment; but it is a judgment that must have some basis. Insofar as Christian experience has some unity, we should not be surprised to detect a common core of concern underlying divergent attempts to conceptualize this experience. Historical studies help to bring these core concerns to the surface. If the analogy that psychotherapy generates cannot address these common concerns, this in itself would tend to make it suspect. But if, on the other hand, the psychotherapeutic analogy that we will develop later in the study does manage to address these concerns, it would qualify in this minimum respect for a serious discussion between this analogy and the historically significant positions that we have set forth in the preceding chapters. If, at that time, marked congruence should develop between this analogy and one or more of these historic alternatives, such a congruence would be a cause for interest. In fact, it is our belief that this analogy will tend to show striking similarity with significant portions of both the dramatic or Classic view and the so-called Moral Influence position. It not only will tend to confirm these theories, it also will help to illuminate their meaning. In view of this, there may be justification for arguing that each of these theories — the Classic, the Moral, and the psychotherapeutically derived analogy — may be pointing to a common structure.

Our task at present, though, is to specify these common characteristics which would constitute the formal criteria for a doctrine of the atonement. Four principles seem to emerge:

1. *The sufficient reason for the atonement must rest in the nature of God.* In each of the theories that we have reviewed, this principle has been present in some sense. In Irenaeus,

God is the supreme giver of life. This is God's self-derived end. He is *a se* in this respect. The perfection and absoluteness of God's capacity to give life does not mean that he will force man to take it. It simply means that all the resources sufficient for life will be given to men. The light will continue to shine. The two hands of God will continue to do their work. All of this will issue ultimately in the fulfillment of creation. The devil, as an obstacle to the inflow of God's life, will be defeated.

A similar ground for the atonement is found in Anselm. Here God's perfection in all respects means that God must remain absolutely consistent with his original intention to create man for a life of obedience. This constitutes the sufficient reason upon which the event of the God-man occurs. God must restore man to his original status.

A similar principle emerges in Bushnell. Here it is seen within the framework of the relational law of love. Since the law of God's nature is such, the sympathy by which man's atonement is effected is guaranteed absolutely. In each of the cases, the sufficient reason for the atonement is rooted in the very nature of God.

2. *Atonement must come in such a way as not to jeopardize God's basic order and structure of the world.* This principle appears in each of the theories studied above but in different ways. In Irenaeus and Bushnell, God does permit a margin of dislocation in the order of justice, but he guarantees a general limit beyond which this dislocation cannot proceed. For Irenaeus, the basic structure upon which the order of the world rests is God's primordial relationship of creative love and fellowship. This primordial relationship contains within it certain natural precepts that continue as implicit in the work of the two hands of God. In addition, God further integrates and disciplines the world in his con-

tingent demands expressed in the Mosaic law. Law, in this secondary sense, guarantees a basic order of justice, and it operates as a background for and complement to the law and grace of God's primary creative fellowship with the world. God's law and grace, in this primary sense, cannot be made less than sufficient for the salvation of man. But the grace of God's primary relationship does not require a perfect compensation of the law. Certain infringements can remain uncompensated as long as this is consistent with God's ultimate intention to fulfill creation.

The relationship between the order of justice and God's primary and secondary law is essentially the same for Bushnell. The ultimate order of the world depends on the bedrock character of the relational law of love. Contingent, governmental structures of law appear and operate on a provisionary basis to integrate and discipline man so that God's relational law of love can better move man to redemption. For both Bushnell and Irenaeus, God's atoning activity does not eliminate completely these structures; but neither is his atoning activity completely measured by them.

For Anselm, there is no discontinuity in the structure of justice whatsover. God's administrative law is not a contingent, means-end, or secondary feature in the nature of God. It is absolutely fundamental to the nature of God. In fact, God's forgiveness and compassion are defined in relationship to it. Sin must be met either by retribution or compensation. Forgiveness can come only if God's law receives adequate compensation. Regardless of this difference between Anselm on the one hand and Bushnell and Irenaeus on the other, for all three a basic structure of justice is maintained — absolutely for the former, but only sufficiently for the latter.

3. *The event of Jesus Christ must add something new to*

effect man's redemption which is not otherwise available. In Irenaeus, the two hands of God always have been at work. The event of Jesus Christ is continuous with the working of the two hands. But in Jesus Christ, the work of God's two hands (which is the work of God himself) is manifested unambiguously in the person of the man Jesus. In doing this, God accomplishes several things: he conforms himself to the level of human comprehension, and in the Second Adam, God's strength and faithfulness become the obedience that finally effects the defeat of the devil.

In Bushnell, God's sympathetic participation in the distortions of sin is a primordial fact. But the man Jesus unambiguously manifests this divine sympathy at the level of one human being. Since it is the very nature of sin to be bound to the world of sense, there must be some point in the world that unambiguously shows forth this divine sympathy.

Anselm, on the other hand, believes that the disobedience of man requires an obedience that will pay back to God what man cannot pay. Hence, the God-man must be born, suffer, and die, and in dying return to God more than what is required of him. In each of the above theories, the event of Jesus Christ represents something new that is not available otherwise for the salvation of man.

4. *The atonement of Jesus Christ effects real redemption.* Some attempt to establish this principle can be found in each of the above three theories. For Irenaeus, real redemption consists of being freed from the captivity of the devil. *What is not always clear in Irenaeus is the relationship of the fact of this defeat to the decision on the part of man to actualize the freedom that has been given him in fact.*

For Anselm, real redemption consists of having the guilt of one's sin removed through the payment and compensation of the death of the God-man. *What is not clear within*

Anselm's thought is how the objective fact of the removal of guilt before the eyes of God enables man to accept subjectively the fact that he is no longer guilty before God.

For Bushnell, real redemption consists of the subjective acceptance by man of God's love. *What is not clear is how man's subjective response to God's enduring love frees him from (defeats) the organic forces of evil that imprison him.*

V

THE ESSENCE OF THE
PSYCHOTHERAPEUTIC RELATION

Since the presupposition of this study is that there is a proportionality between any finite healing-producing structure
and God's infinite healing activity, it follows that our concern with the psychotherapeutic process must direct us to
search for its essence. It is because we must be interested in
what is essential to healing that we have chosen to inspect
the Rogerian client-centered theory of psychotherapy more
closely than other theories of current prominence. It is both
the strength and weakness of client-centered psychotherapy
that it has concerned itself primarily with the essentials of
psychotherapy. It is its strength in that client-centered theory
can speak with more specificity than other positions about
the invariant conditions prerequisite for personality change.
It is its weakness in that such an exclusive concentration on
the essentials sometimes eclipses concern about the accidental aspects of doing therapy in specific contexts and situations. Other theories about psychotherapy, in speaking,
thinking, and theorizing about the full range of particular
behaviors characteristic of good therapy, have tended to lose
sight of the essentials or have substituted the contingent and
accidental aspects of good therapy for the essential and invariant aspects. Such a confusion ultimately is detrimental to
good theory about therapy.

The purpose of this chapter is to set forth the client-centered understanding of the psychotherapeutic process from the standpoint of four issues that are analogues to the four issues used to analyze the theories of the atonement considered in an earlier part of this study. These issues are: (1) the essential structure of the therapeutic relationship (the theological counterpart of which dealt with the essential structure of God viewed soteriologically), (2) the nature of human brokenness (the theological analogue — the nature of sin), (3) the character of the psychotherapeutic agent (the theological counterpart — the person of Jesus Christ), and (4) the dynamic employment of the structure of the therapeutic relationship by this agent (the theological counterpart — the work of Jesus Christ).

In setting forth the client-centered position on these four issues, I will be taking a *particular* approach to this view of therapy. Client-centered psychotherapy has grown up in close relationship to certain centers of academic learning — Ohio State University, the University of Chicago, and the University of Wisconsin. Rogers, as the leader of this movement, must be seen also as its most significant follower. On the one hand, he has been the chief stimulus to research. On the other hand, he has been the chief integrator and synthesizer of this research.

Let us reverse our procedure and first discuss the client-centered vision of man.

THE CLIENT-CENTERED VISION OF HEALTH AND BROKENNESS

It has been one of the persistent objectives of this study to ask the question, What is the nature of human brokenness in relation to which God's soteriological activity proves efficacious? In order to fulfill our purposes, the same question must be put to psychotherapy. The structure of healing, whether it refers to God's infinite healing activity or man's finite and limited healing activity, must be understood in the light of the nature of human brokenness. Healing and brokenness are interdependent concepts and their link, on the psychological level, is *cure* or *change,* and on the theological level, is *salvation* or *redemption.* In addition, the nature of human brokenness, whether psychologically or theologically conceived, must be understood with some reference to what is normative for human existence. Before we can discuss the client-centered view of psychological brokenness — what it calls " incongruence " — we must attempt to understand the concept of health which lies behind it.

For the client-centered tradition, the psychologically immature adult is an infant with an adultlike power to symbolize his experience. Four theoretical constructs will focus our attention adequately on the client-centered view of health. The four constructs are: (1) the *actualization* tendency, (2) the *organismic valuing process,* (3) *congruence,* and (4) the *need for positive regard.* These four constructs provide a full view of the principles relevant to the neonate which, when interpolated to the adult and his advanced powers of symbolization, provide the framework for articulating the client-centered theory of psychological maturity or psychological health.

The Actualization Tendency

Rogers writes in his theoretical section of *Client-centered Therapy* that " the organism has one basic tendency and striving — to actualize, maintain, and enhance the experiencing organism." [1] Rogers borrows this particular phrasing of the actualization principle from Snygg and Combs, but feels that Goldstein, Angyal, Sullivan, Horney, and Maslow have also developed similar concepts.[2] This basic drive, or actualization tendency, is seen as a forward-moving force that propels the individual toward ever-increasing autonomy *and* socialization.[3] In short, the actualization tendency can be seen as the striving of the organism toward ever-expanding areas of *socialized autonomy*. The actualization tendency is thought to have a kind of inner homeostasis which, in the long run, will keep social and individual values in a proper balance. It should be pointed out that this basic actualization tendency refers to the *organism as a whole,* is not limited to one specific organ or tissue need, includes segmental or deficiency needs, but also transcends them.[4]

A more differentiated and scientifically specifiable version of the actualization tendency has been developed by Laura Rice and John Butler. In a 1960 statement entitled " Self-Actualization, New Experience, and Psychotherapy " they register essential agreement with the actualization principle as developed by Rogers, but demonstrate some dissatisfaction with its vagueness.[5] Although the paper uses the term " self-actualization " rather than just " actualization tendency," its remarks are applicable to the latter concept. For their thought, self-actualization includes the general actualization tendency.

Butler and Rice believe that the actualization tendency of the human organism is a drive and has a primitive base. It is independent of the so-called " physiological drives " such as the drives for food and for sex.[6] It has no specific bodily locus, is not a tissue need, and cannot be subsumed under the coping behavior in behalf of maintenance needs or pain avoidance of the human organism. At the same time, it does provide the primitive basis upon which the " social nature " of man can be asserted. Rice and Butler specify this primitive, nonlocalized drive of the whole organism as *stimulus hunger.* In its behavioral form, the drive of stimulus hunger issues in *adience* or *approaching behavior* on the part of the human organism in an effort to gain novel and complex patterns of experience. The authors define the concept in the following quotation:

This drive (or requirement) which we call stimulus hunger or adience shows in behavior as an ever-present tendency for the organism to get *new experience* [italics mine], either in the form of new stimulus objects or in the form of change in the level of stimulation. . . . The tendency is present before birth and is evident shortly thereafter. One of the unique features of this drive, or requirement, is that it elicits *orientation* or *approach* [italics mine] behavior almost immediately. The evidence suggests that, on the average, stimulus hunger is stronger than the other drives which in turn suggests that more adient behavior occurs among healthy infants than does other kinds. For the tendency is ever present whereas the usual drives are rhythmical or rise suddenly and subside abruptly. . . . We emphasize the expression "experience" in our statement of adience because we do not accept current views that coping with the environment is the fundamental element in motivation. . . . We believe, rather, that experience and experiencing is fundamental in human motivation.[7]

In addition, it should be noted that by the term "experience" or "experiencing," the authors do not mean "information," nor are they emphasizing the "sensorium."[8] Instead, they are emphasizing a real "commerce with the stimuli."[9]

Rice and Butler refer to a whole range of experimental and clinical evidence to document the presence and predominance of this drive. It is too varied and too numerous for us to recount in detail. A short summary will have to suffice. Experiments by Carmichael and Corionos with cats in the fetal stage demonstrated that the cats always will *move toward* light strokes by a bristle. The general exploratory activity of the infant and child and their universal tendency to heightened physical contact with the environment is seen as evidence for the existence of this drive. On the other side of the coin, experiments in sensory deprivation tend to show that the human organism becomes disoriented if stimuli are absent. Butler himself has demonstrated that when new stimulus objects are introduced to children manipulating their genitals, they always cease their genital activity and reach for the new object, suggesting that stimulus hunger is not reducible to the sex drive.

Rice and Butler point with some interest to the theoretical work of E. B. Holt, who in 1931 developed the concept of adience and its role in governing behavior. He contended that " the initial response of the organism to any stimulus is to get more of it, to respond positively." Furthermore, he regarded avoidance responses as a consequence of a prior approach response met by " strong stimulation." [10] It is clear, then, that this drive of stimulus hunger (this drive for experiencing), which issues in adient or approach behavior, constitutes the basis for the social nature of man, as Rice and Butler see it. It is also the basis of man's creativity in that with the development of symbolic activity, one's own thoughts can constitute a source of new experience.[11] The authors observe that, for the child, punishment is received most often in connection with adient or approaching behavior. The consequence of this punishment is to inhibit the social outreach of the child as well as to inhibit the creative self-development of new thought stimuli.[12]

It is not clear whether Rogers will incorporate the concept of stimulus hunger into his own understanding of the actualization tendency. It is quite likely that he will. The concept sacrifices none of the original meaning of the actualization concept and goes far toward giving the actualization tendency clearer empirical specificity.[13]

The Organismic Valuing Process

The organismic valuing process refers to the client-centered conception of how the human organism, especially the very young infant, experiences and knows its world. It is a construct descriptive of the physiological process whereby the organism evaluates experience with regard to its relevance for the actualization tendency. But since the overall direction of the actualization tendency is toward ever-increasing areas of socialized autonomy, the organismic valuing process will evaluate, in the long run, its experiences of the environment, both in terms of how they enhance autonomy and how they enhance socialization.

The organismic valuing process, as a bodily process of balancing and synthesizing needs and environmental stimuli, is related closely to the concepts of *experiencing* and *feeling*. Rogers sees these terms as practically synonymous. They refer to the combination and inseparable interlacing of stimuli and the physiological response to that stimuli. They are constructs designed to hold cognition and emotion together.[14] When organismic experiencing is functioning fully, it cannot be seen as simply a subjective process. This is implicit in Rogers' statement that if the psychologically mature person " follows his feelings," he will find them reliable guides to an adequate appreciation of social values.[15] Gendlin, the philosopher of the client-centered school, points out that " Rogers must assume that 'feelings' implicitly contain social and moral meanings and values. Without a theoretical statement of implicitly meaningful experiencing, 'following one's feeling' can be misunderstood as impulse ridden and selfish." [16] Organismic experiencing is trustworthy not only because the actualization tendency in part has a social direction; it is trustworthy because, in addition, it is receptive and, when operating fully, can contain within it the meaning of the social realities that it experiences.

Congruence

The concept of congruence is a construct descriptive of the *integrity* of the neonate and the psychologically mature adult. It describes a situation of being in contact with and reliance upon the organismic valuing process.[17] It is descriptive of a process of spontaneously living and acting out of the depths of organismic experiencing. (The infant, in his immediate and spontaneous experiencing of his likes and dislikes, is the paradigm of this concept. Popularly understood, congruence refers to the process of "following your own feelings.") A person is said to be congruent if he can admit, in principle, any of his organismic feelings into his self-awareness for symbolization.[18] *Incongruence* is understood to be a situation in which organismic experiencing is denied or given only distorted admittance and symbolization in awareness because the self-concept subceives the experience as threatening or contradictory.[19] The incongruent person is not in spontaneous reliance upon his organismic experiencing process because some of his feelings are inadmissible to awareness. In contrast, the psychologically mature or adjusted adult is like the infant in that he has full access to the flow of this experiencing process with the *added* capacity to symbolize this experiencing and incorporate it into his self-concept.[20]

The concept of congruence is related closely to the concept of *openness to experience*. Openness to experience is descriptive of the process of allowing the fluid and ever-changing process of organismic experiencing to flow into awareness.[21] When a person is open to experience, the organismic valuing process more adequately conforms to the datum of external reality than when it is encumbered by constructs imposed by a rigid self-concept. When a person is congruent, psychologically mature, and open to experience, he tends to perceive the world " extensionally," i.e., more in terms of reality itself.[22] When a person is incongruent, he tends to perceive the world " intensionally," i.e., he tends to " see experience in absolute and unconditional terms." [23] The incongruent person tends to overgeneralize in an effort to force reality to conform with his self-concept.

In general, client-centered theory claims that the more congruent a person is, the more integrated as well as socialized he will become by virtue of his closer reliance upon the *actualization* tendency and the process of *organismic experiencing*. For the client-centered school, the roots of the individual's capacity for autonomy, as well as his capacity for vicarious experiencing of others, are grounded directly in these two primitive realities of the human organism.

The Need for Positive Regard

The need for positive regard points to the relational and environmental prerequisites that must be present if the actualization tendency and the organismic experiencing process are to function fully and if the state of congruence is to be maintained. Drawing on the work of Stanley Standal, Rogers presents this concept as referring to a learned, but universal, need on the part of the small child to perceive that his experiencing makes a positive difference in the experiential field of another person.[24] Standal believes that a theoretical statement to this effect is needed on the basis of certain unsystematic statements made by Rogers in *Client-centered Therapy*. At several places in this earlier work,

Rogers asserts that an attitude which conveys a deep respect for the worth and dignity of each individual is necessary for positive personality development and change. Standal points out that Rogers' specification of this attitude as an important prerequisite for change and development seems " to assume the existence and potency of various tendencies or ' needs' in the client." [25] Hence, he posits the need for positive regard as defined above.

Generalizations About Man's Capacity for Wholeness

Our consideration of the four client-centered constructs discussed above issues in certain generalizations about the essential nature of man. In general, these principles suggest that the neonate and the psychologically mature adult are both basically *trustful* and *trustworthy*. Man is basically trustful of his environment and the " others " in his environment. The actualization tendency, when understood under the rubric of " stimulus hunger," demonstrates that adient or approach orientations (trust) are prior to and more fundamental than coping behavior (manipulation) or abient (avoidance) orientations (distrust). In addition, the human organism is trustworthy in that it can avail itself adequately of resources for growth and change, i.e., positive regard, when these conditions are sufficiently present.

Human Brokenness: The Nature of Incongruence

It is against this background of the client-centered vision of health and wholeness that we can begin to understand its view of human brokenness or incongruence. The state of incongruence can be looked at from the standpoint of (1) how it arises, (2) how it is maintained, and (3) its general morphology.

The Rise of Incongruence

Before we can discuss the rise of incongruence, we must discuss the *rise* and *elaboration* of awareness and the self. Rogers suggests that the portion of the infant's total experiential field which seems to be under the control of the infant becomes symbolized by the pronouns " I," " me," or " myself." [26] This is how self-consciousness arises.

Although the self may rise with a primitive sense of autonomy, the self gains its *elaboration* in interaction with a social context. With the development of the awareness and symbolization of self comes the development of the need for positive regard. Since the satisfaction of this need is based upon an inference from the experiential field of the significant other, it is, as Rogers says, " often ambiguous." [27] When the infant or small child perceives that some of his self-experiences are " discriminated by significant others as being more or less worthy of positive regard," the infant tends to incorporate this evaluation into his own *regard complex.*[28] The positive regard complex of significant others can become prepotent over the organismic valuing process simply because the infant, to a large extent, is dependent upon significant others for the satisfaction of certain maintenance needs.

When the infant perceives that some self-experiences are discriminated by others as being worthy of more or less positive regard, the infant's own " self-regard becomes similarly selective." [29] As the infant grows older, his own self-regard complex tends to become independent of the significant others in his environment. Nevertheless, it still will reflect the valuations of the significant other, only independently so.[30] When this happens, it can be said that the individual has taken on the " conditions of worth " of the significant other and made them his own.[31] This often is referred to as the process of introjection.

It is easy to misunderstand this series of theoretical formulations. A clear understanding of it is dependent upon making a separation between feelings and behavior. Rogers is not suggesting that parents should have no values and make no attempt to guide or correct children. If a parent feels that a certain behavior of a child is wrong or harmful, the parent should not deny this feeling but should act on it by expressing the feeling and prohibiting the behavior. Rogers could easily agree with Dorothy Baruch's dictum that parents should accept feelings and guide behaviors and action.[32] Had Rogers devised more of his constructs in the context of child-rearing rather than therapy, he might have made more of the ego or self-building efficacy of actions firmly and warmly guided toward socially acceptable ends. But his point still is well made and valid. Value discriminations in connection with actions should not be used as conditions judging and rejecting the worth of the basic emotional equipment undergirding these behaviors.

Maintenance of the State of Incongruence

The incongruent person maintains and defends his sense of worth by selectively distorting or denying symbolization to all experiences that seem to contradict his conditions of worth.[33] Rogers' theory of defense has been influenced by the research of R. A. Hogan. On the basis of Hogan's work, Rogers uses the word " threat " to refer to the objective situation that exists when a person perceives or subceives an experience as incongruent with the structure of the self.[34] Anxiety is the subjective *inner* state of uneasiness about which the person is aware when an objectively threatening experience is subceived. In defining anxiety as a threat to the self's conditions of worth, Rogers is agreeing with Adler, Goldstein, Horney, and Rollo May in their tendency to see anxiety as a result of a threat to a value that the self holds as necessary for its existence rather than a threat to an instinctual impulse. Rogers has made even more explicit than these writers the idea that anxiety is a response to a threat not only to a value associated with the self's " existence " or " safety " but also to a value associated with the self's " worth." This will have important implications for later discussions of the relation of incongruence, as Rogers defines it, and sin.

Rogers' theory of defense entails a differentiation between subception and perception. *Subception* is an experimentally based construct formulated by McCleary and Lazarus to signify discrimination without awareness.[35] Rogers defines it to mean " that the organism can discriminate a stimulus and its meaning for the organism without utilizing the higher nerve centers involved in awareness." [36] *Perception,* on the other hand, occurs when an organismic experiencing receives symbolization in awareness.[37] Hence, anxiety may be the only thing *perceived* by consciousness when organismic experiencing discriminates an experiencing that is threatening to the self's conditions of worth. The defensive maneuvers of the self only reduce awareness of the threat. They do not reduce the threat itself.[38] When the tension between conditions of worth and denied experiences becomes too great, the gestalt of the self may collapse and a psychotic break occur.[39]

General Structure of the State of Incongruence

In more general terms, incongruence seems to be a matter of *estrangement, death, bondage, justification,* and *idolatry.*
Incongruence, as a discrepancy between the self-concept

and organismic experiencing, is a matter of *estrangement*. It is an estrangement of the self from the larger experiential life of the organism as a whole. There is an estrangement between the "owned" and "disowned" aspects of an individual's experiential field. For example, the self may own its experience of love but disown its experience of anger. The reverse may be the case. The result of this selective symbolization is conflict and estrangement. Incongruence always leads to estrangement between people. When experiences of other people seem to contradict present conditions of worth, the self will defend against the experiences and either deny or distort the experience, and in so doing, deny or distort his relation to the other person to which his experience refers.

The estrangement of incongruence leads to a modified duality of energy systems within the individual. Energy that would have been used for the actualization of the organism as a whole is diverted from this source and channeled into the actualization and defense of the self and its conditions of worth.[40] Such a diffusion of energy that results from the maintenance of two motivational systems and the utter burning off of energy that results from the tension between them leads to a kind of psychological *death*, a depletion of energy and the source of life.[41] Examples of this kind of psychological death are seen in therapy where highly incongruent clients often demonstrate a dearth of spontaneity both in their actions and their symbolizations.

Incongruence is also a matter of *bondage*. The organism as a whole becomes, in a sense, bound to the self and its conditions of worth. The conditions of worth must be maintained if the self is to appear acceptable to itself. Life becomes an endless round of threat, defense, and perceptual distortion. The energy that would be used normally for the actualization of the organism as a whole becomes rechanneled and put into the service of the self and its conditions. This power and energy, in turn, is used to "fend off" experiences that are contradictory to these conditions of worth. Experiences that would reshape the self and its conditions are never allowed to gain undistorted admittance into awareness. The perceptual distortions of the defenses make it impossible for the individual to avail himself of resources for growth because they are misperceived before they can be used as such.

And lastly, incongruence is always a matter of *justification*. This is to say that incongruence is always a result of an attempt on the part of the self and its conditions of worth to render itself worthy and acceptable. It is precisely the character of the incongruent person to believe that his existence is justified only under certain conditions. In reality, a particularly incongruent person may feel very unacceptable. Holding certain conditions of worth and feeling that he does not measure up to them, he may feel quite unworthy. But it is precisely in the light of the conditions that he does hold that he feels himself to be so unjustified.[42]

Finally, this attempt to justify oneself through one's conditions of worth is always a matter of absolutizing something finite and relative. This is the essence of the meaning of "intentional" perception. Absolutizing relative values, as we will see later, is always a matter of *idolatry* from the perspective of Christian theology.

THE STRUCTURE OF THE HEALING RELATIONSHIP

The task of this section of the chapter is to set forth the client-centered view of the essence of the psychotherapeutic relationship. By the word "essence," I mean to refer to the invariant elements in any relationship between two people that are prerequisite for favorable personality change. By "invariant," I do not mean static or unchanging. The essential elements of therapy are invariant in the sense that they are invariably present in every healing relationship. The word "structure" could just as easily be used as the word "essence" and would suggest that these always-present elements have some pattern, form, inner relationship, or inner gestalt, which is in some way intelligible, discernible or analyzable. At the same time, the word "structure" does not imply quite all the meanings of the word "essence." The word "essence" does suggest that there is or may be a difference between what is fundamental, or basic, in the sense of indispensable and that which is less than fundamental, or basic, and therefore, in some instances, dispensable. To illustrate this, let me give an example. If, in a certain psychotherapeutic relationship, the patient or client were to get violent and attack the therapist with the intent to hurt the therapist physically, the therapist might in this instant have to resort to defending himself with such vigor that he would in turn do physical damage to the client. Hurting the client, it might then follow, would not be necessarily an essential element in any good psychotherapeutic relation. It would only be a provisional, means-end element designed to keep the client from finally, if not fatally, dissolving the relationship. In view of this, the essential element of the relationship might be the therapist's strength and commitment to endure the attack of the client and keep the relationship intact. His defense and the physical damage that follow it would be only a peripheral and provisional element of the relation that might be *totally absent* from the next relationship. Hence, it would not be an invariant or always-present element in the psychotherapeutic relationship in that it is not present in some instances of healing. In view of these distinctions, it must be said that we will be attempting, in this section of the chapter, to discern the *essential structure* of the therapeutic relation, i.e., the pattern, form, or inner gestalt of those absolutely necessary (in the sense of always present) elements in every healing-producing relation. The methodological importance of this approach to the psychotherapeutic process for the explicit purposes of this study will become clear in Chapter VI.

Is There an Essential Structure to Therapy?

Within recent years certain empirical studies have been made which suggest that there may be an essence to the psychotherapeutic relation, an essence that underlies all the best therapeutic relations, regardless of school, be it Adlerian, Freudian, Rogerian, etc. These studies suggest that all good therapeutic relations tend to be more alike than different. Fred Fiedler's 1949 study discovered that representatives from different therapeutic schools tended to establish about the same kind of therapeutic relationship. When representatives from the Freudian, Adlerian, and client-centered school threw a Q-sort according to their understanding of the ideal therapeutic relationship, the results demonstrated a high correlation. And when the correlations were factor analyzed, only one item emerged as characteristic of the ideal relationship — " the therapist is able to participate completely in the patient's communication." In the second half of the study, it was found that experts from different schools were more similar in the kind of relationship they developed with their clients than were nonexperts from the same school. This seems to suggest that there is one truly therapeutic relationship which all good therapists develop regardless of different theoretical formulations about the process of therapy.[43]

Necessary and Sufficient Conditions for Personality Change

Such studies as Fiedler's have convinced Rogers and his school that therapy is an orderly process and that the necessary and sufficient conditions for favorable personality change can be specified. Rogers lists six conditions for personality change, five of which are descriptive of the therapeutic relation and can be understood to represent what we have referred to as the essence of the therapeutic relationship. These six principles are set forth in shorthand form as follows: [44]

1. That two persons are in *contact*.
2. That the first person, whom we shall term the client, is in a state of *incongruence*, being *vulnerable*, or *anxious*.
3. That the second person, whom we shall term the therapist, is *congruent* in the *relationship*.
4. That the therapist is *experiencing unconditional positive regard* toward the client.
5. That the therapist is *experiencing* an *empathic* understanding of the client's *internal frame of reference*.
6. That the client *perceives*, at least to a minimal degree, conditions four and five, the *unconditional positive regard* of the therapist for him, and the *empathic* understanding of the therapist.

Proposition two does not concern us directly because it does not deal with the therapeutic relationship. Yet it points to the fact that, unless the client *feels anxious* to some degree, he is not likely to seek a helping relationship. Such a principle suggests that in the background of every candidate for therapy there is some kind of judgmental experience which has converted his vulnerability to overt anxiousness. This will have important implications for later developments of our argument.

When Rogers says that for therapy to occur, two people must be in " contact," he means by this that they must be in " psychological contact." [45] This principle is significant because it serves to emphasize the importance of the human relationship for therapeutic change. Rogers considers that two people are in contact when " each makes a perceived or subceived difference in the experiential field of the other." [46] This suggests two important concepts to be referred to later in our study. First, a relationship cannot exist unless there is a felt difference in the experiential field of both the client as well as the therapist. Second, a relationship can exist between two people, even though it may be unconscious and only subceived by one or the other party.

Proposition three deals with the congruence of the therapist. Since the concept of congruence refers more to the therapist's relationship to himself than it is descriptive of his relationship with the client, we will discuss it under the fourth question to be brought to Rogers' constructs — the question of the character of the therapeutic agent.

The Relationship as Positive Regard

A person is receiving unconditional positive regard if he perceives that of his self-experiences " none can be discriminated by the other individual as more or less worthy of positive regard." [47] By self-experience, Rogers means any experience the organism is having that is also an actual or potential datum of symbolization by the self.

Positive regard does not entail the attitude of approval. To illuminate the concept of unconditional positive regard further, Rogers also refers to the concept of prizing — a term borrowed from Dewey and introduced into client-centered theory by John Butler. Prizing is differentiated from the attitude of appraising. To appraise is to evaluate some of another person's experiencings as more praiseworthy, more important, more valuable, and more worthy of concern and interest than other of his experiencings.[48] An attitude of prizing is an active and spirited process of valuation that values by discriminating *all* of another's self-experiences as important and worthy of respect.

Both prizing and unconditional positive regard are later refinements of the concept of *acceptance*. Acceptance often was defined ambiguously in early client-centered literature, and in spite of Rogers' own specific protests, tended to conjure up images of permissive, uninvolved, almost laissez-faire passivity. If interpreted in the light of these later constructs, acceptance is still a respectable term to describe the therapeutic relation.

An additional facet of the nature of acceptance is brought out in one of Rogers' essays in *On Becoming a Person*. Here he talks of acceptance as the client's perception that he is " fully received." A client is received psychologically if he senses that all that he is and feels at any one moment, whether it is " fear, despair, insecurity, or anger," is being admitted into the experiencing of the therapist.[49] A person is receiving unconditional positive regard when he is being received into the organismic experiencing of the therapist without being misperceived by the secondary distorting and denying operations of the conditions of worth. If the therapist has unacknowledged and uncontrolled conditions of worth, he may subceive a feeling that the client expresses but he will not be able to *receive* the feeling fully into his own experiencing processes, both at the organismic and conscious level.[50] Hence, acceptance or unconditional positive regard is a process of relating fully (in the sense of experiencing fully) the feelings that the client expresses.

Standal asserts that the possession of conditions of worth is the most basic block to the right discrimination or full experiencing of the client's feelings. But there are also other blocks or impediments. It may be difficult for the therapist to grasp the feelings of the client because the therapist lacks appropriate *evocable responses* — experiences that the therapist has had himself which would enable him to capture and symbolize what the client is expressing.[51] The therapist might have difficulty symbolizing the client's feelings if he lacked appropriate *inferential signs*. An example of this might be seen in the case of an English-speaking therapist talking to a French-speaking client. The therapist might not know how to match feelings and signs, or how to infer feelings on the basis of signs or signs on the basis of feelings.[52] The therapist might have difficulty symbolizing the experiences of the client if he lacked the appropriate *expressive signs,* which might occur, for example, if a therapist understood French but could not speak it.[53] As crippling as these handicaps might be, it is possible for the therapist to be conscious of these limitations and to work to overcome them. Then he can refer to those feelings of his client with which he is unfamiliar as " this feeling " and be open to further references to it. Or he may attempt to learn the private language of the client.[54] The ultimate barrier to a full experiencing of the client is having conditions of worth that always will lead the therapist to experience the client ambiguously, either by feeling one thing and symbolizing another or by feeling one thing and ignoring, disowning, or denying it in awareness.

Unconditioned positive regard, as a refinement of the

earlier concept of acceptance, is a construct descriptive of a mode of relationship that will acknowledge the client as a person of " worth and significance." In *Client-centered Therapy,* Rogers calls this assumption about the worth of the individual the " philosophical hypothesis " upon which the client-centered counselor works.[55] The concept of acceptance or unconditional positive regard, understood as a nonselective, nonevaluative, nondistorting, and full experiencing of the feelings of the other person, is thought to communicate best such a faith in the client's worth and significance as a person.

The Relationship as Empathy

In order to understand the concept of empathy, we must first understand the concept of " internal frame of reference." Rogers defines this to mean the subjective world of an individual which is " available to the awareness of the individual at a given moment." [56] It includes the full range of stimuli, feelings, and meanings perceived or perceivable in awareness.

Rogers defines empathy as a process of perceiving " the internal frame of reference of another with accuracy, and with the emotional components and meanings which pertain thereto, as if one were the other person, but without ever losing the ' as if ' condition." [57] It is important to emphasize the feeling or experiencing element. Rogers writes that the therapist must be " *experiencing* an empathic understanding of the client's internal frame of reference." [58] Empathy has a peculiarly emotional and vicarious character in which, as Rogers puts it, we " sense the hurt or pleasure of another as he senses it." [59] Knowing the client empathically is distinguished sharply by the client-centered school from knowing the client from an " external frame of reference." Knowing the client externally means knowing him from the standpoint of some preestablished theoretical framework or set of diagnostic categories.[60]

There is some discussion in the client-centered school as to the exact meaning of empathy. Gendlin believes that a good client-centered response is one that gives some symbolization to a feeling which the client can refer to consciously but to which he cannot give conscious and/or adequate symbolization.[61] This is to say that a good response, one that still stays within the individual's internal frame of reference, attempts to name the *implicit meaning* in an unsymbolized but consciously referred to feeling. By reflecting the implicit meaning of the feeling, Gendlin can say that he is still within the internal frame of reference of the client. But internal frame of reference has grown to mean " consciously felt but not necessarily consciously symbolized."

Gendlin's formulation has the advantage of being reconcilable with the implication of the concept of acceptance and unconditional positive regard. According to this construct, because the therapist has few or no conditions of worth, the therapist can accept *more* of the client's experiencing than the client can accept himself.[62] Otherwise, if the therapist stays solely within the client's valuations conveyed in his consciously held sign behavior, the therapist would reflect the client's experiencing according to the client's conditions of worth. This implies that the therapist actually would identify with the client's conditions of worth and would support them. And if this were the case, the therapist subtly would be helping the client disown or continue to distort his experiencing. Although Rogers does not address the issue explicitly, he seems to side with Gendlin when he suggests that the therapist brings a " new quality " to the denied and distorted experiences of the client — a new quality that simply accepts that which to the client has seemed " threatening, impossible, disorganized." [63] Gendlin's way of formulating therapy does not go so far as to introduce external categories of interpretation. In accepting the feeling that the client can accept only partially or distortedly, the therapist still attempts to accept it according to the feeling's own implicit meaning. But, as Gendlin points out, this becomes very close to what many analytically oriented therapists believe to be the character of a good " interpretation." [64]

It is clear that when unconditional postive regard and empathy are brought into proximity, their distinction nearly disappears. To empathize with another's feelings *is* to affirm one's interest in and positive regard for the other person. It communicates the idea that " I care enough for your feelings to attempt to share them with you." On the other hand, unconditional positive regard is receiving the feelings of another without blocking this reception with inhibiting or rejecting defensiveness that would obscure their uniqueness. Although the Rogerians do not do this, for our purposes, to point to this close relationship between these two constructs, we often will refer to them with the phrase " unconditional empathic acceptance."

Of course, it should go without being said that in a real-life therapeutic situation, we do not find unconditioned empathic acceptance. All too often the therapist does have conditions of worth that qualify his capacity to so receive the client. In addition, the limitations of finitude, the phasic rise and fall of our own maintenance needs, and limitations in time are qualifying factors. It is true that the structure of unconditioned empathic acceptance could be descriptive only of a superhuman person. The point of adding the term " unconditioned " is to demonstrate that the extent to which empathic acceptance can remain invariant and constant is the extent to which it can be efficacious. It is precisely the concept of perfection which it suggests to us that we want to consider for the purposes of this study. Certainly a good therapist is one who would admit that such a perfect unconditioned empathic acceptance is not a possibility for him. To act as though it were would render the therapist pompous and unrealistic. But this does not negate the facts that empathic acceptance is the " model " for a proper understanding of the healing relationship and that the kind of perfection it suggests is precisely what we mean to apply to our understanding of the nature of God upon which an adequate doctrine of the atonement can be based.

The Necessity for Congruence: The Character of the Therapeutic Agent

Now it is time to turn to the question of the " character " of the therapeutic agent. The third proposition in Rogers' list of necessary and sufficient conditions for therapeutic change best addresses this issue. The proposition states that for therapy to occur, " the second person, whom we shall term the therapist, is congruent in the relationship."

Congruence in Absolute Terms

If a therapist is absolutely congruent, all his feelings or experiencings, whether actual or potential, can be integrated, in principle, into conscious symbolization. The thrust of this construct is to suggest that there is no artificial way in which a therapist can develop a relationship of acceptance and empathic understanding. Acceptance and empathic understanding must flow from and be rooted in the foundation of all psychological life — organismic experiencing. When the concept is understood in absolute terms, it suggests that the nearer the therapist gets to a total reliance upon organismic experiencing uninterrupted by conditions of worth in the self, the nearer one will get to a full acceptance and empathic feeling of the other person. The more congruence, the more *openness to experience* and the more *extensional* are our perceptions. This means that the fewer our conditions of worth, the more we tend to see the other in terms of his own uniqueness rather than according to our own constructs.

A recent book by Robert L. Katz entitled *Empathy: Its Nature and Uses* agrees with the client-centered position that empathy correlates with the extent to which one relies on the more primitive bases of psychological life. Empathy, he asserts, entails lowering ego defense. It involves a regression of the ego to include more primary process, or what Rogerians would call organismic experiencing. The empathic person must assimilate a degree of childlikeness.[65] This corresponds with the Rogerian assertion that congruence is characteristic of both the neonate and the psychologically mature adult, the difference being that the adult — although like the child in that he must be low in conditions of worth — would have an autonomous self-concept.

A self-concept with no conditions of worth would specify the character of the ideal therapist. How this kind of self-structure or character aids therapy may become more intelligible if we recall the concept of stimulus hunger. According to Rice and Butler's interpretation of the actualization tendency, stimulus hunger is the persistent drive for new experience which is the primitive base of all approach behavior and social interaction. What these authors fail to point out, but is implicit in their formulation, is that stimulus hunger is also the primitive base for the kind of full experiencing characteristic of unconditional positive regard. In addition, because stimulus hunger is an end in itself and not a means to the satisfaction of a deeper need, perception dominated by it is less selective and more open to the uniqueness of other objects than is perceptual activity dominated by survival needs and conditions of worth. Hence, when stimulus hunger is uninhibited, perception is more empathic.

There is a great similarity between the concept of stimulus hunger and what Maslow calls growth motivation. Perception motivated by growth motivations is more ideographic, more extensional, more world- and self-validating, and therefore, more empathic.[66] In the light of these concepts, it becomes clear how an autonomous self-regard complex, with fewer conditions of worth and more congruence with basic organismic experiencing, can heighten unconditioned empathic acceptance. It also becomes possible to understand the motivation the therapist brings to his work. Since the therapy entails a deep commerce with the feeling of another person, it would be profoundly fulfilling to the therapist's own hunger for new and varied experience.

Congruence Viewed in Relative Terms

Although unconditioned positive regard and empathy should increase as congruence increases, it may well be that at certain midpoints along a continuum, congruence would lead to the experiencing of rejecting and nonempathic feelings. The therapist's attempt to be congruent means attempting to symbolize these feelings too. This does not mean that the therapist should express these feelings in open communication with the client. Rogers suggests that these feelings should be expressed only if the therapist finds himself persistently focused on his own feelings rather than on those of the client.[67] The important point is that, in general, client-centered theory suggests that although the therapist's attempt to be congruent may lead him to experience and symbolize rejecting, threatening, and nonempathic feelings, the more perfectly he approaches pure congruence in a relationship with a client and eliminates his own conditions of worth, the more completely will he accept and empathize with the client.

Condition Six: The Client's Perception of Acceptance and Empathy

Rogers' last proposition about the necessary conditions for personality change states that for therapy to occur, the client must " perceive, at least to a minimal degree," the unconditional positive regard and empathy of the therapist for him. The important point of the proposition is its emphasis upon the perception of these elements by the client. It is not enough to say that these elements must be communicated; to some extent they must be perceived by the person needing help.

It is not altogether clear as to the importance of verbal communication in client-centered theory. Earlier client-centered theory was characterized by a great emphasis upon a nondirective " reflection " of the client's feelings and verbal expressions.[68] This is still very much a part of client-centered thinking, but its importance has tended to become subordinate to the relationship itself. Experiences in play therapy and experiences with highly inarticulate people have tended to suggest that therapeutic change may occur even though verbal communication can be minimal or nonexistent.[69]

The Essence of Therapeutic Change

The essence of therapeutic change is the conscious *experiencing* and symbolization of denied, distorted, rejected, and disowned feelings. In an article entitled " The Essence of Psychotherapy," Rogers lists four characteristics to this moment of experiencing around which personality change occurs. First, it occurs "in this existential moment." It is not a thinking about something; it is an "experience of something at this instant, in the relationship." Second, "it is an experiencing which is without barriers, or inhibitions, or holding back." Third, it is an experience that "has been repeated many times in [the] past, but which has never been completely experienced." Fourth, "this experience has the quality of being acceptable." [70] Rogers calls this moment of experiencing a "molecule" of personality change and believes that there are series of such moments strung out through the therapy process.

Gendlin, in a paper entitled "A Process View of Relationships," sets this moment of experiencing in the context of the therapeutic relationship in which it occurs. He starts out with the principle that a person is a "process in interaction with an environment." [71] He defines a process as a flow of energy with an open end so that the energy can go someplace. The feelings that an individual has are always feelings toward something or someone. These feelings can be in process and flow if the "further end" of the process, i.e., the object or person toward which the feeling is expressed, will receive it. If the further end of the process is closed, the feeling tends to become blocked up, inhibited, and is what Gendlin calls a "potential feeling." It is within this framework, Gendlin believes, that the efficacy of the therapeutic relationship becomes clear. He writes:

Seeing the client as a "separate" individual denies the importance of human experience in relationships. It conceives of feelings and experiences as if they were about nothing and toward nothing. Real feelings are organic and in interaction with something real. Most relationships don't permit the expression of feelings or when they do, the difference in reality that the feeling makes is different than was intended.[72]

Change in the self-structure results from *feeling a feeling through*. The therapist, as the further end of the process, can facilitate this process if, with empathic acceptance, he feels *with* the client in this process of feeling through. The therapeutic relationship will be efficacious to the extent that the therapist can receive *unconditionally* any and all of the client's feelings with empathic acceptance. *In this way the therapist helps the client accept that about himself which the client cannot accept by himself.*

Experiencing and Negative Feelings Toward the Therapist

Theoretically, no self-experience of the client should qualify the therapist's capacity to receive unconditionally with empathic acceptance the feelings of the client. This includes the negative and hostile feelings that the therapeutic situation may provoke.

How do negative and hostile feelings arise in the therapeutic situation? What causes them? How does their proper handling contribute to the success or failure of counseling? Negative feelings in the client can be provoked in a variety of ways. First, the client will react in a negative and hostile way to any event that tends to threaten his conditions of worth. This means that he will react to any word or gesture on the part of the therapist which appears to judge him. Second, the client will react in a hostile and defensive way to his own denied and distorted feelings or anything which draws them to invade his consciousness. This means that if his therapist's acceptance activates his denied experience, he will react negatively to both his disowned feelings and the therapeutic relationship that aroused them. Third, the client will respond with hostility to the therapist's unconditional positive regard. Although from one perspective the client may appreciate the safety of this acceptance, from another perspective he will experience it as quite threatening. The unconditional positive regard of the therapist contradicts the client's conditions of worth.[73] The *no* conditions of unconditional positive regard contradict the very fact that the client has conditions; it contradicts the client's conditions of worth by failing to support them. The case of Mrs. Oaks, to be analyzed later, will provide several instances of hostility illustrating these dynamics.

The negative feelings in the client, stimulated by therapy, might be explained by analytically oriented practitioners as a phenomenon of transference and resistance. Rogers agrees that even client-centered counseling can induce *transference attitudes* in the client.[74] Transference, as the generalization of attitudes held toward another important person in the client's early environment to the person of the therapist, often occurs to some degree. Rogers feels that these attitudes seldom develop into full-scale transference neuroses because they are accepted empathically in the same way that all other feelings are received.[75] In this way, it is thought, the client's attitude is reflected for what it really is — an attitude in the client and not necessarily a fact about the therapist.[76]

The resistance of the client to the therapist's unconditional positive regard is, in some sense, a transference attitude. It is a generalization to the therapist of a learned mode of defense designed to " fend off " experiences that contradict the client's own conditions of worth. As a learned mode of defense, it is not based on mechanisms like the repetition compulsion or death wish. It is a learned response to long years of experience in having one's relationship with other people qualified by conditions of worth.

Since one's conditions of worth and their defensive maneuvers are learned, to be saved from them they must be unlearned. Butler points out, in learning theory terms, that the only way to overcome the client's tendency to react with defensive hostility toward experiences which contradict his conditions of worth (including the therapist's relationship of no conditions) is for the therapist's unconditioned empathic acceptance to remain "absolutely constant." [77] It is only in this way that the client can gradually unlearn his belief that there are conditions of worth according to which he must deny and distort his experiencing.

This unconditioned and constant acceptance of the client can be based on nothing less than understanding in the sense of empathy. If the client is to be convinced that this relationship can endure even his negative reaction toward the therapist, he must perceive that this acceptance is based upon a real empathic understanding of the depth of his hostility. Otherwise, the client only can conclude, on the basis of past experience, that when the therapist does begin to understand the depths of his hostility, the relationship will be withdrawn or qualified.

An interesting example of resistance to the empathic reception of the therapist can be seen in the following description by a client of her relationship to her therapist. This excerpt came from a log the client kept during her therapy.

My first reaction to you, I think, was one of surprise at your sensitivity and awareness of what and how I was feeling, even when I expressed it very inarticulately or not at all. I knew you were quick and sensitive, but I didn't think that anyone could be *that* understanding.

Then I began to get the feeling that not only were you sensitive to and understanding of my feelings, but you also *cared* and cared very much. This is the feeling which I think I fought vigorously for the whole time. It simply emanated from you — from your hands as you handled the cigarette lighter, from your foot as you stretched it out in front of me and moved it back and forth and particularly from your eyes. . . . Because of the strength of this feeling, I usually found it necessary to talk to the wall or the window, but I was always painfully and acutely aware of you. . . . Throughout all my sessions I was focused on my relationship with you. Whenever I made any attempt to pull away from it, to discuss other relationships on an intellectual plane, I felt compelled to come back to you. I simply could not shake you. I was firmly convinced that to give love meant to sell my soul, to become completely dominated by and dependent upon the loved one, and that love could not be received without paying this high price. Therefore, I fought desperately against any love you might give me. I tried telling you how unworthy I was — how selfish, inadequate, nasty. I tried hating and attacking you. You could not possibly love me; therefore you were being deceitful and cruel in pretending you did. I even tried " curing " myself and raving about how wonderful it was. But you were always there, like a firm rock which I beat upon to no avail and which merely said clearly that your love did not control me and I could not control it.

Later on she describes further her discomfort in perceiving the empathic acceptance of the therapist and her final breakthrough in accepting this acceptance.

Gradually the goal or end of my search became a light which was working its way to the surface (as I worked down to it). Last week it was right under the surface. I had one more layer to remove. I talked, intellectually, of my feeling of being unloved from birth. I gave several examples and tried to pin down and explain my feelings in relation to these examples. As I talked I kept getting more and more uncomfortable because you seemed to be *feeling much more strongly than I did* [italics mine]. Then I began to feel that you weren't even listening to what I was saying, *but you were feeling all the things I was feeling, even more than I was* aware of feeling [italics mine], and you were *caring*. Suddenly I felt as if I had become a baby and was being held comfortably, securely, with warm understanding and a great love in my mother's arms. Then I realized that that was what I had missed and that was what I wanted now and had wanted all my life. I also realized that I had just been loved that way and that I could never have discovered what was lacking until I had experienced it — completely. Now I could stand on my sand dune and reach across to you on your dune, my father on his dune, my mother on her dune, and all the others in my life that I wanted to love. We could all join hands and run down into the lake. However, the feeling I felt was one of joy, not the desperate ecstasy previously felt when I was alone on my dune.[78]

The therapist's capacity to remain constant like a " firm rock " and receive the negative feelings of the client with empathic caring, to feel these feelings even more deeply than the client, was a crucial factor in helping the client continue in her experiencing process. These two aspects are an *active-passive* process. The therapist's unconditional positive regard emerges as an *active* process of positively caring for what the client is feeling. Empathy emerges as a *passive* process of participating in and feeling with the experiencing of the client. The two together combine into a single relationship to which the term " unconditional empathic acceptance " can be applied.

The Outcome of Experiencing

In Rogers' chapter in Koch's symposium he lists fifteen different aspects of the outcome of a successful therapeutic experience. All these outcomes follow from the client's increased capacity to experience fully, both at the organismic and the conscious level, those aspects of himself which were formerly unacceptable. Nearly all of these fifteen outcomes have been measured operationally by various objective mea-

sures. The client-centered school probably has done more research than any other school of psychotherapy. Much of this
research can be found in the Rogers and Dymond volume.[79]
TAT, Rorschach, self Q-sorts, counselor and client ratings,
Willoughby Emotional-Maturity Scale, have been admin-
istered to great numbers of clients to determine what kinds
of changes actually take place in therapy. In general, when
the client, through the therapist's empathic acceptance, learns
to accept and experience what was earlier unacceptable, the
deeper actualization tendencies of the organism are liberated
from the self and its conditions of worth; the self becomes
more congruent with experience; physiological and psychological tensions are reduced; anxiety and threat are lessened;
the locus of evaluation tends to become more autonomous;
self and ideal self move closer together; perceptions are
more realistic, extensional, less defensive; positive regard and
acceptance of others increase; more positive self-regard is
experienced; and more creativity and problem-solving capacity are present.

Rogers does not always make clear the extent to which his
therapy becomes ego or reality therapy toward its later stages.
The client begins to do away with maladaptive ego functions and starts learning new ones. Therapy becomes a place
where he rehearses behaviors and evaluates consequences.
Conditioning therapists would insist that there must be a
subtle process of extinction and reinforcement operating in
client-centered therapy which is not acknowledged in the
theory. Of course, it can be said that unconditioned positive
regard is a kind of operant conditioning, prizing (reward-
ing) the client as he faces and symbolizes denied experiences. To some extent this may be true, as Sidney Jourard
has suggested.[80] But it is important to realize that this prizing
behavior is unselective, except insofar as it attempts to stay

on the growing edge, constantly moving into wider and wider areas of denied and distorted experience. Client-centered therapy's faith in the capacities of the self to symbolize experience makes it feel that the self can accomplish its own relearning process. It is the therapist's task, through his positive regard and empathy, to help the client have sufficient data (feelings and accurate symbols) with which to pursue his job of learning appropriate ego functions and behaviors.

The Case of Mrs. Oaks

The case of Mrs. Oaks is something of a classic in the literature of the client-centered movement. Rogers gives an extensive commentary on a verbatim report of the case in *Psychotherapy and Personality Change.* On the basis of measures derived from the TAT, Willoughby Emotional-Maturity Scale, Q-sort, and other tests, her therapy was considered a clear success. Growth was evident in all areas except with regard to some difficulties with sexual constriction, and movement was discernible even here. Her presenting problem was a psychosomatic illness in her daughter for which she felt responsible. Mrs. Oaks is described as a person with little formal education, though intelligent and widely read.[81]

First Through Sixth Interviews

In these early interviews we will notice the rather dramatic and rapid way in which Mrs. Oaks moves from merely talking about her problems in an intellectual way to a direct experiencing of denied and distorted feelings. By the third interview, we see an example of how a client can experience an old feeling, but more fully and with greater vividness than before. She discovers a new sense of "feeling sorry" and compares it to former feelings.

C.: . . . I — I really felt terribly sorry for something, a kind of grief. And found myself comparing it with, with things I had felt before, I — I . . . When Peggy was ill and I had felt this terrible anxiety and what I thought was a terrible kind of grief, I realize now it wasn't. It was a kind of hysterical feeling.

Within a few interviews, Mrs. Oaks describes this process of feeling or experiencing new aspects of herself as something almost physical, something very different from an intellectual process.

(Fifth interview) C.: . . . And I mean I pick up little pieces [of her self-experience] with absolutely no meaning except I mean the — the feeling that you get from simply handling them without seeing them as a pattern, but just from the touch I probably feel, " Well, it is going to fit some place here."

In the sixth interview she compares the physical and sensuous aspect of this experiencing process to the way blind people learn to read Braille — with " their fingers."

Eleventh and Twelfth Interviews

In the eleventh interview, Mrs. Oaks expresses some real resentment toward the therapist. It is interesting to note that her resentment toward him is tied up closely with her fight to keep from facing her feelings. This is an excellent illustration of our earlier point that negative reactions toward one's own feelings and toward the therapist are tied in closely together.

T.: Therefore you'll forget all this first, but it kind of refuses to stay forgotten. (Long pause.)

C.: Well, it certainly refuses to stay forgotten, that's for sure. (Pause of several minutes.) You're not being very helpful.

T.: (Laughs.) You say I'm not being very helpful. Hardly fair to have you look at your feelings, hm?

C.: (Pause.) Well, actually for the sake of getting . . . I was actually really sitting here just pushing feelings away, sort of catching onto little bits of nothing.

T.: Really quite busy pushing out the feelings, keeping them from flowing in.

C.: M-hm. I mean that is something that just happened now.

T.: Yeah, that's what I mean.

C.: I was feeling a mild resentment because you weren't being very helpful. (A moment after this exchange she continues on the same theme.)

C.: (Several minutes pause.) This is a bad day. One of these days when (words lost) I don't want the responsibility and you won't take it.

T.: M-hm. Kind of rough going, and you feel it should be, whatever takes place should be deep. And yet here I don't take the responsibility for guiding that. And you're fearful of taking it on yourself.

C.: Yeah, I—I . . . that's a little mild. I don't want to take it.

T.: Don't want to.

C.: I don't want to. And I—I'm just resentful that you . . .

T.: M-hm. Really more the feeling toward me, "You *ought to* take this over."

C.: Yeah, that's right. You don't help one damn little bit.

T.: Feel really quite deeply resentful that I don't . . . (Yeah) . . . take it on.

C.: That's right. Probably do me good. I don't know. (Pause.) I think it would be very nice if I could just dump the responsibility . . . you see today I just do not *want* to accept responsibility for my own feelings. I just don't *want* to examine them.

T.: To hell with being responsible for my feelings today. I don't want to look at them. I don't want to be responsible for them. Somebody else can do it.

The therapist's response to this hostility and resentment is one of empathic reception. Mrs. Oaks is angry with him because his constant attentiveness to her feelings has led her to experiencing her feelings more fully than before. But when she expresses the feeling of resentment toward him for being so constantly attentive, he attends to, positively regards, and empathizes with this feeling also.

It was close to this period that Mrs. Oaks felt most disorganized and most incongruent. In theoretical terms, her vulnerability had developed into consciously felt threat and anxiousness. The "disorganization of structure" she referred to would be considered as the breaking up of the self's conditions of worth. It is in passages such as this that we can gain some idea of the process of judgment. It appears that judgment is being felt by Mrs. Oaks in two ways. First, there is the internal contradiction between her felt experiences and her conditions of worth. Second, there is the contradiction between the self's conditions and the felt experience of the therapist's acceptance in which there are no conditions placed on the relationship.

Twenty-sixth Through Thirty-fourth Interviews

One of the turning points in Mrs. Oaks' therapy comes in the twenty-sixth interview, when she discovers how deeply the therapist *cares*.

C.: Well, I made a very remarkable discovery. I know it's . . . (Laughs.) I found out that you actually *care* how this thing goes. (Both laugh.) It gave me the feeling, it's sort of well . . . maybe-I'll-let-you-get-in-the-act sort of thing. It's . . . again you see, on an examination sheet, I would have had the correct answer, I mean . . . but it suddenly dawned on me that in the . . . client-counselor kind of thing, you *actually care* what happens to this thing. And it was a . . . revelation, a . . . well . . . the closest I can come to it is a kind of relaxation, a . . . not letting down, but a . . . (Pause) more of a kind of straightening out without tension if that means anything. I don't know.

T.: Sounds as though it isn't as though this was a new idea, but it was a new *experience* of really *feeling* that I did care and if I get the rest of that, sort of a willingness on your part to let me care.

But this very meaningful interview is followed by one in which Mrs. Oaks again expresses her anger at the therapist. It should be noticed that she accuses the therapist of adding " nothing to her status." In theoretical terms this seems to be saying that the therapist's relationship fails to support and therefore, in some sense, contradicts her conditions of worth. This is a striking instance in which the therapist's relationship of " no " conditions contradicts and puts a judgment upon her conditions.

(Thirty-first interview.) C.: You know, I sort of have a feeling that . . . (Pause.) I'm sort of in the middle of . . . an experience, of a growth process. Well, not of conflict. There's a feeling that . . . I've got to go forward simply because I can't go back. But if I . . . were given a choice . . . I mean, if it were something of more or less . . . well, something I were buying, I might very much be tempted to go back.

T.: You feel very betwixt and between them. It somehow seems almost impossible to go back. Yet, if that were really a free choice between going backward and forward, there's lots to be said for going back. (Pause.)

C.: M-hm. (Long pause: 2 minutes, 15 seconds.) I don't know. I'm aw — quite upset. I just can't look at it yet. (Pause.)

A minute later.

C.: I don't know just why this comes out, but maybe if it's out, maybe it'll help. Maybe it'll be just curtains. Mean, I am sure

I never did . . . t-tell you my past . . . I mean, I just realized it myself . . . weapon that I had. I mean my surefire resistance that always worked for me. And it's that fact that I can say this, this proves what a . . . the kind of climate this is. But I always get the feeling, and it's . . . always directed to you. You don't add a damn thing to my status. And it's always helped me to . . . now that I've said, maybe it just won't work any more, you see.

T.: At this point there's always very strongly the feeling, "You don't add a damn thing!"

C.: That's right. Not a damn thing to my status somehow to . . . (Pause.)

T.: Sounds like a feeling of annoyance and pulling away.

C.: M-hm.

T.: A little bit of resentment.

C.: Course, now that I've caught on to it, it's not going to work too well.

T.: Kinda spoils it as a weapon.

This section clearly illustrates many of the points made in our theoretical discussion. First, it demonstrates that the resistance to growth, as far as Mrs. Oaks' experience goes, is in the self and its conditions of worth rather than in deeper mechanisms of repetition compulsion or death instinct. According to her experience, at this point, she is *unfree to stop growing*. She experiences something deeper than the self which is forcing her onward. Directly after this, she attacks the therapist and expresses hostility toward him. Why is she angry? Because he adds nothing to her status. This status factor, the things she has been attempting to do to justify herself, is called to her attention directly after saying that she feels that if it were up to her, she would not grow. Closely related to this status factor is her "surefire resistance " that seems to be her tendency to " pull away " in " annoyance " from those things which do not add to her status, i.e., contradict her conditions of worth. Her attack on the therapist is experienced in an ambiguous way. On one hand, she feels that it may mean " just curtains." Her attack may cause the therapist to withdraw his relationship, or in some way it may dissolve the situation. Yet she has some intimation that it won't, because, as she says, " the fact that I can say this, this proves what a . . . the kind of climate this is." But because she can admit her tendency to be " annoyed " and " pull away " from things that don't add to her " status " without disintegrating the therapist's relationship, she feels that maybe this " weapon " (defense) won't work anymore. It is in this way that she becomes freed from this weapon, this device for closing herself off to other people. In the very *same* interview she seems to be able to accept into her experiencing some of her most deeply disowned feelings. She " owns " and accepts her deep feeling of hurt and self-pity.

C.: And I have the feeling that it isn't guilt. (Pause.) (Weeps.) So . . . course I mean, I can't verbalize it yet. It's just being *terribly hurt!*

T.: M-hm. It isn't guilt except in the sense of being very much wounded somehow.

C.: (Weeping.) It's . . . you know, often I've been guilty of it myself, but in later years, when I've heard parents . . . say to their children, "Stop crying," I've had a feeling, instead I've thought it through, so that . . . I mean . . . a hurt as though, well, why should they tell them to stop crying? They feel sorry for themselves, and who can feel more adequate-a-a-adequately sorry for himself than a child. Well, that is sort of what . . . I mean, as — as though I mean, I — I thought that they should let him cry. And . . . feel sorry for him, too, maybe. In a . . .

rather objective kind of way. Well, that's . . . that's something of the kind of thing I've been experiencing. I mean, now . . . just right now. And in — in —

T.: That catches a little more the flavor of the feeling, that it's almost as if you're really weeping for yourself. . . . .

C.: And then of course, I've come to . . . to see and to feel that over this . . . see, I've covered it up. (Weeps.) But . . . and . . . I've covered it up with so much bitterness, which in turn I had to cover up (Weeps.) *That's* what I want to get rid of! I almost don't *care* if I hurt.

Two interviews later this deep feeling of hurt has been replaced partially by much more positive feelings about herself.

(Thirty-third interview.) C.: One thing worries me . . . and I'll hurry because I can always go back to it — a feeling that occasionally I can't turn out. A feeling of being quite pleased with myself. Again the Q-technique. I walked out of here one time, and impulsively I threw my first card, "I am an attractive personality"; looked at it sort of aghast but left it there, I mean, because honestly, I mean, that is exactly how it felt . . . a . . . Well, that bothered me, and I catch that now. Every once in a while a sort of pleased feeling, nothing superior, but just . . . I don't know, sort of pleased. A neatly turned away. And it bothered me. And yet . . . I wonder . . .

In the next interview, Mrs. Oaks goes beyond this feeling of being pleased with herself and talks of her experiencing of her most basic nature. As she digs deeper into herself, she just cannot find that something " terrible that she thought she was supposed to find there."

Forty-first Through Forty-eighth Interviews
    Toward the end of her therapy, Mrs. Oaks makes some remarks about the therapeutic relation that deserve looking

at. She observes that the love she has found in therapy is not a love that tries to find its justification in the object.

T.: What it really means is that . . . that love as it is culturally defined and understood is for you really fallacious because it means finding the — the reason or the justification for *yourself* in this other person.

C.: And that isn't really possible, I don't think . . . it isn't possible. Now isn't that true of therapy, am I wrong? See, I found that here somehow. Now isn't that true? . . . There might, there might be something I don't know what it is. It means there might . . . there might be a communication . . . rather than " I love you " . . . now I'm thinking, I'm talking about a therapeutic situation, I don't know . . . There might be a recognition . . . a projection . . . of this, of this, of this bit of self love that one has . . . this secretness . . . so that rather not " I love " but that " You are my love." I think that there might be something to that. I don't quite know.

This is what Mrs. Oaks thinks is crucial to therapy. The therapist does not find his justification in the client. The therapist does not say, " I love you " as if this is something that his self accomplishes. Instead, in ideal therapy, the therapists admits, " You are my love." It is something that simply is the case and something that the conscious self can neither create nor manipulate.

Other Theories of Psychotherapy

The presupposition of this review of other theories of psychotherapy is the work of Fred Fiedler referred to above. If he is right that experts of different schools are more alike in their therapeutic relations than novices of the same tradition, then there ought to be some way in which this underlying similarity, or essence, is conceptualized in the systems of the various schools. We concede that there are important and distinctive elements which the proponents of the respective traditions would not want minimized. Admitting this to be the case, let us examine some representative theories of therapy for evidences of the essential structure of psychotherapeutic relation as we have defined it with the phrase " unconditional empathic acceptance."

Freud

Freud's understanding of psychoanalytic therapy is rich and complex and has many features to it that are not emphasized in the client-centered tradition.

His early theory of analytic technique emphasized the recall of repressed memories associated with forgotten traumatic events. He employed hypnosis to facilitate recall and saw the emotional catharsis, which occurred as a consequence of this recall, as the curative event. Dissatisfactions with this approach appeared when Freud discovered that all patients were not equally susceptible to hypnosis and that the cure effected by this procedure often proved to be only temporary.

The importance of these early approaches largely lies in the discoveries that evolved from them. Freud noticed that there were resistances to the recall of traumatic memories. Secondly, he observed that thoughts tended to occur in a sequence at the end of which a disturbed content might appear. This led to the fundamental rule of therapy called free association. For analysis to proceed, each patient had to agree to verbalize every thought and feeling that came into consciousness, with no special effort to control, guide, or select which one he would discuss with his doctor. The method of free association demanded a certain corresponding attitude in the therapist designed to facilitate this process in the patient.

Freud referred to this attitude in the doctor as a kind of " evenly-hovering attention." [82] In order to encourage free association in the patient, the doctor should maintain a non-deliberate, unselective, and evenly distributed attentiveness to the totality of the patient's verbalization.

It would seem that within this attitude are rudimentary evidences of both unconditional positive regard and empathy. Certainly this kind of " hovering attentiveness " would be experienced by the patient as a kind of nonevaluative prizing. In addition, as Medard Boss has pointed out, there is something decidedly empathic and phenomenological about the unselective attitude that both doctor and patient attempt to take toward the patient's thoughts and feelings. [83] Of course, there were times when Freud recommended getting outside of the patient's internal frame of reference with responses that would interpret the patient's resistances. But he coupled this recommendation with another regarding timing. An interpretation should be made slightly prior to the moment when the patient was nearly ready to come to the insight himself. As we observed earlier, this is surprisingly close to Gendlin's recommendation that a good therapeutic response is one that symbolized what the client can feel and refer to consciously but not symbolize adequately. The end, or goal, of the two approaches is essentially the same, i.e., to help the client symbolize and bring under conscious control of the self (or ego) thoughts and feelings that formerly were rejected, repressed, or avoided. The issue becomes a matter of distinguishing between what is fundamental and what is peripheral to the therapeutic process. What heals the person — the hovering attention and prizing that frees the patient to attend to his own denied and distorted feelings, or the occasional interpretation of superego and transference resistances that further helps the patient remove momentary blocks to this process? Client-centered counseling has demonstrated that therapy can occur without interpretation, but neither school has denied the importance of the persistent, evenly distributed (unconditioned) and unselective listening that Freud called " hovering attentiveness " and that we have called " unconditioned empathic acceptance."

Adler

Even though Adler had much to say about general and special diagnosis and strongly emphasized the importance of " explaining " to the patient the meaning of his " life style " and finding convincing ways to get him to accept it, he also articulated elements similar to those we have been stressing. Adler explicitly referred to the process of empathy as a method for coming to understand the structure of a patient's style of life.[84] But upon occasion, Adler seems to go beyond this. Not only is empathy a tool for understanding, it has a certain therapeutic efficacy in-and-of-itself. Empathy is a part of man's general capacity for " social interest " and must be employed by the therapist to awaken a similar social interest in the patient. Adler writes: " We can succeed only if we are genuinely interested in the other. We must be able to see with his eyes and listen with his ears." [85] In another place he writes, " The task of the physician or psychologist is to give the patient the experience of contact with a fellow man, and then to enable him to transfer this awakened social interest to others." [86] He goes on to compare this attitude with the function of the mother whose role it is to provide a person with " the greatest experience of love and fellowship that the child will ever have." [87] This basic attitude works to give the patient an experience of " encouragement " to undergird his faltering self-esteem. We can see that this attitude functions to accomplish much the same thing as does that which the client-centered school calls unconditional positive regard. It serves to give the patient a bedrock of support (or what we will later call justification) as he ventures forth to face the unacceptable and threatening within himself.

Karl Menninger

Menninger sets forth a basically Freudian theory of the therapeutic relationship in his *Theory of Psychoanalytic Technique.* His distinctive contribution is the elaboration of a transactional model that conceives analysis as occurring in the context of a contractual relationship between doctor and patient in which both give something to the other. The doctor gives his time and expert knowledge, and the patient gives the doctor financial remuneration. This vendor-buyer contractual relationship is often confused because the patient frequently does not want from the doctor what the doctor is prepared to give, and, conversely, the doctor cannot give what the patient appears to want.

In the context of this contract, the patient is asked to free associate. The doctor's response to this is one of abstinent, yet interested, attention. The abstinence of the doctor is one that refuses to gratify the neurotic transference demands of the patient. This frustration of his transference expectations incites the patient to resort to more and more deeply regressive coping devices designed to wrest gratification and approval from the doctor. When the frustration tolerance of the patient mounts almost to the breaking point, the doctor may venture an interpretation designed to illuminate the meaning of his regressive behavior and his resistances invoked to maintain them.

All of this sounds different from the approach we have been discussing. But there are elements within Menninger's theory that appear similar to client-centered views. The attitude of unchanging interest, characteristic of unconditional positive regard, seems to be implicit in the following description of the therapist's behavior in the midst of the patient's various coping maneuvers:

All the while the analyst remains (or attempts to remain) in a detached, unchanging, stable position, so that whether the patient is up or down, whether the patient is provocative or seductive, whether the patient is angry or gay or flippant or sad, the analyst remains as he was. This constancy on the part of the analyst is unhuman, to be sure. It constantly surprises the patient because in ordinary life people respond to the behavior of others by corresponding changes. It is reassuring and encouraging to find someone who is both *interested in* [my italics] and yet unaffected by one's mood swing and one's confessions.[88]

Note that Menninger says that the analyst is supposed to be " detached " and " unaffected " but yet " interested." He goes on to say that the detachment and neutrality of the therapist does not mean " wooden aloofness." He uses Freud's own terminology to call it " a hovering attention." [89] Quite clearly, whatever Menninger may mean by detachment, he does not mean emotional disengagement. It is quite clear that analytic language does not always successfully communicate the best in analytic practice. As Medard Boss has suggested, the analytic emphasis upon objectivity and detachment is in reality its way of conceptualizing how the therapist respects the individuality of the client.[90] It must be considered as the analytic equivalent of empathy — allowing the analysand to stand before the doctor in all of his uniqueness. Hence, once again we find elements of the underlying, ever-present structure of all therapy, a subtle and dynamic interrelation of empathy and unconditional positive regard.

Daseinsanalysis

Medard Boss, in his book entitled *Psychoanalysis and Daseinsanalysis,* has discussed the nature of the psychotherapeutic relationship in some detail. A leading proponent of existential analysis, Boss draws heavily from the philosophy of Martin Heidegger and serves as a significant example of a broader movement including men like Ludwig Binswanger, J. H. Van Den Berg, F. J. Buytendijk, and, in the United States, Erwin Straus.

Although Boss is critical of Freud's biological determinism, he feels that the analytic method of free association, and the attendant attitudes it requires from the therapist, is " intrinsically harmonious " with Daseinsanalytic procedures. Existential analysis believes that healing is a matter of regaining one's capacity for " world openness." Man's humanness is composed of his capacity to be open and aware of his relations with the world — allowing these relationships to disclose themselves and come into being in the light of man's illuminating and meaning imparting consciousness. Boss believes that Freud's procedure of free association was designed to facilitate a basic attitude of " world openness " in the patient. Both the Freudian and Daseinsanalytic therapists, he believes, promote this openness in the patient with an attitude, to use Freud's phrase once again, of " evenly hovering attention." [91] The analyst must himself have a profound openness to *Beingness*. He must be able to allow relations to emerge into *Beingness* in himself as well as in his patients. Boss insists that the doctor must undergo analysis himself so that all obstacles to his own " world openness " can be removed.[92]

The unconditional openness and receptivity of the Daseins-analytic therapist functions, I would say, much like Rogers' concept of unconditional positive regard that " discriminates none " of another's feelings as being more or less worthy of positive regard. Certainly the client-centered attitude of " evenly distributed " positive regard facilitates the emergence into awareness of relations from which the patient was formerly disassociated. The similarity between the two characterizations of the therapeutic relationship can be seen further when Boss maintains that the good analysis " demands above all selfless care and cherishing of the patient " — a caring that not only " accepts the other fully the way he is " but gives the " patient's possibilities . . . a chance to emerge." [93]

In addition, this attitude of " world openness " in the therapist contains an empathic quality as well. It attempts to understand the patient's emerging world as it discloses itself to the patient. This world openness is phenomenological in character and refrains from imposing reductionistic and externalistic categories on the patient's experience. Of course, the emphasis is upon empathically understanding the patient's *emerging* world — both that which he can accept presently and that which he may be having difficulty accepting. Since the therapist's openness must exceed the patient's, the analyst is not unambiguously within the patient's internal frame of reference; the analyst will be open to relations to which the patient only partially will be open. The similarities between client-centered and Daseinsanalytic approaches promise a rich field of research that should be looked into with more detail than can now be done here.

Whitaker and Malone

We look at the views of this team of authors because their thought serves to illustrate, in a different theoretical framework, several points we have been making as to the essential structure of the therapeutic relationship. The task of therapy, according to them, is not cure but rather the catalyzation of a person's innate growth processes. Therapy catalyzes the growth processes by providing a deeply emotional human relationship that breaks through the incrustations of culture which block these deeper sources of energy. Therapy is a place where a patient can bring his " symbolic affect " (his childhood transference needs) and project them on to the person of the therapist so that they can be " lived through " to a different outcome.[94]

Therapy proceeds by the doctor maintaining an " intractable interest " and participation in the patient's symbolic affect while at the same time integrating this affect into his own maturity.[95] But Whitaker and Malone bring in an additional feature at this point. This sharing and participation in the symbolic affect of the other is done by both therapist and patient. It is both an interpersonal and intrapsychic process. The interpersonal aspect involves an unconscious and non-verbal interchange of massive proprioceptive and exteroceptive stimuli.[96] The intrapsychic aspect involves an introjection by each party of the other into his own intrapsychic society.[97] This means that the patient becomes the therapist's child-self and the therapist becomes the patient's intrapsychic parent. To say that the patient becomes the therapist's child-self, is to say that the therapist identifies the patient's immaturity with his own residual infantile needs. It is in this way that the therapist resonates with and shares in the symbolic affect of the patient.[98] At the same time that the patient's infantile needs become the therapist's child-self (his own residual infantile needs), the therapist attempts to accept these needs and integrate them into his own mature body-image.

In this way, the therapist becomes the patient's intrapsychic parent. As the therapist cathects and shares in the patient's symbolic affect, this calls forth more of the patient's infantile transference needs. If the therapist is able to accept and integrate his own residual infantile needs (that is, if his own transference needs are minor and he has learned to face them), he appears in the patient's intrapsychic structure as the good and loving parent.[99] When the patient has incorporated this image of the good and loving parent into his intrapsychic family, it becomes possible for the patient to start releasing the growth energy bound up with his transference needs. He no longer needs to repress them.

In summarizing the efficacy of this process, the authors say that through " this kind of relating," the patient finds an " acceptance of his own fantasies and unconscious experiences because he has them in the presence of one who implicitly participates in them, and thereby accepts them. Thus, the therapist not only symbolizes the parent who forbade these fantasies earlier in life, but also represents the total culture." [100]

We cannot fail to notice the similarity between what Whitaker and Malone call " intractable interest " in the symbolic affect of the patient and what the Rogerians call unconditional positive regard. In addition, what the client-centered school calls empathy is very similar in function to what these authors call the therapist's " participation in the symbolic affect " of the patient. Yet empathy always has an " as if " quality, according to the Rogerians. " Symbolic sharing " does not have the " as if " qualification for Whitaker and Malone. According to them, the therapist shares by having his own residual transference needs activated by the patient's transference. Yet there is a definite difference between the client's transference needs and the therapist's. As they point out, the therapist does not project his needs back upon the patient. The patient does not become the doctor's symbolic parent. The patient's transference simply activates the therapist's residual child-self which the therapist then attempts to integrate and accept into his mature body-image. There is an " as if " quality to this sharing for the reason that the patient's needs do not become the therapist's needs in the *same sense* as they are needs for the patient. The function of this sharing is the same as the function of empathy for the Rogerians. The therapist accepts and integrates what he " shares " with the patient, while the patient, by himself, is unable to do this.

The structure of the therapeutic relation, in actuality, is quite similar for both schools. Where they differ most profoundly is in the way they relate this structure to the character of the therapist. For Whitaker and Malone, it is the therapist's own residual transference needs plus his desire for growth that motivate him to cathect (show interest in, relate to) and participate in the patient's symbolic affect.[101] It is assumed that were the therapist without residual infantile needs he would not be motivated to continue doing therapy. For the client-centered school, the fewer conditions of worth the therapist has, the better therapist he will be. Ideally, the best therapist would have *no conditions* of worth that would cause him to deny or distort his or the client's feelings. Such an ideal therapist would be motivated to continue to do therapy by virtue of the very nature of the actualization tendency itself when understood in the sense of stimulus hunger. The actualization tendency itself impels man toward experiential concourse with his social environment. Hence, he would seek to grow, not so much through integrating his "infantile selves" into his self-concept, but in an effort to gain new experiences. The client-centered school recognizes that having lived through experiences — independent of the therapeutic experience — similar to those of the client may be helpful in being able to empathize with the client. This is what Standal means by the "evocable response" with which the therapist can understand the client's feelings. But for the Rogerian, these evocable responses should not serve as the basis for the motivation to do therapy.

The point is, even though there may be some difference in their understanding of the dynamic emergence of the essential structure of the therapeutic relationship, there is considerable agreement between them as to its nature. The extent to which the therapist can receive into his own feeling processes the feelings of the client and accept these feelings is the extent to which he is helpful. It is only in this way that the client or patient learns to accept those feelings which he formerly denied and rejected as unacceptable.

VI

SOME METHODOLOGICAL CONSIDERATIONS

We must consider more systematically the basis upon which our program is based. In order to make our method clear, we will have to give attention to two concerns. First, we must develop an understanding of analogical thinking. Second, we must set forth an ontological and epistemological framework in the context of which our theory of analogy can be further supported and which will be compatible with the nature of the therapeutic process, helping to further clarify and order it.

ONTOLOGICAL ACCEPTANCE AND THE NATURE OF ANALOGICAL THINKING

The possibility of using for explicit theological purposes the so-called secular healing disciplines such as psychotherapy may be predicated on the fact that these disciplines are not as secular as they represent themselves. There may be hidden assumptions in their work without which their success would be impossible and which make them, whether consciously acknowledged or not, implicitly theological and even churchly in their functions.

There is one major assumption that has been neglected by all but a few writers.[1] The assumption is this: the client's acceptance in therapy is predicated upon an ontological acceptance that transcends the therapeutic situation to which the therapist's acceptance witnesses. What does this mean?

It is becoming increasingly clear that the therapist occupies a representative role. He represents more than just himself. The Freudians have shown how the therapist can sometimes represent members of the client's family. Jerome Frank has gone farther than most writers in emphasizing that the therapist is a socially sanctioned expert whose healing power rests in part on his symbolic role as a representative of society.[2] It is obvious, then, that when a therapist successfully implements a relationship of empathic acceptance, more is implied than simply that *this* therapist has accepted *this* client. His acceptance is a representative acceptance.[3] It witnesses to a larger context of empathic acceptance. This larger context includes his social environment — his parents and the larger community. Although this larger context of acceptance may include the social environment, it also transcends it. It only dialectically includes the social milieu. It includes it with a " yes " and a " no." Certainly, both client and therapist only too clearly are cognizant of the many ways in which the client is not and has not been accepted by his social matrix.

This larger context of acceptance to which the therapist's acceptance witnesses is the ground of all effective social acceptance, but it is a ground to which the social environment does not always conform. In brief, the therapist's empathic acceptance announces, proclaims, and witnesses to the fact that the client is truly acceptable, not only to him as a therapist, but to some structure which transcends all finite referents, i.e., to the universe and whatever power that holds it together. And similarly, the client does not come to feel that he is acceptable simply to the therapist, but accepts the fact that he is acceptable in an ontological sense. Without this broader context of meaning operating in the therapeutic situation, it is doubtful whether the fruit of therapy would have any generalized consequences outside the narrow confines of the therapeutic situation. Successful therapy rests upon a *generalization* of an experience the client has with the therapist. The fact that the therapist may never name this larger structure does not negate the fact that his attitude implies it.

That this larger ontological structure of acceptance is a hidden presupposition of most secular therapy can be seen in the thought of Carl Rogers. Rogers has contended that the therapist must confront the client as a person of *worth* and *dignity*. Rogers admits that such an attitude on the part of the therapist is basically a philosophical attitude. It is a presupposition of all successful therapy.[4] It is a presupposition that, Rogers tells us, is being tested constantly in the counseling situation. According to our experience, this so-called philosophical and humanistic assumption needs to be supported by ontological roots. To say that each individual has an intrinsic worth and dignity is to say, in addition, that each individual has it irrespective of particular attitudes which fellow humans may hold toward him. It suggests that ultimately the individual's worth and dignity is measured by a structure which transcends all finite attitudes. If every individual has an intrinsic worth and dignity, the best my attitude can do is acknowledge and witness to what is the case irrespective of my idiosyncratic likes and dislikes. Hence, this humanist affirmation pushes us toward an ontological principle or reality by which all worth, value, and significance is measured ultimately.

Various theologians have discerned, in one way or another, the existence of this larger ontological structure of acceptance operating in therapy. Daniel Day Williams, with reference to pastoral counseling, has called it the Third Man who is Christ.[5] Wayne Oates [6] and William Hulme,[7] once again with pastoral counseling largely in mind, have called attention to this larger structure of acceptance. Before we had met each other, my former colleague, Thomas C. Oden, and I had concluded, independently and almost simultaneously, that secular therapy also contained this implicit assumption of a larger ontological structure of acceptance. Dr. Oden developed his thinking within the context of a dialogue between Rogers and Barth and sees this larger ontological structure in terms of Barth's Christological formula *Deus pro nobis*.[8]

Of course, within the context of Christian theology, it is entirely appropriate to give this larger ontological structure of acceptance a Christological articulation as have Oden and Williams. Even Oates has done this, in effect, since the work of the Holy Spirit — with which he associates this larger structure — always must receive, within Christian theology, a basically Christological interpretation. Without denying the validity of what has been suggested by these men, we need to say more. We need to ask additional questions. Is there an analogical relation between the therapist's acceptance and the larger structure it assumes? If there is, which way does the analogy operate? This is to ask, Which structure is the measure of the analogy, the smaller or the larger? Finally, can the therapist's acceptance become a source for theological statements? The following propositions will attempt to discuss these questions:

1. There is an analogical relationship between the therapist's empathic acceptance and the larger structure that it implies. By "analogical relation," we mean what has been meant traditionally by the term in Thomistic literature. It

implies *proportionality*. This means that, although two structures may be different with regard to quantity and degrees of perfection, they can have a similar basic essence. The therapist's empathic acceptance must have an analogical or proportionate relation to the larger structure or it could not effectively indicate, symbolize, or witness to it. It must somehow or other reproduce the form of that to which it witnesses if it is to indeed symbolize *that* thing and not something else. The analogical base of all symbols will be discussed in the context of Dorothy Emmet's epistemology to be set forth within a few paragraphs.

2. The larger structure of acceptance operating in the therapeutic situation is the presupposition, measure, and ground of the smaller structure and constitutes the possibility of the smaller structure. The same principle, expressed more concretely, can be said the following way: The *possibility* of the therapist accepting the client is based upon an intuition of a *prior* or *a priori* ground with reference to which the client is *actually* ontologically accepted. It cannot be properly said that we infer the larger structure on the basis of the existence of the smaller. Rather it should be said that we imagine the possibility of accepting the client because of a prior intuition that he is acceptable to something that transcends us both. If it seemed, in our earlier discussion, that we inferred the larger structure on the basis of the existence of the smaller, we now want to say it more correctly. The possibility of accepting the client is based upon the actuality that he is accepted. Imperative follows indicative. Because the client *is* (indicative) acceptable, the therapist can or *should* (imperative) accept him.

That analogical thinking within a theological context is always basically a matter of moving, so to speak, from the top downward (deductively) instead of from the bottom upward (inductively) is an insight shared alike by such divergent thinkers as Charles Hartshorne and Karl Barth. Both clearly recognize that theological thinking is not just a simple process of applying pieces of finitude analogically and symbolically to God. Barth expresses this when he says that we do not come to a concept of the Fatherhood of God on the basis of an imaginative expansion of the best in human fatherhood. Rather, we come to know what is the best in human fatherhood because of a prior revelation of the perfect Fatherhood of God.[9] It is interesting to note that Hartshorne, whom many regard as an advocate of natural theology, agrees. In the context of his brilliant critique of Tillich's doctrine of God, Hartshorne points out the following similarity between Barth and himself. Hartshorne criticizes Tillich's contention that predicates characteristic of finite objects can be only *symbolically* true of God. Hartshorne reverses the procedure. He insists that no predicate can ever be literally true of any finite entity. Statements pertaining to finite objects are symbolically true of them. Only God can be the subject of statements that are literally true. And then he brings Barth into the discussion by writing:

Concerning the question of literalness in theological concepts, I wish (with apologies to him) to urge Barth's procedure (when taken to task for treating God in terms of personality). He said, I believe, something like this: We know what personality is because we know God; our understanding of human " personality " is derivative from revelation. Similarly, I suggest, we know what human temporality is because we have (to use Tillich's word) an " ecstatic " sense of divine temporality.[10]

The last sentence of the quotation uses the category of temporality as an example. Other examples could be mentioned. Only God literally " loves." Finite humans only symbolically

love, for they never love completely, perfectly, or unambiguously. Only God literally " knows." All finite creatures
know only partially or incompletely and therefore nonliter-
ally. Hence, Hartshorne and Barth agree that finite goods
are known and nameable because of a prior " revelational "
or " ecstatic " confrontation of the divine and perfect instance of that good.

This basically similar understanding of the analogical procedure held by these two thinkers will be surprising to some.
It is important to comprehend their position for an understanding of the proper methodological procedure in the dialogue between Christian theology and psychotherapeutic psychology. The similarity between Hartshorne and Barth rests
in the basically Anselmian backgrounds to their thought.
Hartshorne's entire career has centered around both a critique and defense of Anselm's ontological argument.[11] The
debt that Barth owes to Anselm is clearly admitted in his
Fides Quaerens Intellectum.[12] Both Hartshorne and Barth
appreciate and uphold the Anselmian insight that all relative
judgments about the good assume an ultimate standard of
perfection. In terms of the counseling relationship, this
means that all relative or finite instances of empathic acceptance assume and are predicated upon an ultimate and perfect standard and measure of all acceptability. In addition,
both believe that this prior intuition of perfection that measures all finite goods is rooted in a faith or revelational event.
Of course, their understanding of faith and revelation will
differ, but not as much as we might think.

Let us turn to these differences. They will have crucial implications for the ground rules of the dialogue between theology and psychotherapeutic psychology. The first difference
relevant to our discussion centers around their divergent understanding of the nature of faith and revelation. For Barth,

revelation is a Word spoken by a self-disclosing God in the person of Jesus Christ.[13] Knowledge of God is dependent upon his self-disclosure and God chooses to disclose himself in the person of Jesus Christ. Faith is a matter of hearing and believing that Word which is spoken in the person of Jesus and witnessed to by the Scriptures.[14] Hence, within the Barthian framework, the ultimate revelation of the perfection which is the measure of all finite goods is in the person of Jesus Christ. For Barth, the basic intuition of an a priori perfection (that is the presupposition of Anselm's ontological argument) now receives a specifically Christological rootage. Jesus Christ concretely manifests this perfection. Jesus Christ becomes the measure of all perfection. Jesus Christ becomes *the analogy*. Jesus Christ reveals God's Fatherhood which becomes the analogy by which all human fatherhood is measured. Jesus Christ reveals God's love which becomes the analogy by which all finite expressions of love are measured. Hence, Barth proposes an *analogia fide* rather than an *analogia entis*.[15] Within the context of our discussion about psychotherapy, this means that Jesus Christ reveals God as *Deus pro nobis* (God for us) which becomes the perfect analogy that supports, makes possible, and measures all lesser instances of human positive regard or acceptance.[16]

For Hartshorne, faith is a prerational perception of God's perfection — a perfection that intersects and participates in the depths of every actuality. Hartshorne freely admits that the intuition of a perfection which is the ground of the so-called ontological argument and the measure of all relative goods is a prerational, faith perception.[17] Hartshorne does not localize exclusively this a priori perfection in the Christ event as does Barth. Yet Hartshorne can imply that it is received through a revelational experience. He borrows Tillich's concept of " ecstatic naturalism " to express the kind of revelational experience that he has in mind.[18] Within the context of Hartshorne's ontology, "ecstatic naturalism" would mean two things. First, it means that God at all times and at every place objectifies himself into the depths of every actuality. Second, it means that the datum of God's perfection is not equivalent to an actuality's center of consciousness or subjectivity. Man experiences God's perfection at the level of what Whitehead would call "causal efficacy" or Dorothy Emmet would call the "adverbial mode of perception." Hence, the word "ecstatic" is appropriate. Man does not build up a concept of perfection through rational, self-conscious processes. Man perceives perfection when he ecstatically transcends rational and self-conscious processes and experiences God's inflow at a prerational level.

But there is another difference between Hartshorne and Barth. Hartshorne believes that this faithlike experience of perfection is also subject to demonstration by the neutral laws of logic.[19] For instance, he believes that he can prove the ontological argument. The intuition of perfection originates within a faith experience, but its ultimate verification can be accomplished on grounds outside the circle of faith. Barth clearly disagrees with Hartshorne at this point. Statements about the perfection revealed in Jesus Christ are verifiable only within the circle of faith by the principle of coherence.[20]

Both of these positions are right in many ways. As we have seen, on many points they are quite similar. They have, at least in part, a mutually supporting understanding of analogical thinking. The dialogue between theology and psychotherapeutic psychology can best proceed in a context that synthesizes these two positions. The Barthian Christological emphasis needs to be balanced by a Hartshornian understanding of the general ontological relation that exists between God and man. The Hartshornian ontology needs to be balanced by Christian understanding of sin and its effects on man's capacity to perceive and know the good. This leads us to our third proposition.

3. The a priori standard of perfection assumed by all finite judgments about the good is both Christologically revealed as Barth maintains and ontologically present as Hartshorne maintains. The Christian will finally have to agree with Barth that the a priori standard of perfection which measures all finite goods is supremely revealed in Christ. But even though it is supremely revealed in Christ, the Christian can affirm that God has a general relation with the world in the natural processes of creation and providence. This general relationship gives all men everywhere an intimation of God's perfection. Informed by the revelation of God in Christ, the Christian can then look to all the concrete processes of the world to ask what they intimate about their ground, God. The Christian, with his mind oriented toward that larger standard of perfection, that ultimate analogy in Jesus, can then look to the world for smaller, concrete, empirically describable examples of the larger structure. Then, after analysis of the smaller instance, an empirically describable analogy can be generated and used to bring clarity to the larger, molar, mythological analogy revealed in Christ. We are clearly transcending the exclusively Barthian Christological stance. Although we begin with it, in the sense that it becomes our primary guide, we believe that positive theological knowledge can be found outside the supreme revelational event of Jesus Christ.

In essence, we are suggesting that the analogical process works both ways. It first works from the top down (a priori), as Barth and Hartshorne both admit. But it also works from the bottom back up to the top (a postiori). This is where

Hartshorne goes farther than Barth. Hartshorne would see the analogical process as working in both directions. We move to an analysis of finite goods with an a priori intimation of perfection in our minds. But the concrete content of this ultimate perfection is gained from an analysis and generalization of the structure of the finite good.[21] I am suggesting a similar process for the dialogue between Christian theology and psychotherapeutic psychology. Let us start with the revelation of perfection known in Jesus Christ. Let us allow this revelation to guide us to smaller goods. Then, with the help of scientific observation, let us make an analysis of the structure of the smaller good and use the results of this analysis as a clarifying analogy with which to sharpen our understanding of the ultimate standard of the good as revealed in Jesus Christ.

Something very close to the position I am advocating can be seen in John Baillie's *The Sense of the Presence of God*. He explicitly agrees with Barth that the revelation of God's perfection in Jesus Christ constitutes the a priori analogy by which all finite goods are measured. But Baillie goes farther than Barth. Baillie admits some appreciation for Brunner's distinction between special and general revelation.[22] He believes, along with Brunner, that it is legitimate to talk about "revelation in creation" as well as special revelation in the historic man Jesus.[23] He therefore sees the need for inductive analogies. Indeed, he believes that Jesus himself used them. Note the following quotation:

A difficulty with this teaching [Dr. Barth's] may perhaps be found in the fact that Jesus, in his parabolic discourses, constantly appeals to the analogy between human and divine fatherhood, and uses indeed a certain argument *a fortiori* from the former to the latter. "Or what man is there of you, whom if his son ask bread, will he give him a stone? Or if he ask a fish, will he give him a serpent? If ye then, being evil, know how to give good gifts unto your children, how much more shall your Father which is in heaven give good things to them that ask him? " [24]

The analogy can work both ways. This Baillie clearly saw. But what does not occur to him is that scientific analysis of certain concrete processes of healing which operate between human beings can engender analogies that can constitute a positive clarification of man's interpretation of the a priori perfection revealed in Christ.

It is this kind of procedure that Seward Hiltner has in mind in his concept of " correlation of perspectives." [25] Hiltner proposes that pastoral theology use this method. He also proposes that theology's dialogue with secular disciplines use this method. With regard to pastoral theology, the method means that the pastor brings theological questions to bear on the study of concrete, empirically observable pastoral practices and draws theological answers from his reflection on those processes. With regard to the dialogue between theology and psychotherapy, it means that theology would bring theological questions to the study of the psychological material and then draw theological conclusions.

Hiltner's method is difficult for some to understand. This is true because he has been a bit too indirect about communicating his ontological assumptions. It is easy to miss the Whiteheadian and Hartshornian metaphysic that undergirds his thought. A study of concrete empirical processes, be they pastoral or psychotherapeutic, can reveal positive theological truth, for Hiltner, because finally all of reality is undergirded by God's relationship. The way in which God operates in and through these concrete processes can be seen by the person who asks theological questions of these processes. This is not natural theology that he is recommending. One can bring theological questions to concrete processes because of a prior confrontation with the revelation of God in Jesus Christ. But the perfection revealed by Jesus Christ is also a perfection that intersects the depths of all empirical realities. Hence, theological truth can be found in both places.

Let us return to our major question: Can the therapist's empathic acceptance be a "clarifying analogy" with which to interpret the nature of God's acceptance? The answer is "yes," but with the following qualification. It must be remembered that God's acceptance precedes and constitutes the ground, possibility, and ultimate measure of the therapist's acceptance even though analysis of the smaller, empirically discernible acceptance of the therapist may serve to sharpen our understanding of the actual structure and dynamics of God's acceptance.

An Ontological and Epistemological Framework

To understand what has been said about the nature of the analogical process, a full ontological and epistemological framework must be set forth. The onto-epistemological framework most helpful for our purposes is that of Dorothy Emmet. Emmet's position is a simplification and slight reinterpretation of the philosophy of Alfred N. Whitehead. Since Hartshorne is a Whiteheadian, it will give insight into the ontology behind Hartshorne's concept of analogy. It will help us understand how analogical thinking goes in two directions. (It will also help us develop an epistemology of empathy.)

Emmet makes a distinction between two kinds of perception — adverbial and accusative modes. The adverbial mode is an "integral feeling, qualifying a state of experience." [26] It is a physiological response to the energetic shocks from our physical environment. This physiological response sets up affective tones, or bodily feelings, that constitute the subjective forms of the energetic processes transmitted to us from our environment. The accusative mode of perception abstracts and differentiates certain simplified symbolic forms from the affective and molar responses of the adverbial mode, and in turn, projects these forms onto the external environment.[27] Perceptions in the accusative mode are always inferences built up from the way things affect us at the adverbial mode.

Basic to an understanding of these two modes of perception is her concept of rapport or preanimistic relatedness. Emmet's concept of rapport seeks to assert and point to a basic "continuity of our functions and activities with those of the environing world."[28] At the adverbial level of perception the continuity of functions between us and the world is *felt* as patterned qualities. The adverbial mode of perception must be understood as a wholistic response — a response that has identity or correspondence with the patterned processes playing upon the organism but that, at the same time, is not unambiguously reproductive of these energetic activities.[29] Some selective activity occurs at this level as well as at the accusative level. Although perceptions in the accusative mode are abstracted from the more wholistic perceptions of the adverbial mode, they can still be said to have a participative relation with the organism's *response* and the energetic patterns to which this response at least in part conforms or corresponds. Only at a later and more refined level in the symbolic process can it be said that symbols become arbitrary and have no participative relation to the processes they symbolize. At this level they are called signs.

Insofar as the event in the external world at least in part

forms the adverbial response, the event can be said to be *in* our experiencing, but at the same time the event *transcends* our experiencing. To symbolize the event means to symbolize what transcends our experiencing on the basis of what is *in* our experiencing. As Emmet states, " indirect inferences as to the transcendent character of these events are built up from our responses to them." [30] Emmet calls this an " analogical " process.[31] She suggests that since all perceptive activity involves a process of projecting on to the transcendent aspect of events interrelations within and between our own responses to these events, the symbolic process itself is necessarily an analogical process.

The history of science points to innumerable instances in which analogical models drawn from within experience have been constructed to represent realities partially transcending experience. The planetary theory of atoms, the mechanical model, field theory, and organic models are well-known examples. The possibility of the method of analogy rests on the assumption that there is, at least, a partial identity of structure between the qualitative pattern of the event and our response to it.[32] Futhermore, the analogical method rests on the principle that in the concepts of rapport and adverbial response, ontology and epistemology meet. The analogy participates in the reality it represents.

How does Emmet's understanding of analogical thinking square with what we said earlier? First, it would be at the adverbial level of perception that man has his a priori experience of God's perfection. This primary intuition of God, although experiential, is a priori in the sense that it is prior to any inference. It is not a product of an inference. It is a given. Yet our symbolization of this a priori experience is inferential in character. Any effort to give this a priori experience any specific content would take part in an inferential analogical process. The symbolization of the immanent and transcendent aspects of our adverbial experience of God must be done in terms of interrelations or models which are within experience.

This means that, although God's justification and acceptance is prior to all interpersonal acts of acceptance, our symbolization of God's acceptance, at least in part, depends upon interpersonal analogies. God's acceptance is an a priori experience at the adverbial mode of perception. But only one term of this relation is in experience. We only know this relation of acceptance directly in terms of our response to it at the adverbial mode. We do not know how to symbolize this acceptance in and of itself. To symbolize this a priori fact of God's perfect acceptance, we must do so in terms of interpersonal analogies that are in all respects within human experience.

This is how therapeutic acceptance may be able to provide an interpretative analogy. Some men are therapists and may be able to symbolize something about therapeutic acceptance from the standpoint of the therapist. Some men are clients and may be able to symbolize something about therapeutic acceptance from the standpoint of receiving it. All aspects of the experience of therapeutic acceptance are in someone's experience. All aspects of the experience of therapeutic acceptance can be observed and analyzed by someone. All perspectives can be pooled and a clear analogy can be generated. And this analogy can help give clarification to the specific character of the a priori experience of God's acceptance.

The same process is the case even if we work within the traditional Christian assumption of a specific revelation of this a priori perfection in Jesus Christ. Jesus was a historical figure. But most contemporary Biblical scholars agree that our report of him is limited to the response of the church.

This response was not always consistent and complementary. In the early response, there are rudimentary beginnings of at least three different and not easily reconcilable understandings of the work of Christ which later hardened into *Christus Victor,* satisfaction and moral theories of the atonement. Even within the context of Biblical revelation, we need to bring empirically describable analogies in tension with Scriptural witness as a means for bringing clarity to those points at which the Bible may be contradictory, diffuse, or simply global. As Whitehead, Emmet, and Meland all point out, the dramatic and mythical form in which Biblical truth is expressed, although essentially true, may be at least somewhat vague and molar. Hence, for the purpose of bringing clarity to theological speech and for the purpose of reducing internal contradiction, the analogical process must operate in both directions.

All theological thinking must operate with a twofold process of verification. First, it must use the principle of *internal coherence*. This means that first it must be basically confessional. It must measure the adequacy of its speech in terms of its internal consistency with the entire Biblical and historical witness. This is basically Barth's position. But secondly, it must use the principle of *external coherence*. Daniel Day Williams has both argued for and effectively used this principle.[33] Verification by external coherence assumes the principle that truth is basically one and that all perspectives seeking truth eventually will and should cohere with and confirm one another. Williams asserts that although each perspective or discipline seeking truth has its own internal standards of verification, each discipline needs, finally, to test itself against other perspectives. When different perspectives, using different methods and employing different internal standards of verification, begin to cohere, this in itself is a criterion of verification. Of course, the theologian always stands within the circle of faith as he looks for clarifying analogies outside this circle.

The position of this chapter falls in line with the theological methodology of men like Schubert Ogden, John Cobb, Daniel Jenkins, and John Woelfel.[34] This method asserts the priority of revelation and, at the same time, attempts to find empirically testable analogies in the light of which Biblical language can be clarified and in terms of which it can be expressed. This method will have the twofold virtue of giving Biblical and theological language more clarity, specificity, and verifiability, as well as presenting a new secular language in terms of which the gospel can be communicated. But a secular language for the proclamation of the gospel is of little interest for purposes of communication unless it provides some added clarity which Biblical categories may not have in and of themselves. If the secular language to be used is not intrinsically clarifying, it may have no potency at all for the communication of the gospel. There are different kinds of secular languages, and some of these languages are as unfamiliar and strange to certain people as Biblical categories are to others. The language of psychotherapy may sound utterly bizarre to an Oklahoma wheat farmer or a New York dock worker. Unless this language is clarifying, more intelligible, and therefore communicative, there is no reason to take the time to introduce it. This is the major difficulty with the program of my former colleague, Thomas C. Oden, who, in his book *Kerygma and Counseling,* looks to psychotherapy not for clarification but for a new language, a secular language that will help give the gospel a secular form.[35] Supposedly, clothing the gospel in this secular form will enable us to sell or communicate this gospel to modern man. But this presupposes that modern man already knows the language of psychotherapy, which, of course, is not widely the case. Not being able to admit that the empirically discernible structures of psychotherapy actually contribute anything substantive to our understanding of the Christian faith, he has involved us in unnecessary additional linguistic baggage as well as two jobs of translation instead of one. My position, to some extent, does the same thing, except it is justified insofar as I assume and attempt to demonstrate that substantive clarification can be gained from psychotherapy and, for this reason, is therefore worth the time, trouble, and momentary confusion. In addition, I do not share the contemporary loss of faith in the communicative capacity of Biblical categories. Biblical categories are suggestive to many people, and to this extent are communicative if only in an evocative sense. The difficulty is that they are not always sufficiently clear to serve as effective guides to thought and action. In addition, it is often difficult to decide on grounds completely internal to the Bible, which one of many different competing and somewhat contradictory Scriptural ideas is the most true or sound. For this reason an analogical method is needed to supplement specialized Biblical and historical scholarship.

Psychotherapy and This Ontological and Epistemological Framework

The psychotherapeutic process is a process between human beings. As such, it is characterized by processes of *knowing* and *relating* typical of all human transactions with the world. There is a sense in which the therapist and client know each other. Therefore, the psychotherapeutic process must take part in the common elements characteristic of any act of knowing. There is a sense in which the therapist and the client are related. Therefore, the psychotherapeutic process must take part in the common elements that mark all relationships. Research into the nature of the psychotherapeutic process has itself yielded insights for both of these issues.

How do we order the psychotherapeutic relation in the light of Emmet's ontological and epistemological framework? First, the concept of rapport is crucial for our discussion. The concept of empathy in the Rogerian view of therapy demands it, but there is only a vague acknowledgment of the need for such a principle in the literature of this movement.

Empathy — defined to mean a feeling of the client's feeling " as if " it were one's own — would be impossible to conceive without the concept of rapport understood as the interchange of affective, qualitied patterns of energy; it is only through such a process that our feeling toward another person can be thought to include the datum of the other's feelings.[36] As we have already seen, Gendlin asserts that our feelings can include the meaning of the other's feelings, but does not assert *how* this can be thought to be the case. At one place Rogers himself acknowledges Angyal's concept of the *biosphere* that also asserts an interrelation of processes similar to the concept of rapport, but nowhere has he tied it into his total theory in a systematic way.[37] In another place, Rogers quotes a report of O. H. Bown, who refers to the therapeutic relation as the transmission of an " energy which can be picked up by another person only through his feeling, rather than through the intellect." [38] But Rogers does not express a direct opinion on the issue. Regardless of this failure to make explicit use of such a concept, the concept of empathy seems to demand the concept of rapport.

Whitaker and Malone explicitly seem to acknowledge such a concept. The symbolic affect of both parties is delivered to the other through massive proprioceptive and exteroceptive subliminal stimulation. But these authors confuse the significance of this process by stating that the capacity of the therapist to share in this affect depends upon his having minor residual transference needs that will be stimulated by the patient's affect. But there must be some way for the form or pattern of the patient's affect to be conveyed into the feeling processes of the therapist before these residuals can be activated. What these authors should say is that these residuals must be present before the therapist's feeling of the client's feeling feels *familiar*, i.e., feels like a feeling the therapist has had before. Then the question becomes, would the therapist be interested in new feelings and would he attempt to integrate them into his mature body image? Whitaker and Malone seem to think that the therapist *would not* be interested and that he would not be motivated to integrate them into his mature body image. The growth motivation for Whitaker and Malone seems to be limited to the desire to better integrate "old selves," or old affects into the mature self-concept. According to Whitaker and Malone, completely new feelings would be of no interest to the therapist.

The present direction of the client-centered school does not seem to be limited by this difficulty. The therapist could share in a completely new feeling, i.e., a client's feeling that in no way resonated with a therapist's conditions of worth. The therapist might have difficulty grasping this new experience, but according to client-centered theory he would still be interested in it. The drive for stimulus hunger gives the therapist the desire to feel, differentiate, and integrate new feelings as well as old, unresolved ones. The point is, though, that the client-centered school as well as Whitaker and Malone needs an onto-epistemological principle such as the concept of *rapport* to understand how the therapist can share, participate, or empathize with the client's feelings.

It is clear that the distinction between adverbial and accusative modes of perception can also help order the psychotherapeutic process. The adverbial mode of perception contains the unsymbolized affective responses of the organism to the patterned energy of the other event. These adverbial responses contain, at least in part, the form of these patterned energies of the other. Even though unsymbolized (meaning preconscious or not yet conscious), these adverbial responses contain latent symbolic forms and are therefore meaningful. Client-centered theory recognizes this in its theory of implicitly meaningful but unsymbolized feelings and experiencings. These feelings are implicitly meaningful, but are often denied symbolization by the defensive measures of the self and its conditions of worth. The whole concept of subception implies that there is a preconscious adverbial mode of perception. Consciousness, for the Rogerian school, involves a process of making explicit the implicitly meaningful forms of our feelings. Hence, the client-centered theory of consciousness is very similar to Emmet's understanding of the accusative mode of perception.

SEPARATING THE FUNDAMENTAL FROM THE PERIPHERAL

A finite structure can conform to the pattern of an infinite structure only in a fragmentary and ambiguous way. First, there would be the ambiguity consequent upon the difference between the infinite and the finite itself. Whatever can be predicated of the infinite structure is completely and absolutely true of it. Whatever can be predicated of the finite structure can be true only partially of that structure. For instance, if it is said of God that he *knows,* it means that he does so completely and unambiguously. To say that some finite man *knows* is to say he knows only partially. He knows some things and not other things. He knows some things well and other things poorly. Hence, if one were to predicate the capacity to " know " to God, it would be completely, unambiguously, and hence literally true of God. If the same were to be predicated of a finite being such as man, it would be ambiguous and partial and hence nonliteral or symbolic. Only God can *know* in the full literal sense of the word.[39]

But there would be another kind of ambiguity — the ambiguities consequent to the difference between the holy and the sinful. For instance, if it were predicated of God that he knows, it would also mean that he *knows* with *holy righteousness* since his infinite perfection also would include his moral perfection. But not only do finite men *know* partially and incompletely, they also know sinfully. The incompleteness of finite categories would also be further distorted by the corruptions of sin.

Any finite structure used to symbolize the nature of God's soteriological activity would have to be analyzed so that that which was relevant to its sinfulness and its finitude could be separated from that which reflected its participation in and proportionality with this ultimate structure.

Let us illustrate how the limitation of finitude manifests itself with regard to the essence of the psychotherapeutic relationship — unconditional empathic acceptance. It will be remembered that empathic acceptance must go hand in hand with congruence. The congruence principle means that empathic acceptance must spring from the integrity of the whole organism. It also means that it must not outstrip this integrity. Hence, the congruence principle forces the recognition of the limitations of finitude. For example, most therapy is structured so that physical violence to the therapist will not be permitted. Often this arises as an explicit rule only in play therapy with children, but it is held as an operating principle for the therapist in other kinds of therapy, even though not explicitly stated.[40] Such a structuring is an acknowledgment of the therapist's finitude — the fact that the client could, if he had the strength, seriously qualify the therapist's acceptance by rejecting the therapist through killing him or badly injuring him. Also, the limitations that the therapist places on his time is a similar example. Limiting therapy to fifty minutes acknowledges and clarifies the therapist's temporal limitations.

As an aside — not directly relevant to our present point but yet important for our future argument — it should be mentioned that the presence of structure in therapy acknowledges not only the therapist's finitude, it has an additional value for the client. Limiting destruction to physical property or to the therapist's person helps provide a security factor for the client; it helps protect the client from destructive guilt reactions, a consequent decline in self-regard, and as Bruno Bettlelheim points out, lowers anxiety about the counter aggression of others as well as lessens possible delusions of omnipotence.[41] But the use of structure and law in this sense must be placed in perspective. By itself, it has no therapeutic efficacy. It serves to *integrate* a situation so that empathic acceptance can accomplish its work. In some situations the emphasis on structure is very minimal, if not completely absent. Hence, it is a secondary factor in therapy. It is a means-end aspect designed to serve the essential and always constant element of empathic acceptance. This will have implications later when we address the relation of God's *administrative justice* to God's love and forgiveness.

Other aspects of therapy are acknowledgments of the therapist's character deficiencies (acknowledgment of these, from a theological perspective, would be called the therapist's sinfulness). To be congruent in the relationship, the therapist must be willing to admit — at least to himself and in some cases to the client — his own conditions of worth, his own defensive anxiety resulting from them, and his own rejecting attitudes. He owns these conditions, i.e., he confesses them to himself, in order to remove them, as nearly as possible, as blocks to his empathic acceptance. He acknowledges the *limitations* of his empathic acceptance in order to increase empathic acceptance. Or he acknowledges them in order to clarify to himself (and possibly to the client) just *wherein* the therapist can be empathically accepting. The important point, though, is this: the use of any finite structure of healing as an analogy for the healing activity of God necessitates isolating and eliminating the elements of finitude and sin that characterize it.

VII

EMPATHIC ACCEPTANCE AND THE DOCTRINE OF THE ATONEMENT

The purpose of this chapter is to construct a theory of the atonement based on the concept of unconditioned empathic acceptance. I will attempt to use this understanding of the essential structure of the therapeutic relation as an analogy to interpret the meaning of the central events referred to in this doctrine — man's redemption through the cross and the resurrection of Jesus Christ. Once again, the doctrine of God will be the controlling issue.

EMPATHIC ACCEPTANCE AND GOD IN HIS SOTERIOLOGICAL ESSENCE

The essential steps that we have taken in arriving at this point should be reviewed. We have (1) tried to isolate the necessary and essential structure of the therapeutic relation, (2) separate it from qualifications of finitude and sin, and (3) set it in the context of certain contingent or means-end accessories. It now becomes time to attempt to conceive this structure without the limitations of finitude and sin and the contingent elements that accompany it in this form. Then we must maximize these essential features of the therapeutic relation to the limits of perfection. In this way we will arrive at an analogy applicable to the nature of God.

The thesis of this section is that the cross represents a crucial element in the structure of God's love which symbolizes the fact that God fully feels the depth of sin's hostility. His love overcomes this hostility by enduring it, and he remains unqualified in his capacity to receive sinful man into relation with himself. The two aspects of being fully qualified by sin's hostility and then remaining unqualified in his capacity to accept sinful man into relationship constitutes the full cycle of God's redeeming activity, symbolized respectively in the cross and the resurrection.

Empathic Acceptance and Absolute Relativity

Empathic acceptance undistorted by sin would be empathic acceptance without inhibiting and distorting conditions of worth. For, as has been pointed out, conditions of worth tend to cause us to reject, deny, or ignore experiencing that encounters us. Secondly, ideal empathic acceptance would be empathic acceptance devoid of the limitations of finitude. Included among these limitations are those of time, physical strength, and language differences.

Let us review the structure of empathic acceptance in its most abstract form before we attempt to conceive it in its most ideal form.

Empathic acceptance refers to the capacity of the therapist to enter into an *active-passive* relationship with the client. It is an active relationship in that it conveys a positive regard or caring for the feelings of the other. Yet it is a passive relationship in that it conveys this caring by receiving or feeling the feelings of the other as the other feels them. Hence, it is a relationship that demonstrates concern, caring, positive regard, adience, and warmth by receiving the feelings of the other as if they were one's own, and possibly, in some instances, receiving and owning the feelings of the other which the other cannot own. To have empathic acceptance, the therapist must allow his own feeling processes to be qualified by the feelings of the client. This relationship can be called an *internal* relation in the sense that what the client feels helps to define what the therapist feels. Through empathic acceptance, the therapist attempts to be adequately *relative* to the feelings of the client in that he attempts to *conform* and *relate* adequately his feelings to the feelings of the client. The nature of this internal relation can be seen more clearly if it is contrasted to a definition of external relation. An external relation would exist between them if, somehow or other, the client's feelings in no way altered, defined, or helped constitute the feelings of the therapist. If this were the case, the therapist in no way would be relative to the client. This is to say that the feelings of the therapist in no way would be affected or qualified by the client, and would draw their content and form from some source independent of the client.

Let us now look at the structure of empathic acceptance in ideal or maximal proportions. The individual exhibiting empathic acceptance is relative to any and all feelings that the other may have. There is no feeling that he does not relate to in the sense of receiving it, empathizing with it, and being internally qualified by it. But there is one sense in which the maximally empathic individual is not relative in the sense of being qualified or qualifiable. This is precisely in his ability to be completely qualified by and relative to the feelings of the other. This is to say that the individual with maximum empathic acceptance would be *unqualifiable* in one respect — in his ability to remain supremely qualifiable. In the ideal case, there would be nothing that others could do or say that would cause this individual to withdraw or put conditions on this capacity empathically to accept and receive the other.

This would be the nature of the ideal instance of *unconditioned empathic acceptance*. It would be that structure which is unqualified in its capacity to be qualified by the object of its relationship, absolute or constant in its capacity to relate to and empathically receive any particular other.

This means that the supreme example of empathic acceptance would be *absolutely relative* to all finite actualities and their feelings. It would be *absolute* in the sense that nothing could qualify or condition its capacity to know and feel the other. It would be supremely *relative* because the content of its feelings would conform maximally to all other feelings. Absolute relativity is the abstract essence of the ideal or maximum structure of empathic acceptance. By abstract essence I mean its purely formal character from which all its concrete actions would issue and through which the range and depth of its concrete feelings become possible.

In more straightforward terms, this absolutely relative or empathic individual would be supremely social. The social awareness of all " others," in the sense of feeling their feelings, would be his *end*. It must be remembered that empathic acceptance, to be therapeutic, must spring from an individual's own congruence — from the deepest strivings of his nature. The extent to which such an individual conformed to this end would be the extent to which he remained consistent with his own character. To feel the feelings of the other empathically would be the *law* of his nature. This would be his *eternal obligation*. This eternal obligation would govern all his deeds and all his transactions with other beings. This eternal obligation would not constitute a law standing *above*, or *over*, the life of this supreme individual. It simply would be the law of his own nature with which he must conform if he is to remain consistent with himself.

It should be remembered that the therapist's acceptance witnesses to, and is grounded in, a larger structure of justification. We simply are investigating what sense we can make out of the larger structure when it is interpreted in the light of the structure of the therapist's attitude that seems to imply and reflect it. The attitude of the therapist further implies that the larger structure infallibly and perfectly accomplishes what the therapist only partially and incompletely accomplishes. Hence, to symbolize the larger structure in terms of the smaller one means pushing the categories of the smaller structure to maximal and perfect proportions. Empathic acceptance has engendered the principle of absolute relativity. Now we must ask, what would absolute relativity mean for the perfect knowledge, the perfect power, the perfect righteousness, the perfect justice, and the perfect love of this supreme individual?

The perfect *knowledge* or omniscience of this supreme individual would be empathic knowledge. Anything less than knowing another object in the sense of feeling what it feels is something less than perfect knowledge.

His perfect *power* would refer to his "unconditioned" capacity to know, feel, and relate to all other beings. Such perfect power would not include, necessarily, the power to force the other to acknowledge this supreme individual's capacity to so relate to him; nor would it mean that this supreme individual had all the power there is. There would be other powers, and these other powers might resist acknowledging the power of the supreme individual to relate to him empathically. The model of psychotherapy helps illustrate this. The therapist cannot determine the client's acceptance of the therapist's empathic acceptance. The therapist's empathic acceptance is the condition or occasion providing the possibility upon which the client may come to accept his acceptance. But the therapist's attitude cannot determine in all respects the client's acceptance of this relationship.

The client's refusal to accept, acknowledge, or admit the *de facto* existence of this empathic acceptance does not impugn or qualify necessarily in and of itself the capacity of the therapist to so accept him. It is conceivable that the therapist would have sufficient power to so relate to the client. But this sufficient power would not include also the power to determine, in all respects, the client's acceptance of this acceptance. Later, though, we will see what this understanding of God's power (what theologians have called God's " own pleasure ") means for the effectual transformation of that man who refuses to acknowledge the *de facto* existence of this perfect empathic acceptance.

What would perfect *righteousness* mean within the framework of this eminent instance of empathic acceptance? It would mean that it is the *eternal law and obligation* of this supreme individual perfectly to receive and care empathically for every particular thing. His righteousness would be found in his infinite capacity to relate adequately and *equally* to each creature in this manner. Whatever is meant by God's *justice* would be subsumed under the rubric of God's righteousness. God's righteousness provides a bedrock of justice in that it guarantees that all men will be equally and adequately loved, empathically received, and positively regarded. This is the primary sense in which the word " justice " will be applied to God in this study. Later, we will make a careful distinction between God's justice, understood in this primary sense, and God's *administrative justice*. And finally, it is under the rubric of righteousness understood in this way that we can specify the meaning of God's *honor*. God's honor simply refers to God's unconditioned capacity to remain consistent to his own basic nature. It refers to God's capacity to conform to the structure of his own righteousness. His honor would mean that nothing can cause God to fail in the equality and adequacy of his righteousness. But once again his honor, just as his power, would not depend entirely upon the extent to which this capacity was acknowledged by his creatures. For instance, it is conceivable that God could know and feel perfectly the feelings of all creatures, while these creatures would acknowledge inadquately that they were so known and felt.

And finally the perfect love of this supreme individual would refer to his unqualified capacity for empathic *fellowship* with all finite creatures. It would mean that the possibility for perfect fellowship and communion between God and his creatures would be assured, at least from the standpoint of God. God would be infinitely adjustable to the felt needs of the other. No felt need would go unattended, unrecognized, unappreciated, without the concern of God. Through this perfect fellowship, God would live active positive regard into the world which every creature, at least in its adverbial depths, would feel.

Such a view of God's perfection has several implications. It would mean that God is *a se* in some respects, but not in all respects. God would be *a se* and immutable with regard to his power, his righteousness, his knowledge, and his love, but *not* with regard to the concrete content of his own feeling and experiencing of the world. For the concrete content of his feelings, he would be dependent upon the variety of feelings resident in the world at any particular moment. It would also mean that God is not above the temporal process. The events of the temporal process would evoke variations in the content of God's own life. In his concrete life God would be infinitely complex rather than supremely simple. Instead of being in a state of self-identical perfection, God would be an integration of the full range of diversity resident in the totality of finite beings and their feelings.

The Structure of Sin and Incongruence

We need to examine the similarities and differences between sin and incongruence. If there appears to be a formal similarity between them, then it makes sense to infer that the kind of efficaciousness which empathic acceptance has with reference to incongruence also will be the case with reference to man's sin. Since we are interested only in demonstrating a formal and structural similarity between them, our discussion will not be exhaustive and many questions will go unanswered.

Our study will reveal the following: that the understanding of human brokenness evolving from the social and psychotherapeutic sciences has more in common with that view of the human condition associated with the *Christus Victor* image of the atonement than it does with those views of man connected with the Latin or Moral Influence theories.

From the client-centered perspective, incongruence is caused by the presence of conditions of worth. Conditions of worth are absolutized values (taken over from the environment) that one uses to validate one's worth; they tend to defensively inhibit contradictory values from being experienced fully and symbolized adequately. Quite clearly, Rogers wants to distinguish heuristically held values from conditions of worth and understands the latter as values that are characteristically overdetermined. He agrees with Adler, Jung, Horney, Fromm, May, and many existentialists that man's brokenness is due to value conflicts, one side of which is rigidly and defensively overemphasized and absolutized. Adler's " neurotic life style," Jung's concept of " bias " or " one-sidedness," Horney's " neurotic trend " and " devil's pact," and Caruso's explicit appropriation of Kierkegaard's concept of " absolutizing the relative " as characteristic of the neurotic reaction, are different expressions of what Rogers is describing by his concept of conditions of worth.[1] The conditions of worth try to gain justification through certain value absolutes and confront the world with " intentional " and overgeneralized modes of perception that attempt, in effect, to reshape the world in their own image.

Two similarities between incongruence and sin are immediately discernible. Both sin and incongruence entail an idolatrous overreliance upon finite values for one's justification and worth. Rudolf Bultmann suggests that this is what Paul meant when he described sin as anything that man does to justify himself by the created order (*sarx*), the realm of finite values.[2] Secondly, absolutizing finite values through conditions of worth leads to estrangement. Values that contradict these conditions of worth are denied, disowned or distorted, and to this extent, we become estranged from them. This points to another similarity between sin and incongruence. Paul Tillich has pointed to the element of estrangement in sin and characterized it as a state of being turned away " from that to which one belongs." [3] Although theology would differ from psychology in including God (and our feelings toward God) as a referent to which man belongs, they both agree that brokenness involves a rigid and idolatrous dependence on some values and feelings at the cost of estrangement from others.

But there are different understandings of the nature of sin, and the one which the concept of incongruence most clearly resembles is that associated with the *Christus Victor* drama of redemption. The self's conditions of worth, when seen in terms of the energy they divert from the more fun-

damental processes of the organism, can be compared fruit-
fully to the function of the devil in the thought of Irenaeus.
It will be remembered that the function of the devil is to
offer man certain ways to justify himself externally to his relationship to God. In our terms, Irenaeus' devil is both the
author and embodiment of the conditions of worth by which
man attempts to find his security and justification. Furthermore, the devil is an objective power that holds the deeper
growth forces of man in bondage. At the same time, even
though the devil is an objective power, it is not metaphysi-
cally independent of God, and no ultimate dualism is implied. The devil is parasitic in nature and derives its strength
from a source more fundamental than itself. Even though it
is opposed to God, it lives off the very life of God.

In a sense, the conditions of worth of Rogerian psychotherapy are also objective powers. They contain a power of their
own, but this power is not independent or self-derived. The
power of the self's conditions of worth is parasitic and derived from a source more fundamental than themselves.
They gain their power by " robbing " or " diverting " energy
from the deeper actualization tendencies of the organism. At
the same time, they gain control of these deeper growth motivations, thereby binding and thwarting them. The point is
that both Irenaeus' concept of the devil and the psychotherapeutically derived conditions of worth constitute real " powers " from which man needs to be " freed " if he is to be
saved.

There are certain differences between these two orders of
conceptualization that bear further discussion. So far we have
said that the devil lives off the power of God and that the
conditions of worth live off the deeper growth potentialities
of the organism. In addition, although Irenaeus strongly emphasizes the external pressure of the devil, he never relieves

man completely of his freedom, whereas the determinism of the psychotherapeutic view tends to mitigate freedom almost to the vanishing point. And lastly, the devil clearly is represented as a supra-individual structure of evil, whereas the conditions of worth, so far as Rogers is concerned, are defined individualistically. Let us discuss the first difference.

Although for Irenaeus, the devil lives off the power of God, God is seen as the source of all life and the efficient cause of man's capacity for growth. Irenaeus could identify what the Rogerians have called the " actualization tendency " as the continuation of God's creative activity working in and through man. For Irenaeus, this impulse toward growth was the very image of God in man, was derivative of man's relationship with God, and was nothing that man owned in and of himself. It was a " gift " from God, a matter of God's grace. The devil lives off the power of God. Yet Irenaeus identifies God's creative power quite closely with the growth forces of man. He baptizes these growth tendencies and puts them in a theonomous context. Psychotherapy and the ancient view are closer together in their understanding of the sources supporting the forces of evil than we first thought. Psychotherapy contends that the conditions of worth of the self live off the deeper growth tendencies of man. Irenaeus could agree quickly. The difference between them lies not in this, but in Irenaeus' further identification of these growth energies with the creative fellowship of God. The difference between them lies in the fact that Irenaeus sets man's capacity for growth in a theonomous context.

Secondly, although Irenaeus believed that the devil existed before the fall of man and constituted a pressure prompting man to disobedience, he still insisted that man partially was responsible for his own fall. In fact, Irenaeus, as was pointed out earlier, thought there were three reasons for man's fall — the temptation or pressures of outside forces (the devil), the misused freedom of man, and the immaturity of Adam (the first man). Rogers would specify only two of these reasons as operative in the rise of incongruence — the pressures of outside forces (introjection) and the infant's immaturity and dependence. By immaturity, Rogers means the infant's lack of an autonomous self-regard complex.

For two reasons, Rogers' understanding of the role of introjection in the rise of conditions of worth may be unsatisfactory. The first reason is psychological. Quite clearly, children do not always unambiguously reduplicate within themselves the values of their parents. Often the process is more complex. Under the threat (subjectively experienced as anxiety) of parental conditions of worth, the child may evolve compensatorily (Adler and Horney) a different set of conditions of worth that he dogmatically adheres to in order to survive.

The other reason is philosophical. A rigid determinism is as philosophically untenable, whether one speaks of human or subhuman events, as is indeterminism. Simply because an individual's incongruence may be built around conditions of worth introjected from environmental pressures, it does not follow that the individual has no responsibility for "accepting" these conditions. Freedom and responsibility never can be eliminated completely, no matter how dominant the external determinative factors seem to be. A thoroughgoing determinism seems to be scientifically and philosophically as indefensible as a thoroughgoing indeterminism. Charles Hartshorne has pointed out that each event is more determinant than the totality of factors constituting its causal environment. This means that even at subhuman levels each event has a *uniqueness* which transcends the totality of causal factors operating on it.[4] This element of uniqueness may be the element of freedom and responsibility resident in every creature. Whether or not a man's incongruence and estrangement is seen as " sin " or " sickness " depends upon whether it is viewed from the perspective of the freedom and responsibility involved in its development or from the perspective of the environmental pressures involved.

It is interesting to note that psychology invokes freedom at the point of doing therapy when it insists that the client must take responsibility for his own progress. But to affirm freedom as a factor in the possibility of recovery must also necessitate its inclusion as a factor operating at the onset of illness. Psychotherapy, as did Irenaeus, also must hold in tension the factors of freedom, external pressure, and immaturity in explaining the rise of incongruence.

Psychotherapy and Irenaeus also tend to see the powers that hold man as supra-individual. Certainly insofar as Rogers and others like him use the concept of introjection as an explanation of how conditions of worth arise in the individual, they must admit a continuity between the conditions of worth of a single person and those of the larger cultural environment. Even if, as we have argued, some element of freedom should be admitted, there is still overwhelming evidence that cultures tend to be united by commonly held value structures which become absolutized at certain points and that constitute a context into which each person is born. The work of Erich Fromm has pointed to certain forms of cultural pathology.[5] His concept of the " marketing orientation " plus the work of social scientists such as Vance Packard and David Riesman have given colorful as well as competent documentation of the existence of such supra-individual conditions of worth. Insofar as the collective energies of a culture as a whole become diverted into the support of these conditions of worth, it can be said to be " bound " and in "servitude" to these standards of self-justification. In short, both Irenaeus (in mythological and dramatic terms) and Rogerian therapy (in scientific and almost deterministic terms) see man as under the domination of supra-individual powers by which and through which man attempts to justify himself, which live off man's more fundamental sources of growth, and which lead man into a state of loneliness, stagnation, and loss of vitality (death).

Psychotherapy and Irenaeus contrast sharply with the Latin view of human brokenness. Anselm is an example of a thinker who singles out one factor (human freedom and disobedience) as the chief cause of sin. The factor of original man's immaturity in no way is included. He envisions original man with a fully developed will, sufficiently rational and holy both to know and choose the *summum bonum*. The presence of the devil is admitted by Anselm, but since man had fully developed powers to know and choose the good, the fact that man succumbed to the temptations and pressures of the devil is no excuse. As Anselm writes, " In strength and immortal vigor, he freely yielded to the devil to sin, had on this account justly incurred the penalty of death." [6] Hence, for Anselm, only one factor is an effective explanation for man's fall, i.e., the misuse of man's freedom. The responsibility for human brokenness totally and completely falls upon man. This partially explains why, for Anselm, man's *guilt* is the most crucial factor to overcome if man is to be saved. The great *seriousness* of sin about which Anselm talks is a consequence both of Anselm's understanding of the fully mature and responsible original man and his doctrine of the honor of God. Between these two poles, the problem for salvation becomes a question of how to remove man's *guilt*. For Irenaeus, the problem of salvation is how to *defeat* the devil who once beguiled and now holds captive the once righteous, but childlike and imma-ture, Adam.

The emphasis is different for Anselm. Even if the sinner were to reform and not sin again, Anselm asserts that he could not repay and compensate for the great seriousness of the sin for which the sinner alone is responsible. Guilt, for Anselm, is not an impediment to change; it is an impedi-ment before God's demand for perfect obedience. Guilt, for Anselm, is not so much a bondage from which man must be released; it is a bad record which must be wiped clean if man is to receive immortality once again.

Man's guilt is not played down by Irenaeus, but it is not held *against man*. Guilt need not be fully compensated for in Irenaeus' thought. For Irenaeus, man's main need is to be freed from the bondage in which the devil holds him and for which man is, to some degree, responsible for placing himself. The psychotherapeutic view of human brokenness is closer to Irenaeus' emphasis upon bondage than it is An-selm's emphasis upon guilt. It is important to make this distinction clear if we are to gain an understanding of how empathic acceptance proves efficacious in overcoming the brokenness called sin as well as the brokenness called in-congruence.

Certainly the factor of guilt is important in the psycho-therapeutic process. But here guilt emerges as an inhibitor to change rather than an objective fact that condemns the client even if he were to change. Psychotherapy is closer to Irenaeus at this point. For both, guilt is not held against the broken man. Guilt must not be compensated necessarily. For Irenaeus, God continues in his creative fellowship in spite of man's guilt. For therapy, unconditioned positive regard and empathy continue in spite of the client's guilt. Cer-tainly, Irenaeus' God sees guilt, takes it seriously, is not blind or amoral about guilt. Neither does the therapeutic agent blind himself to guilt. The point is, that for both, the problem is not the objective fact of guilt so much as it is man's subjective *bondage* to guilt. For psychotherapy, it is man's subjective bondage to his own conditions of worth, which in turn judge him and make him feel guilty, that constitutes the major block to change.

The guilt that man has before his conditions of worth is a *false* guilt. He may feel that he is not living up to his conditions of worth. But in reality, he should not be placing his justification and worth on these conditions to begin with. The guilt, the loss of self-regard, the inconsistency that automatically follows from having conditions of worth is truly senseless, wasteful, false, and needless. And yet, to the broken man, it is real and is the primary obstacle to his salvation. Although man is objectively guilty before God for having conditions of worth, the main obstacle to salvation is not this objective guilt. The main obstacle is man's bondage to his own conditions of worth and the false guilt that they create. For Anselm, as we have observed, the situation is different. For him, even if the person could come to sin no more, he would be objectively guilty before God for past sins.

Excursis

The idea of false guilt has been strongly attacked by University of Illinois research psychologist Dr. O. Hobart Mowrer in his two books *The Crisis in Psychiatry and Religion* and *The New Group Therapy*.[7] Whereas the Freudian tradition developed the idea that neurosis was the result of an unreasonably strong, inflexible, and unconscious superego that produces needless guilt anxiety in the ego, Mowrer believes that neurosis is a consequence of a weak superego which cannot impede dishonest, immoral, or antisocial acts but which is still strong enough to create guilt. Mowrer is convinced that the superego must be fortified by the experiences of history, tradition, and culture. According to Mowrer, the neurotic person is closer to the criminal than to the saint; he is underacculturated and has not learned to live by the rules of society and the wisdom of tradition.

It is clear that Mowrer is as uncritical about his faith in culture and history as the neo-Freudians are in their near contempt for these same expressions of human life. Each person is to be educated, according to Mowrer, into the proven and time-tested ethics underlying his society. The process of education must be accomplished through what Mowrer calls " defensive identification." Moral values are taught through this process. Defensive identification is, in essence, what the Rogerians would call introjection; it is a process whereby the child takes over the moral values of his parent (and culture) as a way of defending himself from rejection, insecurity, or disapproval. Childhood dependence facilitates the process; the child needs the protection and nurture of the parent and learns to do what will please the parent in order to be assured of his continued good favor. It is only against the background of possible rejection, loss of support, and disapproval that the child is stimulated to internalize culture's values. Hence, unconditioned acceptance would, according to Mowrer, produce criminals. The mothering function (with which he associates unconditioned acceptance) needs to be supplemented with the demands and expectations of the father. On the basis of this kind of psychological analysis, Mowrer is critical of the Reformation doctrine of justification by faith alone, the whole idea of salvation by grace, and certainly any interpretation of God's faithfulness that might imply a concept of universal salvation. Instead, he feels more comfortable with the epistle of James, much of the moralism of liberal Protestant theology, and the Catholic idea that satisfaction must precede forgiveness (which, as we have noticed, is consistent with the basic framework of Anselm's atonement theory).

Several comments need to be made about this position, some critical and some appreciative. First, there is room in Rogerian theory for much of what Mowrer has to say. Unconditioned positive regard (acceptance) applies to feelings and not behaviors; it means that " no feeling is discriminated as being more or less worthy of positive regard." Rogers suggests that behavior must be controlled, guided, and channeled. Although he has great faith in the capacity of the self to execute socially acceptable behaviors when all the data is available to it, there appears to be some room for parental and societal disapproval or, what Mowrer might call, defensive identification. But clearly, it would apply to behaviors and not feelings — " you can feel mad, but I forbid you to break the window."

These comments must be coupled with a theological critique of Mowrer's view of culture and tradition. In brief, such a position is dangerously close to absolutizing culturally relative values; it appears to approach a position of idolatry. False guilt is guilt produced by the idolatrous adherence to false absolutes. Most of us would appreciate our Western approach to the importance of work even though it is a culturally relative value, as is physical cleanliness, home ownership, large breasts, narrow hips, masculine aggressiveness, and bright children. If cultural values are relativized — as they must be from the standpoint of the Bible's judgment on all man's idolatries — then it becomes possible for us to use disapproval, reward, and controlled punishment in guiding our children into culturally valued behaviors. We can expect our children to behave within the acceptable limits of their social context, not because their justification and worth depend on it, but because it does not depend on it. Learning social values and behaviors is a *game* which, although important, is nonetheless a game. When cultural values and behaviors are relativized, we can expect our children to learn them; we grant them differential doses of recognition or reward (reinforcement) and disapproval (extinction) simply because it is now clear that their ultimate justification and validity as persons does not depend on either the success or failure they experience in confronting these tasks. According to this view, Christian child-rearing would involve a multilevel approach. Peripheral adaptive habits, socially relative values, and behaviors reflecting social convenience receive conditioned approval or disapproval because they are themselves conditioned or relative goals. Basic feelings and attitudes — which underlie peripheral adjustments and which get to the heart of one's personhood — receive unconditioned positive regard and empathy. Theologically, this means that creation in all its basic aspects is to be affirmed and positively regarded (by both God and man) while certain of the specific expressions to which creation is directed must be met with differential judgments, restraint, and control.

Mowrer is right insofar as he sees a place for conditioned approval. He is wrong in absolutizing cultural values (although he is right in taking them seriously). He is wrong in failing to see the importance of unconditional positive regard as a substructure on the surface of which differential judgments come and go. The kind of conditioned and differential judgment Mowrer is talking about would apply, in terms of God's dealings with man, at the level of what we will later call "God's contingent structures of judgment and integration."

There is a sense in which Bushnell stands midway between Irenaeus and Anselm on these issues. Bushnell emphasizes man's *justitia originalis,* his original receptiveness to the inflow of God's righteousing power. He also stresses the immaturity of the original man. But he understands the devil to be the organic, supra-individual structure of evil *consequent* to man's sin rather than *prior* to it. But from a standpoint of man's fallen situation, the problem for salvation becomes very similar to what it was for Irenaeus. It becomes the problem of how to save man from bondage — bondage to his own self-created structures of evil.

In spite of this implication toward which we have seen Rogerian psychotherapy, Irenaeus, and Bushnell converging — e.g., that bondage rather than guilt is the problem to be overcome if man is to be saved — this is not meant to imply that the problem of guilt can be overlooked. Anselm is right in this respect. Salvation cannot be a simple matter of forgiving sin if forgiveness is thought to mean " letting sin go." Guilt both in its objective and subjective sense must be taken seriously. As we will see later, there is little place for permissiveness in that relationship which will overcome sin if permissiveness is to be interpreted to mean moral disengagement. Our point is simply that, from the standpoint of the actual dynamics of change, bondage rather than guilt becomes the crucial problem for salvation.

Empathic Acceptance and God's Relation to the World

Earlier in this chapter, the concept of unconditioned empathic acceptance was used as a model to interpret the nature of God's soteriological activity. Let us set down in propositional form some implications that this model holds for the nature of God's relation to the world whether seen from the perspective of soteriology or cosmology.

1. *It is God's primordial nature to be related to the world in the sense of feeling its feeling.* According to the principle of congruence, empathic acceptance must spring from the basic motivational processes of the personality if it is to be therapeutic. This means that it must be fundamental to the character of God, just as it must be fundamental to the character of the therapist. This would mean that God's basic essence is such that he would be empathically related — without exception, i.e., without condition or qualification — to all other individuals. No experience or feeling coming from the empiric world could contradict God's self-image. God's self-image (God's self-understanding of himself) would reflect adequately and unambiguously his fundamental essence, which is to feel empathically all feelings. Hence, in a technical sense, it cannot be said that God is sympa-

thetic, if sympathetic is thought to mean the experiencing of another's feelings with the other's conditions of worth attached to them. If this were the case, God would be accepting our conditions of worth as his own. This would mean that God would become alarmed and attempt to fend off and reject the same feelings that we would be attempting to fend off and reject. Therefore, he would be of little help in enabling us to overcome the brokenness resulting from the denials and distortions of experience affected by our conditions of worth.

2. *This primordial relationship would partake of the nature of rapport.* The concept of rapport must accompany any application of unconditioned empathic acceptance to God as an interpretative analogy. If God can feel the feeling of the world, there must be an interchange of patterned energy between God and the world. But since the concept of rapport implies that the interrelation of processes flows in both directions, it follows that each individual's feelings are felt completely and unambiguously by God; in turn, each individual at least in some limited (finitude) and distorted (sin) sense will feel the form of God's essence. It is possible for an individual to feel the form of God's love at the level of adverbial experiencing while failing to acknowledge it at the accusative level. Just as the client in the therapeutic situation can deny, distort, or reject the therapist's empathic acceptance, it would follow that, in the same manner, the sinner can deny, distort, and reject God's love and unconditioned empathic acceptance, even though it is the most persistent and pervasive datum of his experiencing.

When unconditioned empathic acceptance is abstracted and maximalized into the principle of absolute relativity, it means that God is the *ultimate object* of the feelings of every finite individual. God is the "open-end" (Gendlin) receiving all feelings into his experiencing, thereby perfectly feeling even that about ourselves which we cannot accept.[8] It is in this way that God integrates the world and perpetually is in the process of overcoming human brokenness. All feelings in the world happen to God just as they happen to the finite individuals first having them. But since God has no conditions of worth that would cause him to distort his experiencing, all feelings that first happen to other individuals finally happen more completely and fully to God than they do to the individual first having them. (Something like this may happen occasionally in psychotherapy when the client reports that the therapist seems to be feeling the client's feelings more deeply than the client himself.) But we must be cautioned against looking at this process in entirely passive terms. It is an active-passive process. By receiving the feelings of the world, by being the final object of every change, he also actively conveys unconditioned care, concern, love, and interest in the world. It is precisely in his passivity that God also constitutes the most determinative active influence on the world.

3. *The concept of unconditioned empathic acceptance also has implications for an understanding of God as creator.* If God is one God, what is typical of his character in his soteriological, saving, or healing activity ought also to be characteristic of his activity as creator. In the process of psychotherapy, the active care, concern, adience, or love that is conveyed through the therapist's empathic acceptance has a creative function. It tends to create a new self-understanding in the client. Although there are other individuals whose knowing of us helps create our self-understanding, God's empathic acceptance is unconditioned, complete, and per-

fect, and he is preeminent among individuals in creating, forming, and shaping the world through the way in which he knows the world.

4. *Whether empathic acceptance is seen from the perspective of creation or soteriology, it follows as an implication of this analogy when applied eminently to God that empathic acceptance should be the most pervasive datum impinging upon each individual's experiencing, and for this reason the form of empathic acceptance should constitute the image of God in man.* According to the concept of rapport, God's empathic acceptance is conveyed to man through an interchange of patterned and qualitied energy. But subception, defense, denial, and distortion can cause us to fail to recognize consciously this datum which constantly pervades our adverbial experiencing and which constitutes the most determinative motivational factor in human experience. As an element in human motivation, it should reflect the form and pattern of empathic acceptance. Such a motivational factor would be thought of as the image of God in man. It would not be something that man " owns " or " possesses " in and of itself. Man's response to this experiencing of God would bear at least a partial identity to the pattern of God's empathic acceptance. Limitations of finitude and, after the fall, the distortions of sin would operate to make our response to the inflow of God's empathic acceptance only a partial correspondence.

The concept of " stimulus hunger " recommends itself as a positive and empirically specifiable referent for such a motivational factor. Stimulus hunger was seen as the basic actualization tendency of the organism manifesting itself in adient behavior, the drive to enter into real experiential " commerce " with surrounding stimuli, and the impulse to feel feeling as an end in itself. This we saw to be the motivational foundation for the empathic acceptance of the therapist.

But we have pointed out already that, even though stimulus hunger can be identified as this image of God in man and seen to be operating even in the youngest infant, we still must make a distinction between its mature and immature manifestation. As we indicated above, in the immature infant this datum is the most dominant element in his experiencing, but there is no developed self-concept so that the individual understands or perceives himself as dominantly influenced by this experiencing. In the sinful, there is a developed self-concept but the datum of this experiencing is not symbolized or, if symbolized, it is not central to the gestalt of this self-concept. For the religiously mature, there is not only an organismic experiencing of this datum of God's empathic acceptance, but there is a symbolization of this datum in awareness and an integration of this datum into the self-concept so that it becomes its most central element. The mature man (who also would be the religiously mature man because of our theonomous rootage of the concept of stimulus hunger) would know and understand himself as one whose end is to enter into increasingly larger circles of empathic concourse with the events of the external world.

5. *Applying the therapeutic relation to God means that not even the fall of man can qualify God's capacity to be empathically accepting.* This principle is simply a special application of the *unconditioned* character of optimal empathic acceptance. Even man's fall into sin cannot qualify God's empathic acceptance. Even here, God empathically feels the depths of man's fallenness. The fall can be no more than an ontic alienation. It cannot constitute a separation between God and man. A real separation would mean that

God no longer feels the feeling of the fallen man. This would imply that God's essence had been qualified.

Since a total ontological separation would be unthinkable from the standpoint of our understanding of the nature of God, what would be the nature of man's alienation subsequent to his fall? His alienation would have the character of the estrangement between self and experiencing typical of incongruence. God's unconditioned empathic acceptance would be a datum in the experiencing from which the self is estranged.

Empathic Acceptance, Judgment, and the Law

It is time to specify the various ways in which elements of judgment and law seem to be ordered within the framework of this analogy.

What does judgment mean within the context of this analogy? *Judgment occurs in any interhuman situation when there is a conflict and contradiction between experience and our conditions of worth.* There are four ways in which judgment operates in the therapeutic situation. Also, there are four senses in which law can operate in the therapeutic situation. *Law is a structure of judgment that seems to have intractable and inescapable character to it.* In the therapeutic situation, each of these elements of judgment also constitutes a structure of law because of its *relatively* intractable and inescapable nature within this context.

The intractability that renders a structure of judgment also a structure of law is discernible even more readily when the analogy of empathic acceptance is applied to God. In the therapeutic situation, these structures of judgment often fall short of constituting actual structures of law because of the ease with which the client or patient can remove himself from their presence by terminating the relationship.

First, there is the judgment of the therapeutic relation itself. As was pointed out in Chapter V, the " no conditions "
of the therapeutic relation tend to contradict the very fact
that the client has conditions upon which he believes his
self-justification and worth depend.

God's relation of unconditioned empathic acceptance is
also a structure of judgment. The " no conditions " of God's
empathic acceptance contradict and therefore judge the
sinful self's conditions of worth and acceptability. It is against
the background of man's sin that God's love emerges as
judgment and intractable law. Against the background of
sin's conditions of worth, God's love operates as a plumb
line that judges and exposes the uselessness of man's efforts
to justify himself.

Second, there is the judgment and law that come from the
client's own conditions of worth. When these are applied to
the sinner as he stands before God, his conditions of worth
constantly are judging and finding contradictory certain
experiencing occurring in the larger organism. In turn, the
denied and distorted experiencing of the larger organism
constantly is judging and contradicting the self and its conditions of worth. Hence, the law and judgment of the self
and its conditions of worth are also a law and judgment that
are being judged constantly in return by the incongruent
person's own experience. In addition, God (as does the
therapist), in his acceptance of that about the client which
the client's conditions of worth will not accept, tends to in-
tensify the internal conflict, judgment, and contradiction between the self and the experiencing of the total organism.
But it cannot be said that God's empathic acceptance (nor
the therapist's) *causes* this internal judgment. To say that
God *wills* this internal judgment, in the sense that he permits it, can be asserted if one's understanding of the sov-

ereignty of God demands it. But it is not necessary to invoke this concept to understand how sin immediately involves itself in its own punishment and judgment; this results as a natural consequence of having conditions of worth.

The next two structures of judgment are really the same structures looked at from different perspectives. From one perspective, these structures can be called structures of judgment that recognize the therapist's limitations, especially his finitude. I am referring here to limitations the therapist may put on his time and the freedom the client may take with his person and property. These limitations constitute judgment and law because they often contradict what a client's conditions of worth prompt him to do. Insofar as these limitations stem from the therapist's finitude, they are not applicable to God and need not be discussed further. We will call this third group *judgments of finitude*.

But from another perspective, these same structures often can help integrate the client or patient so that empathic acceptance can be more effective. This fourth group can be referred to as the *judgment of the structures of integration*. The example of such structures, as we gave earlier, dealt with the control of destructiveness so that the client would not experience an increase of guilt, self-depreciation, fear of counter aggression, or delusions of omnipotence. Judgment and law connected with these structures of integration are primarily a means to an end, appear punitive or manipulative when operating by themselves, and should be considered workable and constructive only within a larger context of empathic acceptance.

This fourth structure of judgment and law can be applied immediately to God and his relationship to man. These integrative structures emerge as acts of God performed to actualize an optimum level of integration in the midst of the fallenness of the human situation. They are *contingent* acts that are secondary to the basic essence of God. God first and foremost has a character defined by unconditioned empathic acceptance. As we have indicated already, the concept of unconditional empathic acceptance constitutes the primary sense in which God is love and the primary sense in which he is law. When God's empathic love is viewed from the perspective of its adequacy and equal distribution, it is the primary meaning of God's righteousness and justice; when it is viewed from the standpoint of its self-consistency, it is the primary meaning of God's honor. This primary sense in which God is love and law must be kept separate from other ways of referring to God's law. The secondary sense in which God is law refers to the means-end structures of coercion designed to keep the human situation integrated so that his law and love in the primary sense can operate with enhanced effectiveness. These secondary structures of law attempt to generate a situation of *justice*. This is to say that they attempt to protect individuals from the injustices of conflicting conditions of worth. At the same time, because they put limitations upon injustice (man's inhumanity to man), they help halt the intensification of guilt and the increase of prideful delusions of omnipotence. It will be important for later discussion with Anselm to note that these secondary administrative structures must not be confused with God's honor in the primary sense.

These secondary structures of integration do not contradict God's fundamental essence. Their objective is the same as that of God's fundamental character, i.e., to actualize a situation in which there are no conditions of worth. They are of a piece with God's fundamental character. God is the same God in both instances, demonstrating to man that there are no conditions external to his relationship to God upon which his worth depends.

Of course, it can occur that God's administrative law, his structures of integration, can become the law of the self. Adherence to this law can become the condition around which the self can attempt to justify itself. An instance of this in a psychotherapeutic situation would be certain forms of the institutionalized patient who conforms to the rules of the treatment situation without availing himself of the central resources. This law can be grasped by the self as a condition of worth. This is the essence of Pharisaism. The means-end law of God has been absolutized into an end in itself. But the law of the self may be other than the law of God's secondary integrative and administrative structures. This would characterize the non-Pharisaic sinner, to which neither Paul nor the history of Christianity has given enough attention.

Sin, Incongruence, and Hostility

Incongruence, as was indicated earlier, reacts in a negative and hostile way even to unqualified empathic acceptance.[9] The " no " conditions of complete acceptance contradict and judge the conditions of worth of the incongruent self. Sin, too, reacts in a *negative* and hostile way, regardless of its outward manifestation, to a relationship of complete and unconditioned empathic acceptance. To defend oneself against contradictory experiences, one must either deny or distort the experience.

Both distortion and denial are attempts to be rid of the threatening experience. The ultimate implication of their intent is to be rid of the object that produces the threatening experience. With regard to the threat of God's relation, the ultimate intent of the sinner's hostility is to be rid of God, to reject God, as the client may, time and time again, attempt to reject the therapist.

We have already demonstrated that all men experience God at least at one level of their being, i.e., the level of adverbial, or organismic, experiencing. But just as the client may experience the therapist's empathic acceptance at one level of experiencing and yet reject it at another, so can the sinner feel God's absolute and perfect acceptance at one level but suavely, yet angrily, reject him at the level of conscious symbolization.

God's Relation to the World and the Processes of Atonement

Since unconditioned empathic acceptance implies the principle of *absolute relativity,* what does this finally imply for the doctrine of the atonement?

Not only must the therapist accept and empathize with the client's general feelings, he also must be able to receive empathically those negative feelings which were intended specifically to dissolve his acceptance. The therapist must be willing to be the " further end " of the client's negative feelings as well as all other feelings. This means that the therapist must allow his own feeling processes to be qualified by the client's hostility, just as he would receive all other feelings of the client. The eminent instance of unconditioned empathic acceptance is precisely that structure which is *unqualified* (absolute) in its capacity to be qualified (relative) by the feelings of another — even the other's most negative and hostile ones.

Since empathy is perfect and absolute in God, he truly feels, in the depths of his own being, all hostile and negative feelings expressed toward his acceptance. According to the insights of psychotherapy, anything other than knowing another object in the sense of *feeling* what it *feels* is something less than perfect knowledge. If man perceived that God's acceptance was based on a faulty or inadequate understanding or feeling of the full reality of his hostility, then man would be left to conclude that either God's acceptance would be withdrawn when man's enmity really was understood or that God's acceptance was sheer sentimentality and spineless permissiveness. Sentimentality is sympathy based on a shallow knowledge or feeling for the real feelings of the object of sympathy. God's acceptance is predicated on a complete and absolute empathic understanding of all our feelings, even our negative and hostile feelings toward him. It is because his acceptance endures unqualified *even though* he fully understands (fully feels) our hostility that we are "persuaded" to come to trust him. Or as Butler puts it when speaking of the therapeutic relation, it is only when the therapist's attitude of empathic acceptance remains "absolutely constant" that the client can come to unlearn his expectation that there are always, and will always be, conditions placed upon his worth and acceptability.[10]

The thrust of this is to call attention to the importance of God's *passivity* to the healing process. It is the absolutely unconditioned, intractable, enduring, unqualified character of God's *passive* reception of all of man's feelings, even his most hostile ones, that makes it possible for man to realize that there are no conditions placed on his worth and that he is free to feel and integrate those feelings into his wholeness which he was unable formerly to accept.

The Symbols of the " Cross" and the " Resurrection"

Can the symbols of the " cross " and the " resurrection " take on meaning within the structure of unconditioned empathic acceptance? Referring to the cross and the resurrection as "symbols" is not to suggest that they have a non-historical character. I simply am suggesting that the cross and the resurrection may refer also to something in the nature of God.

The intention is to interpret the cross in the light of God's empathic acceptance of our negative feelings and the resurrection in the light of his unconditioned durability to accept these feelings. The ultimate objective of sin's hostility is to negate empathic acceptance as a threat to its conditions of worth. The "death" of one offering such a relationship is the logical end of these negative feelings. In view of this, the cross represents God's capacity to feel fully the depths of sin's hostility — mankind's collective wish to negate him and the relationship that he offers. At the same time, the resurrection indicates that there is one sense in which God cannot be qualified or conditioned — in his capacity to feel these feelings. The resurrection points to the *absoluteness* of God's relativity, i.e., of God's empathic feeling. The cross points to the *relativity* of God's absoluteness. This absolute relativity, this unqualified qualifiability is the very structure of love. Love is unqualified sensitivity when sensitivity is thought to mean empathy.

Without these two aspects of God's active-passive relation to the world, the way in which God overcomes the brokenness of the world would be difficult to conceive. It is in this never-ending relationship that God lives *justification* into the world. He shows forth this justifying influence through the intractable caring for the feelings of the world — even those feelings which the world cannot itself accept.

It is God's cross-resurrection activity that overcomes the supra-individual structures of bondage (principalities and powers) which intersect, support, and form a continuity with the self's conditions of worth. But God's victory over the self's conditions is a victory that intimately involves the personal cooperation of the self itself. The self is bound to these conditions of worth. But its bondage is a *perceptual* bondage. The self believes that it is precisely these conditions which it must maintain in order to be justified, acceptable, and worthwhile. By remaining absolutely constant in his acceptance, God helps the self to come to learn that there are no conditions prerequisite to God's justifying love. This means that the supra-individual structures of evil are defeated, but not entirely without cooperation from the self.

The principalities and powers (the self's conditions of worth) are directly behind the self's hostility toward God's intractable love. This freely given love contradicts these conditions of worth, and they, in turn, defend themselves with hostile rejection of this love. God makes this hostile defense useless and of no avail by *accepting it.* By still enduring, God demonstrates to man his ultimate acceptability in spite of these powers and their conditions.

As these powers begin to lose their grip, the energy that supports man's conditions of worth is " released " and made available once again to the more fundamental fulfillment of man's basic nature. Creation is fulfilled. Now man is free to grow according to the direction the image of God in man would take him.

We are talking about a general atonement process characteristic of God's general relation with the world. The fall of man did not stop this process. God's atoning love continued, anyway, as an automatic continuation of God's basic nature, operating now, however, against the background of sin. What appeared as God's *creative* caring and fellowship with the world before the fall now appears as God's *graceful* caring and fellowship. In both instances, whether it appeared as creation or grace, it was God's unconditioned empathy and acceptance. Grace is in no way a *contingent* element in the nature of God. Grace is God's creative feeling of our feeling *enduring* as absolute and unconditioned even after the fall. This also gives us our ultimate clue about the nature of *forgiveness*. Forgiveness is the continuation of God's unconditioned empathic acceptance *in spite* of man's rejection of it. Forgiveness is the nature of grace. It is continuous with God's creative fellowship. Yet it is this same forgiveness and grace that constitutes God's *judgment* in its primary sense. Since God's empathic acceptance has no conditions attached to it, the very absence of conditions contradicts and judges sin's conditions of worth and acceptability. It is this same forgiveness and grace that constitutes the primary sense in which the world is measured and found wanting.

The Atoning Process and the Christ Event

Our maximalization of empathic acceptance into a general atonement process has not been done arbitrarily. There are two reasons why it is not arbitrary. First, for empathic acceptance to be effective, it must be fundamental to the character of the therapist. *It cannot be a temporary, occasional, contingent mode of operation.* Therefore, if this concept is to be applied analogically to God, it similarly must be a fundamental, noncontingent, enduring aspect of his character. Second, since empathy seems to involve a real interrelation of processes, its generalization must extend the onto-epistemological principles that it implies.

But there is another basis upon which this analogy can be referred justifiably to God. This had to do with the ontological principle as it applies to the therapeutic relation. Here it was asserted that the therapist's acceptance implies and participates in a larger structure of acceptance to which the smaller structure witnesses and is, to some extent, analogical.

It is on these grounds that we have come to talk about a general atonement process.

What necessity or importance is attached to the atonement worked in the cross and the resurrection of Jesus Christ? It would seem that if this atonement process is going on constantly between God and man, there is no particular necessity for the event of Jesus Christ.

The scope of this study does not permit a full discussion of faith and history, the necessity of the incarnation, and other important questions relevant to Christological issues. But there are two questions that must be raised. First, is there an insight amid our psychotherapeutic analogy as to why redemption must entail a special act of God in Jesus Christ? Second, is not an understanding of God, in the sense of absolute relativity, just as necessary for a proper understanding of the efficacy of the cross and the resurrection of the historic Christ as it is necessary for an understanding of the cross and the resurrection process of the primordial God?

Let us turn to the first question. The psychotherapeutic analogy generates a principle pointing to the necessity of God's special act in Jesus Christ. " Incongruence " constitutes an adequate model with which to articulate an understanding of the nature of sin. According to this model, the self becomes estranged ontically from its adverbial and organismic experiencing — including its experiencing of God's unconditioned empathic acceptance. The self no longer looks to this adverbial and organismic experience of God's love for the basis of its worth. Instead, the self is looking in the *other direction* — toward its conditions of worth. The self's conditions of worth are also continuous with supra-individual structures that the individual has taken over from the *world*. It is the very nature of the sinner to turn away from his direct experiencing of God and to look outward toward the world for the basis of his worth and justification.

The problem of why the incarnation is necessary is analogous to the question of why a therapist is helpful. Our organismic experiencing is always present, always with us. Why does another person in the form of a therapist help us to accept that which is always with us and always pleading, in a sense, to be known and accepted by the self? The answer seems to be this: The self learned to think of some of the organism's experiencing as unacceptable on the basis of standards or conditions of worth taken over from the social environment. In order to *unlearn* this, the incongruent person must do this with reference to *someone* in his social environment. He cannot be freed from his conditions of worth until someone emerges *in the world,* emerges at the place where he is looking, who places no conditions on his acceptance. And the more unambiguous is the witness of this empathic acceptance, the more directly will it refer the sinner to God's unconditioned empathic acceptance felt in the depths of his adverbial experiencing. But it would be impossible for one sinner to witness *unambiguously* to the *justitia originalis* of another sinner. He could not witness unambiguously to it because he has not accepted fully his own *justitia originalis.* Since all sinners look to the world for their justification, must not God provide us with *one* in the world who will witness unambiguously to God's direct justifying influence in the depths of our life?

I am not suggesting that God's direct love in the depths of our adverbial experiencing accomplishes nothing simply because it is the structure of sin to be turned away from these organismic experiencings. Certainly the atonement process goes on. The self may feel a warmth welling up from the depths of its own adverbial experiencing that gives it a sense of worth and justification and frees it from captivity to its conditions of worth. It is not necessary to maintain this either/or attitude in order to assert the uniqueness of the Christ event. Jesus Christ is the unambiguous manifestation of God's unconditioned empathic acceptance at the level of finite beings, but he is not the exclusive means of this love.

The point is (and this addresses our second question mentioned above) that working through a finite person would be a particularly efficacious strategy uniquely adapted to meet the structure of sin. It is conceivable that God could make a contingent and unique manifestation of his love in the person of one human being. Such a contingent manifestation would not be inconsistent with his nature as absolute relativity and, in fact, could occur to and be carried out only by a God possessing this kind of sensitivity and flexibility.

Such a manifestation must be thought to have within it both a dynamic and a noetic element. Its dynamic element means that it takes part in the dynamic interplay between unconditioned empathic acceptance and sin. A historically specifiable group or community of forgiven and liberated human beings springs up around the figure of Jesus of Nazareth. But the life and death of Jesus also have a noetic function. They serve as a symbolization of the character of God. The form and pattern of the events of Jesus Christ's life constitute a symbolization of the form and pattern of the essence of God. In Jesus, this essence of God's fundamental character is expressed noetically and manifested dynamically.

The church's apprehension of the death and resurrection of Jesus of Nazareth represents a basic intuition into the structure and efficacy of acceptance as it exists eminently and maximally in God. The meaning of Christ's death must be seen in the context of the *total ministry of Christ*. In the light of this total ministry, Jesus' death results from an intensification of hostility produced when man is confronted by a relationship of unconditioned acceptance that necessarily contradicts and judges his conditions. The death of Jesus Christ represents God's full and complete empathic reception of this negative reaction and hence the ultimate expression of the genuineness of his forgiveness. Only the extremities of death can represent appropriately the extent to which God is qualified by our enmity. And the extremities of this one man's death both symbolize and manifest God's eternal suffering before the onslaughts of sin.

THE PERSON OF JESUS CHRIST

Although therapy itself, when given a theological critique, affirms the necessity for an unambiguous manifestation of God's love at the level of man's social experience, it also offers a model for comprehending and ordering this manifestation in the man Jesus Christ. Since the attitude of the therapist both participates in and witnesses to a larger structure with reference to which both the therapist and client find themselves acceptable, the therapist performs in this small way a Christological function, limited and ambiguous as it is. It is possible, then, that an analysis of the character of the therapist can offer a model that may aid in the interpretation of the person of Jesus Christ.

In Chapter V we discussed the therapist's character under the rubric of *congruence*. For a person to be congruent and yet experience empathic acceptance assumes that unconditioned positive regard and empathy are fundamental elements of the actualization tendency. Theoretically this is conceivable if the actualization tendency is thought to be rooted in the concept of " stimulus hunger " — the primitive, invariant drive of the organism to enter into wider and wider circles of vicarious experiencing.

We have learned also that both the mature person and the neonate possess a high degree of congruence. The mature person, however, has a self-concept, whereas the neonate does not. Further, the mature person has an autonomous self-regard complex upon which his self-concept rests, whereas the infant is dependent upon others for his self-regard.

In Chapter VI we put the concept of stimulus hunger in a theonomous context. When this is done, not only is it the root of empathic acceptance in human beings, it becomes the objectification in man's adverbial experiencing of the pattern of God's own primordial nature. Looked at theonomously, stimulus hunger is the most determinative datum of man's experience communicated to a man through the processes of preanimistic rapport between God and man. It is the most original and primitive element of the created world. It is the image of God in man. It is the original actuality of man's created existence and thereby presents itself as the original possibility for man to organize his emerging and developing self-concept around.

What does this suggest for the person of Jesus Christ? It suggests that Jesus is the Christ by virtue of his capacity to organize his self-concept around this original possibility of the created order. Just as the therapist approaches a recapitulation of the integrity of the neonate, Jesus Christ recapitulates — completely and unambiguously conforms his self-concept around — the most original possibility of created existence. In this way, Jesus Christ becomes the Second Adam. He possesses the integrity of the original man but in addition possesses a mature self-concept completely and unambiguously conforming to that original vicarious actuality which intersects and undergirds all finite reality. The striking similarity between this view and the understanding of the person of Jesus Christ presented in the thought of Irenaeus will be elaborated in the next chapter.

VIII

THE PSYCHOTHERAPEUTIC ANALOGY
AND THE HISTORIC OPTIONS

At the end of the fourth chapter, four principles were listed that represented the core concerns of all our doctrines of the atonement and the concerns that any doctrine of the atonement should attempt to address. It now becomes our task to determine the extent to which the therapeutic analogy can meet these four criteria. These criteria, it must be remembered, are only formal ones. A particular theory could address each of these principles and still be deficient, in comparison to another position, in its capacity to account adequately for the concerns of these principles. But at least they can serve as minimal standards for judging the qualifications of this analogy for further discussion with the historic options. The four principles are listed below along with a discussion of the appropriate therapeutic analogy.

To what extent does the therapeutic analogy root the sufficient reason for the atonement in the nature of God? It is the inner necessity of the structure of absolute relativity that serves as the sufficient reason for the atonement. God will not allow his relationship to man to be broken entirely. When this relationship is rightly understood, it constitutes an atoning process that is working at all times in absolute and unconditioned terms. The event of Jesus Christ must be considered as the contingent manifestation of a structure that has necessary and unconditioned certainty.

To what extent does this analogy envision the atonement in such a way as not to jeopardize God's basic order and structure of the world? It seems to protect the basic order and structure of the world in two ways. First, God's righteousness means that God distributes his empathic acceptance equally to all without regard to conditions of worth. This in itself constitutes both a plumb line judgment on and contradiction of all of man's self-striving as well as an ultimate and unconditioned structure that constantly is overcoming brokenness and thereby preserving order by accepting about man that which man cannot accept about himself. But, as we have seen, this does allow some margin for dislocation in the order of justice.

Second, against the background of God's unconditioned empathic acceptance are his contingent, means-end structures of law that integrate and administer man in his fallenness for the sake of the purposes of God's ultimate nature. It is within these two orders of law that the atonement takes place. And even though there is some margin of dislocation in the order of justice, the order of the world is basically secure.

To what extent does this analogy provide some framework for understanding the something " new " that the event of Jesus Christ adds to effect man's redemption? Jesus Christ adds an epistemo-soteriological factor to God's primordial relation to the world. In Jesus Christ, God's unconditioned empathic acceptance is manifest *in* the world at the very point toward which sinful man is looking for his justification. This unambiguous manifestation of God's acceptance at the level of the created world (*sarx*) makes it possible to *know* this structure in a way that is more readily available than God's direct manifestation in adverbial experiencing.

As an epistemo-soteriological principle, it must not be construed as overemphasizing the *noetic* function of the Christ event. Christ does not just reveal knowledge. Christ manifests the very structure of God, in all of its power and efficaciousness, in such a way as to make it more available within the perceptual distortions of sinful man. This is the something " new " that the Christ event brings to the human situation.

To what extent does the atonement of Jesus Christ, understood under the rubric of this analogy, effect real redemption? The real redemption envisioned by the atonement when interpreted with the therapeutic analogy is seen when the self's supra-individual conditions of worth are defeated because of the persistent capacity of this empathic and suffering acceptance to receive the very feelings which the conditions of worth are attempting to deny and distort. But the defeat of these conditions of worth which bind man is accomplished through an element of cooperative decision on the part of man. The sinner, realizing that nothing can qualify God's empathic acceptance of him (not even the most violently hostile maneuvers of his conditions of worth), is persuaded finally to trust his justification in God rather than his own conditions of worth.

The shape of this redemption has both *subjective* and *objective* poles. The objective change in the situation is the defeat of the conditions of worth, the supra-individual structures of evil, i.e., a demythologized view of the concept of the devil. The subjective change should be seen as man's acceptance of his being accepted. The subjective change is impossible without God's objective act of participation in our lives. If God could not both positively regard the sinner and at the same time empathize with his distortions, the possibility for such a decision would not exist.

A Prelude to Conclusions

One of the central concerns of this study has been with a doctrine of God adequate for a proper understanding of the meaning of the atonement. The question was asked always of our historical options, " Is this understanding of the work of Jesus Christ based on a concept of God's perfection that sees him *a se* in *all* respects or in only *some* respects? " By definition, the principle of absolute relativity implies that God would be *a se* in *some* but not *all* respects. Naturally, a generalization of any principle descriptive of finite actualities would include a contingent element within it. The passive element in empathic acceptance becomes the relativity principle in the expanded concept. But, an analysis of the therapeutic relation demonstrates that this passive element is crucial to the healing process. Hence, it becomes important to search for a way to include this passive element within an understanding of the *perfection* of God.

Let me give a brief description of some of the points that will be made and supported in the process of this chapter. First, it will be argued that there is a formal similarity between the concept of unconditioned empathic acceptance (the less abstract meaning of absolute relativity), Irenaeus' understanding of " recapitulation," and Bushnell's understanding of " sympathetic suffering." The formal similarity of all three concepts points directly to the idea that God suffers, that he enters into empathic participation with the conditions and consequences of sin, that contingent realities actually touch the Godhead, that God can gather these distortions into his own life and hold them and bear them, but that it is also his unique capacity to endure and remain unqualified, uninhibited, unlimited in his ability to continue his empathic relation with mankind. Second, it will be argued that the concept of unconditioned empathic acceptance, when rightly understood in its operation to overcome sin, suggests the images of a struggle and a victory, the idea of *Christus Victor*.

THE STRUCTURE OF GOD FROM WHICH HIS SOTERIOLOGICAL ACTIVITY ISSUES

With regard to the concept of God as it serves as a substructure for the entire atonement edifice, we find that implications of the therapeutic analogy most strikingly agree with the thinking of Bushnell. Beginning with those points at which the therapeutic analogy shares areas of commonality with the other historic options is not meant to be a device for weighting this task of comparison in favor of the adequacy of the therapeutic analogy. This procedure has two intentions. First, by moving from those areas of obvious commonality to areas of less obvious commonality, the general task of comparison is facilitated. Secondly, there is a sense in which this procedure can serve also as a test for the adequacy of the therapeutic analogy. For if there are large areas of *external coherence* between the constructive position which this analogy has generated and the historic alternatives, this in itself will tend to demonstrate the potency of the analogy to account for some of the central facts that the atonement theory attempts to order.

God's Aseity in All or Some Respects

In comparing Bushnell and the therapeutic analogy, the following generalization can be made. Both agree that it is fundamental to the nature and essence of God to be in relation to his creatures. Bushnell does this when he states that the law of God's own nature is described in the " law of love " and when he contends that love is really the " law relational" and the exact measure of God's righteousness. In psychotherapy, the congruence principle forced us to see the essence of the therapeutic relation (unconditioned empathic acceptance) as springing from the most fundamental strata of psychic life in the therapist. In the expanded analogy we read this to mean that absolute relativity is the *law* of God's nature — a law which, although self-derived, still leads God to have his end outside himself.

It is also interesting to note that both of them use the category of feeling in describing God's relationship to the world. For both, this relationship means, to use Bushnell's words, that God will so "insert himself into miseries" of man "as to have them a burden on his *feeling*" (italics mine). For both, this feeling of the world introduces a conditioned element into the Godhead. In short, it means that for both positions God is completely *a se,* absolute and perfect in his capacity to feel the feelings of all actualities, but that he is not completely *a se* with regard to the content of his own feelings.

Although the conditioned element in the therapeutic analogy is built around the concept of empathy while Bushnell builds it around the idea of sympathy, the two words function in the same way. Sympathy does not mean, for Bushnell, an identification of God through Jesus Christ with the world in such a way that God loses his identity. It is the very nature of God's sympathy, according to him, not to become distorted by the feelings of the other even though God is fully sensitive to them.

When we move to Irenaeus, we see that he is clear about the fundamental relational character of God. Irenaeus spoke about God's relation to the world under the rubrics of " creative fellowship " and the " two hands of God." It is God's self-derived end to " confer His benefits " on a creation external to himself. God's communion and fellowship convey justification, light, and growth.

It is not clear that this relationship implies a conditioned as well as an unconditioned element in the nature of God. Of course, he made several statements that indicate that he believed in the absoluteness and unconditionedness of God. It was our position that these statements should be interpreted in the light of IV.6.2, where Irenaeus asserts that God had worked always for the salvation of man, even before the time of Tiberius Caesar, and that to think otherwise would make God " careless " and " neglectful " and " both change God, and destroy our faith in that Creator who supports us by means of His creation." Here God's immutability serves as the basis for asserting God's ultimate trustworthiness and faithfulness, or what the Old Testament called God's covenantal loyalty (*chesed*).

From another perspective, much of what Irenaeus taught seems to imply — in fact, even demands — some understanding of the conditionedness and passibility of God. Three aspects of his thought seem to converge and demand this. First, there was his identification of the two hands of God with God's own immediate involvement in the processes of creation, revelation, and redemption. This seemed to suggest that anything said about the Son was also a statement about God. Second, there was his insistence that the divine, as well as the human, in Christ suffered. Third, there was his understanding of " recapitulation " not only as a return to the original integrity of the first Adam but as a " summing up " of the conditions and consequences of sin by " stooping low," and taking upon himself " our infirmities " and " our ills." Christ does this not to satisfy God's honor with his obedience, nor to substitute for us in receiving God's wrath. Instead, he stands in the stream of sin's consequences by virtue of his conflict with the hostile powers that hold man in bondage and provoke man to enmity with his God. All of this implies a passivity, a receptivity, a participation very similar to what is conveyed by the concept of empathy in psychotherapeutic terms. That this means a real sharing of the internal frame of reference of all men can be seen in the fact that Irenaeus believes that Jesus Christ lived to be an old man, thereby summing up the predicament of every stage of life, from infancy to old age.

For Irenaeus, God's absoluteness and conditionedness seem to unite in the idea that although God fully takes into himself the enmity provoked by these hostile powers, his creative fellowship still endures unqualified and undiminished. It is for this reason that we have asserted the formal similarity which exists between the concept of unconditioned empathic acceptance and Irenaeus' concept of recapitulation.

Anselm, on the other hand, diverges strongly from the general directions of the therapeutic analogy, Irenaeus, and Bushnell; he does not conceive God's character, or essence, in relational terms, nor is there any sense in which God can be considered to be conditioned. Nothing like the conditionedness or passibility implied by the concepts of empathy (therapeutic analogy), sympathy (Bushnell), or recapitulation (Irenaeus) can be found in Anselm.

Early in *Cur Deus Homo* we discovered that it would be unfitting for God to " stoop to things so lowly " as to suffer on the cross. This major presupposition forces Anselm to eliminate any understanding of the cross that would imply the suffering or passibility of God. Since God is subject to no accidents, he cannot be moved by any consideration external to himself. This means that God cannot be properly said to be compassionate or sympathetic.

There are additional psychological data relevant to this question. Maslow's research into the healthy personality reveals that healthy people are indeed more independent than the rest of the population. They are less " needy " than the average person. This insight constitutes the wisdom behind Anselm's vision into the aseity of God. But what Anselm failed to comprehend was that the independence, autonomy, and lack of " neediness " on the part of the healthy does not exclude passivity and receptiveness. Maslow's research indicates that healthy people are more prone to " Being-cognition " and " Being-love " (as opposed to " deficiency-love " and " deficiency-cognition "). It is the very nature of Being-love and cognition to be more passive, receptive, and open to the world. Hence, independence and passivity are not mutually exclusive. A maximalization of these insights further validates the concept of absolute relativity.[1]

That the question of the immutabiilty of God in all respects is not a dead issue can be seen from a variety of sources. That the Catholic atonement theory still relies on this Anselmian starting point can be seen in Martin Jarrett-Kerr's *Atonement for Our Time*.[2] Tillich's doctrine of God, which has had considerable influence, asserts the immutability of God in all respects — maintaining that language suggesting conditionedness must be thought to apply to God only symbolically.[3] The Tillichian mode of thinking is being strongly advocated by Bishop Robinson (*Honest to God*) as the only acceptable modern way to think about God.[4] The argument of these men is that theism, understood to mean the idea that God is the supreme individual among lesser individuals, needs to be replaced by the concept that God is not a being (individual) himself, but the ground of being. There is much to commend itself in this idea. But I see nothing contradictory about asserting, on one hand, that God is the ground of all finite beings and, on the other, that he is the Supreme Being himself. In addition, if accepting the idea that God is " being itself," or the ground of being, means returning to that aspect of classical metaphysics which asserted the immutability of God in all respects, we will have lost the possibility of developing an appropriate understanding of God for an adequate doctrine of the atonement. The importance for the atonement theory of an understanding of God that allows for his suffering has been discussed at length by Hywel Hughes in his book entitled *The Atonement.*[5]

Nothing like a mutuality of relationship whereby both God and man are affected by the other is envisioned by Anselm. It seems rather that God has made man complete and that man must now stand alone. Let us recall a passage quoted earlier:

Moreover, as Adam and his whole race, had he not sinned, would have stood firm without the support of any other being, so after the fall, the same race must rise and be exalted by means of itself.

God's continuing creative fellowship is not emphasized significantly by Anselm. But because man is supposed to stand alone, it follows that man should make the satisfaction necessary to remove the guilt incurred by sin.

The presence of a relational definition of the perfection of God has an interesting implication for understanding what he expects of man. For the therapeutic analogy, Bushnell, and Irenaeus, man's obedience is a matter of *responsive openness* to God's relationship of love. The goal of therapy is " openness to experience," including the client's experience of the therapist's empathic acceptance. For Irenaeus, man's original uprightness is a matter of " innocence " and his innocence is an unbroken and uninhibited reception of God's creative fellowship. The essence of man's obedience, for Irenaeus, is a " soft and tractable " heart open to " the impressions of His fingers." A very similar view of man's obedience was held by Bushnell.

Since Anselm's God is not defined in relational terms, neither is man's obedience. Man is created with a " rational " and " holy " will so that he can discern and do the good. For Anselm, man was created for self-sufficient moral rectitude. Hence, the implications that the fall of man has for the honor and righteousness of God have a considerably different meaning for Anselm than they do for the other three positions. The issue of the honor of God will be the next topic pursued.

Righteousness, Honor, and Power

The interplay between the righteousness, honor, and power of God are very important aspects of each theory of atonement reviewed in this study, the historic positions as well as the one derived from the therapeutic analogy. In Chapter VII we discussed what the concept of unconditioned empathic acceptance (absolute relativity) implies for God's righteousness, honor, and power. God's *righteousness* was defined as the law of his nature to *receive* and *care* for (show *regard* for) with perfect equality the feelings of each finite being. God's *honor* was defined to mean " the infallibility of his capacity to *conform* to the structure of his own righteousness." God's righteousness and honor stand as the bedrock foundation upon which rests the order of the world. God's justice in its primary sense was subsumed under the rubric of righteousness and refers primarily to the equality of God's relational adequacy.

Whereas God's honor refers to God's propensity to conform to his own basic character, God's power refers to his "unconditioned" and "unqualified" strength to so conform. As was argued earlier (using the model of therapeutic interaction), perfect power need not imply absolute force to determine the creature's acceptance of the love that God offers. The perfection of God's empathic acceptance means that it can stand as the "sufficient condition" upon which man can come to know that he is acceptable. But whether man does so is not determined solely by the power of God's relationship to him. If man does not accept his acceptance by God, his unconditioned love, this does not, as was pointed out earlier, dishonor God — just as in the case of therapy, the client's refusal of the therapeutic relation does not necessarily impugn the capacity of the therapist to accept and relate to the client.

The similarity between this view and that of Bushnell is clear. For Bushnell, God's righteousness is the relational law of love — the law of his nature before the appearance of his governmental will. God's honor is simply his capacity to adhere to the structure of his own nature. In addition, God's immutable adherence to the law of righteousness in his own nature constitutes the basis of his power. It is a moral power. Bushnell identifies God's power with his passive virtues — the utter completeness of God's capacity to be afflicted by our sins and yet to *endure* in the inflow of his righteousing and justifying relationship to man. But the perfection of God's power, as envisioned by Bushnell, does not entail the power to *force* man to accept this justifying relationship. God's omnipotence means that God has all the force to do what force can do. God does not force the inflow of his righteousness, but instead conveys it by means of *persuasion*. The word "persuasion" in Bushnell should not be thought to mean argumentation or propaganda. Instead, it refers to a gentle but immutable interplay between God and man that accomplishes its ends without reducing man to an automaton in the process. The essential agreement between this and the therapeutic analogy is clear.

Irenaeus makes no clear reference to God's righteousness. It seems closely connected with the idea of the sufficiency of God as the perfect giver of life. Nothing seems to be able to condition God's capacity to provide man with the resources for abundant life, be it the fall of man or the hostile attacks of the devil. Irenaeus also states that God's *honor* is not dependent upon man's reception of this life; it is not dependent upon man's obedience. Between the assertion, "They did not glorify Him when they followed Him" and the statement, "Nor has God need of human obedience," we can see that God does not expect obedience for his own sake or his own honor; rather, it is for the benefit of man himself.

At what point, for Irenaeus, could God's honor be impugned? Man's disobedience and fall are not sufficient to do this. It is only if man were "utterly [and forever] abandoned to death, [that] God would [in that case] have been conquered," or, I take it, dishonored. But, the passage continues, "inasmuch as God is invincible and long-suffering, He did indeed show Himself to be long-suffering in the matter of the correction of man and the probation of all." God's invincibility (his power) is seen in terms of his long-suffering; and this long-suffering will eventually work in its own inexorable and patient way to an ultimate victory over the devil. Are we to infer that the long-suffering of God operates in the same way as the "long-suffering, patience, compassion, and goodness of Christ" which Irenaeus sees as the heart of Christ's obedience and which exhibited itself in the fact that "He both suffered, and did Himself exculpate those who had maltreated Him"? I believe so. The measure and meaning of God's power is the long-suffering and patience of the cross. This long-suffering eventually proves victorious in the death of Jesus Christ. For the therapeutic analogy, Bushnell, and Irenaeus, the image of power seems related closely to the passive elements implicit in God's relation to the world.

In all three instances, we receive the picture that God's *honor* is not dependent upon man's obedience. Instead, it is dependent upon God's unqualified capacity to stay in relation to his creatures, providing, through this relation, the means of life and justification. For all three, we receive a picture of God's power as being sufficient to maintain this relation and, through the processes of a persistent persuasiveness, eventually culminating in victory. By the term " persuasion," we do not mean to emphasize rational demonstration or argumentation. We mean instead an interplay of power that accomplishes its end without the use of brute force or fiat. Aulén states well what is intended by this concept when he attempts to set forth the meaning of Christ's struggle with the devil in ransom theories of the atonement. Aulén contends that the purpose of these dramatic transactions is to " deny that God proceeds by way of brute force to accomplish His purpose by compulsion." He continues:

However crude the form, the endeavor is to show that God does not stand, as it were, outside the drama that is being played out, but Himself takes part in it, and attains His purpose by internal, not by external means; He overcomes evil, not by an almighty *fiat,* but by putting in something of His own, through a Divine self-oblation.[6]

For a direct demonstration of how the image of persuasive power is native to Irenaeus, let us turn to his own words.

And since the apostasy tyrannized over us unjustly, and, though we were by nature the property of the omnipotent God, alienated us contrary to nature, rendering us its own disciples, the Word of God, powerful in all things, and not defective with regard to his own justice, did righteously turn against that apostasy, and redeem from it His own property, not by violent means, as the [apostasy] had obtained dominion over us at the beginning, when it insatiably snatched away what was not its own, but by means of *persuasion* [italics mine], as became a God of counsel, who does not use violent means to obtain what He desires; so that neither should justice be infringed upon, nor the ancient handiwork of God go to destruction.[7]

It is interesting to note that in this passage the word " justice " refers to the manner of God's own method of dealing with man and the devil, rather than the certainty of an appropriate system of rewards and punishments. God's righteousness and justice seem synonymous and refer to the manner in which God uses his power, or, as he says later, the way God operates in " not snatching away by stratagem the property of another, but taking possession of His own in a righteous and gracious manner." [8]

A significant point of difference between these positions is the precise way in which they envision the dynamics of God's persuasive power. This difference is heightened further by their differing views of the context in which these dynamics operate. It is at this point that Bushnell begins to emerge as somewhat deficient, or at least, misleading. It is also at this point that Irenaeus and the therapeutic analogy seem to move toward a surprising but important agreement. The development of this aspect of our argument must wait until we discuss the *work* of Jesus Christ. But before this can be done, we must discuss the relation of God's righteousness, honor, and power in the thought of Anselm.

Anselm presents a considerably different view of these subjects. The word "righteousness" is not applied to God in *Cur Deus Homo*. Instead of a concept of God's righteousness, we find a prominent place given to the justice of God. In addition, we find a strong emphasis upon the honor and power of God. God's honor is seen as the *rerum ordo* (the order of things), the will of God that is the bedrock foundation of the world. It is the purpose of this will, this foundation for the order of the world, that man be upright and obedient before God. God's honor is his capacity to fulfill these basic intentions for man and thereby preserve the order of the world. Man's fall into sin is an offense to God's honor. This position contrasts with Bushnell, Irenaeus, and the therapeutic analogy who do not see the fall as an affront to God's honor. Only God's utter abandonment of man to the devil would actually put God's honor in question.

But this is not the case with Anselm. Man, in his createdness, owes everything to God. When man sins, he fails to give God his due and "robs God of his own and dishonors him." Anselm's nonrelational characterization of the nature of God makes God's honor a matter of the completeness with which he can be assured that the created order conforms to his will. For Bushnell, Irenaeus, and the therapeutic analogy, God's honor depends more squarely on how completely God maintains his own loving, life-giving, and righteousing relationship with the created order. Of course, Anselm cautions us to remember that nothing really can qualify God's honor in and of itself. The sinner's disobedience only dislocates his own place in the order and harmony of the world.

Here we confront what constitutes one of Anselm's greatest difficulties. It is clear that if Anselm is to be consistent in his stress on the absolute immutability of God in all respects, there would be no way in which man's sin could actually constitute a *real* lessening (robbery) of God's honor. To speak meaningfully of sin's offense to God's honor and still maintain the immutable perfection of God's honor in itself, we must turn to either Harnack or McIntyre in the interpretative options discussed in Chapter III. We must follow Harnack and push the meaning of God's loss of honor into the arena of public reputation and conceive it in analogy to an embarrassing, but groundless insult which God cannot tolerate. Or we must follow the lead of McIntyre and conceive it as a witness to the fact that sin is an "intensely personal" betrayal of the trust between God and man; but both interpretations lead us to an issue that must be addressed on the basis of modern psychotherapeutic insights. The result of either of these interpretations is to place in the Godhead what would be called, in Rogerian terms, a *condition of worth*. It would, in effect, place within the Godhead a neurotic element that can never serve as a solid presupposition for the salvation of man.

An insult, offense, or affront is possible only against a background of conditions of worth. Frieda Fromm-Reichmann has pointed out that if a therapist goes into a therapeutic situation with the conviction that he must save the client and if, when he notices that the client is failing to respond, he takes this unresponsiveness as a personal affront, the possibilities of good therapy are almost nil.[9] As Dorothy Baruch has pointed out, only the neurotic parent attempts to guide the disobedient child with the idea that the child's behavior has been an insult to the parent's standing as a good and sufficient parent.[10] Likewise the good therapist is motivated for the good of the client and does not take the client's rebelliousness as a personal affront or insult. The good therapist's end is outside himself, just as God's end is outside himself in the case of Bushnell and Irenaeus; the end of both is to feel the feeling of the other as if it were his own. If they do this — the therapist relatively and God absolutely — they maintain their honor. Whether we interpret the " loss of honor " about which Anselm speaks as either an intense personal betrayal (McIntyre) or a public offense (Harnack), psychotherapeutic insights tell us that such action would be interpreted as manipulative and untrustworthy, primarily for the good of the so-called therapeutic or healing agent and not for the good of the broken man.

The difficulty that Anselm confronts with this issue stems from his presuppositions about God's nonrelational absolute aseity in all respects. Since God has all perfection in himself, is in need of no one, and is not influenced by any consideration external to himself, his *ends* are also internal to himself. Hence, God must save man out of an effort to remain self-consistent with his own original intentions. God is motivated to save man primarily in order to save the integrity and dignity of his own life. The *ends* of God's action reflect back upon himself.

For Bushnell, the therapeutic analogy, and, we believe, Irenaeus, God's *ends* are self-derived but external to himself even from the beginning. When man falls, God is secure that by doing his part he will, in good time, become victorious.

A very interesting passage in the case of Mrs. Oaks illustrates my point. The therapeutic experience has given her new insight into the nature of love. She no longer believes that, in true love, the lover can attempt to justify himself by the object of his love. Let us recall what she said:

But the moment you — you accept that concept and the moment you say, " I love," then there's somehow . . . the other person becomes a justification to your own . . . well, for your life . . .

And that isn't really possible, I don't think . . . it isn't possible. Now isn't that true of therapy, am I wrong? See I found that here, somehow. Now isn't that true . . . so that rather not "I love" but that "You are my love." I think that there might be something to that. I don't quite know.

To apply our analogy to God would mean that this is the nature of God's love. God does not save man because, once having decided to create man morally erect, he must now see that man is restored in order to remain consistent with his own intentions. Instead, God is in eternal obligation to be in relation to man. God cannot say, "I love you." He can only say, "You are my love." Since there is nothing that can frustrate or qualify this love, this love continues, not for the self-consistency and honor of its own life, but for the benefit of the other.

If God's immutable intentions are in fact immutable reality, if the "isness" of his will is always simultaneously the "isness" of reality, it certainly is not fitting (*conveniens*, to use Anselm's own words) to envision God with such great concern over an apparent, but not real, loss of honor. If, instead, God's capacity as a creator is sufficient, and his capacity to sustain and bring that which he creates to fulfillment is likewise sufficient, then why should such a perfect God find the fall of man such a personal offense when he knows within himself, is secure within his own self-knowledge, that within good time, the adequacy of his powers and intentions as God will restore man eventually to the place for which he was originally intended?

It might be thought that the position we are supporting, in contrast to Anselm's, does not take sin, disobedience, and the fall of man seriously enough. But in reality it does. Sin is not grave because it is an offense to God's honor; it is grave because it deprives the sinner of the full benefit of the love, the life, and the righteousness that follows from the uninhibited inflow of God's relationship. God hates sin because he hates what it does to his loved ones, not because of what it implies about the inadequacy of his capacities to be God.

In all respects Anselm's presupposition about the immutable perfection of God gets him into further difficulties that center around his understanding of God's power. Since sin is an offense to God's honor, God will maintain his honor either by punishment or by satisfaction. Through the method of punishment, God shows the sinner that he is still subject to the divine will by taking from man what belongs to him, i.e., his happiness. On one hand, God's honor demands that God be paid what is due him. God's power gives God the strength to take " by force " that which the sinner refuses to give him. Not only are the consequences of sin a result of God's active intentions, but the image of power behind this emerges as absolute brute force.

In Anselm's thought, there is another and more positive way for God to maintain his honor. God accomplishes this through saving man, but saving him in such a way as to fulfill God's original intentions for man while satisfying the demands of managerial justice. In order for God's honor to be maintained, God must demonstrate his perfect power (omnipotence) to accomplish his original intentions without lowering the demands of his justice. The power of God, when operating for the purposes of the salvation of man, also operates in a nonrelational, noninteractional manner. Nothing like a persuasive image of power emerges in Anselm's concept. God's immutable power provides a satisfaction in the perfect obedience of Jesus Christ. But the obedience of Jesus Christ is a transaction with neither the devil nor man which can be said to overcome persuasively their resistance to God. The satisfaction is accomplished without reference to the decision of man (Bushnell) or to a righteous defeat of the devil (Irenaeus). And lastly, the power of God which enables him to accomplish his saving deed in Jesus Christ is in no way built around a concept of the passive element in God, as is the case with the concept of sympathy in Bushnell, long-suffering and recapitulation in Irenaeus, or empathy in the therapeutic analogy. It is a concept of power that operates without involvement in the distortions of the human situation. Even though Anselm does not stand with our other positions on his understanding of the honor and power of God, he puts to their positions an important question. The question is this: Can the therapeutic analogy, Bushnell, and Irenaeus adequately account for God's capacity to *order* the world? Is, in the last analysis, Anselm's understanding of God's power and honor the only defensible option if the order of the world is to be secure? We shall attempt to answer this question in the next section.

In concluding our discussion on the honor of God, we need to discuss Bushnell's second theory of the atonement. It attempts to incorporate certain Anselmian elements. In most of its crucial features, it remains similar to his first theory. It does, however, recognize a wrath principle in God, a moral disgust, on his part, toward sin and its distortions, although it is a contingent and secondary quality.

The similarity between Anselm and this revised theory rests with their mutual agreement that forgiveness is contingent upon some element of compensation, although they conceive of this compensation quite differently. For Bushnell, it is a compensation *completely* internal to the Godhead.

The question becomes, though, To what extent is Bushnell's second theory an improvement? Let us look at what this wrath principle would mean from the standpoint of the psychotherapeutic analogy. The critique of this wrath principle, in Bushnell's second theory, will be very similar to the critique of honor in Anselm's understanding of God. To assign wrath to God is implicitly to assign conditions of worth to God. The question becomes, If God becomes angry at sin, what are the conditions of worth in God that sin contradicts? As Fromm-Reichmann has pointed out, anger in the therapist is always a sign that the therapist has a self-investment in the process of therapy which demands that the client conform to the therapist's needs rather than that the therapist conform to the client's needs.[11] If God is secure in his conformation to the law of his own nature, and if he is secure as to the sufficiency of the relational law of love to restore man finally to his wholeness, what place can there be for the idea that God becomes angry in the face of sin? Although it is correct to assert that enmity exists *between* God and man, it is not correct to suggest that God contributes to this enmity with his own wrath.

Furthermore, the concept of congruence has implications for Bushnell's second theory. If the therapist were to become angry in the therapy situation, it would be of little therapeutic value for him to attempt to " move these sentiments " aside. Instead, the concept of congruence suggests that the therapist will be effective only insofar as he fully symbolizes and acknowledges, at least to himself, all his feelings, even his angry ones. If God is angry over sin, it is not very reassuring to hear that he has moved his anger aside. Therapy has demonstrated that this is an artificial process. Bushnell adopted this view because it seemed to fit the analogy of human experience. But he built the analogy without the benefit of the sharpened insights of psychotherapy. In order to become devoid of anger, the therapist must search out the conditions of worth which lay behind his anger. This involves a change of character. But this is precisely what Bushnell refuses to admit, i.e., that God's character ever changes. He wants to set the elements in God that accomplish man's redemption into the mold of eternal obligation. Hence, it is my belief that he has done little to improve his position by adding the dimension of wrath as he does in his second theory.

Justice, Judgment, and the Order of the Word

Bushnell and the therapeutic analogy converge at many points in their respective understanding of the nature of God's judgment and justice. Both tend to conceive of God's justice under the rubric of his righteousness. Both allow some discontinuity in the justice and order of the world, but tend to see it as basically secure. Both make a distinction between the law as the structure of God's primordial relation to the world and law in its contingent, means-end, governmental, administrative, or integrative sense. For both, the basic job of ordering the world is accomplished through God's primary relation with the world where he meets man's profoundest needs through love and acceptance. Punishment and retribution play a secondary role in both theories, although there seems to be more of a place for punishment in Bushnell than in the therapeutic analogy. For both, human brokenness issues in certain natural consequences which judge it and make it painful, although there are important distinctions between them in the way they conceive these natural consequences to operate.

For instance, for Bushnell, God's governmental will works through the causes of nature. God does not inflict the consequences of sin directly, but ordains an order of the world in which sin will involve itself in its own painful consequences.

Such a position is very similar to our generalization of the implications of the therapeutic situation. There we accounted for the natural consequences of sin without positing a direct act of punishment by God. We did not go as far as Bushnell in equating God's secondary law with the working of the natural consequences of sin. But, for Bushnell, as is the case with the therapeutic analogy, God's secondary or governmental will does not insist upon a strict system of rewards and punishments. God may treat the sinner better than he deserves, " since the ultimate purpose of justice is to help the sinner to wish to be saved from sin." Even his second theory expressed in *Forgiveness and the Law,* which includes the idea of compensation, makes the compensation internal to the life of God and not something required of man before forgiveness can be granted.

Irenaeus' understanding of the judgment and justice of God is strikingly similar to that found in the therapeutic analogy and Bushnell. He goes farther than Bushnell (as Bushnell goes farther than the analogy) in admitting that God " provides " an appropriate punishment (consequence) to sin. But at the same time, God provides it in that he " permits " the consequences of sin to go their way; but the fact that sin has consequences does not mean that God withdraws his love, light, and justifying relationship. The point is that Irenaeus (as does Bushnell to some extent) goes farther than we felt it necessary, when developing the therapeutic analogy, in maintaining the principle that God causes something to happen if he " permits " it to happen. Insofar as this principle affirms that God maintains his sovereign rule even over those occurrences which he does not intend or cause explicitly, the principle would represent only a difference in emphasis rather than an attitude essentially divergent from the general thrust of the therapeutic analogy.

That the essential thrust is similar can be seen at several points. As do Bushnell and the therapeutic analogy, Irenaeus believes that there are two types of law. There are the natural precepts implicit in the creative fellowship of the two hands of God and known to man in his original integrity before God. And then there is the law, such as the Mosaic law, which appears and disappears at certain points in history, which serves to " order and discipline " fallen man. Its end is the same as the precepts implicit in God's primary creative fellowship. Its purpose is not to punish but to control man and prepare him for the working of God's grace. *Law in neither sense of the word demands absolute justice and compensation.* The sinner does not get his due always since the purpose of God's law and judgment is to move the sinner toward salvation rather than to distribute an immutable system of rewards and punishments.

The therapeutic analogy provides a proper interpretation. Administrative and integrative measures of limitation and coercion are helpful to the extent to which they operate in the context of a larger structure of empathic acceptance, the goals of which they serve as a means. The continued and enduring creative fellowship of the two hands of God, in Irenaeus' thought, operates as this larger structure in the context of which God's contingent administrative law works as means to an end. Some dislocation in the order of justice is permitted, as with both Bushnell and the therapeutic analogy; but the two hands of God continue their work at all times among sinful man, and God's contingent structures of administrative law integrate man so that the two hands and the *ultimate event* (of Jesus Christ) toward which they move will have some order in which to work.

Anselm's understanding of judgment and justice is strikingly different. There is no sense in which law is considered a contingent aspect of the character of God. God's administrative justice, for Anselm, is fundamental to the nature of God. No transgression of man must go "undischarged." God must not save man in such a way as to jeopardize his "management of the universe." God's managerial justice or honor means, for Anselm, that sin must either be punished or that God's immutable justice must be compensated duly. The punishment of man is something that follows directly from the will of God. The judgment of God's punishment of sin is an expression of his justice — God's giving sin its due. It does not operate simply to limit and control man so that God's grace will have some modicum of order in which to work, as is the case with the therapeutic analogy, Bushnell, and Irenaeus. God's managerial justice is so fundamental to the nature of God that his grace and forgiveness are defined in terms of it; they in fact become contingent and conditioned by the prior necessity that the justice of God be compensated.

Forgiveness and the Nature of God

In contrast to Anselm, where law always is fundamental and absolute while forgiveness is contingent, the formula is reversed for Bushnell, Irenaeus, and the therapeutic analogy. With each of these positions, forgiveness springs forth from the most fundamental aspects of the nature of God and in no way is contingent or conditioned. In each of the three approaches, forgiveness issues from God's primordial relation to the world and the fact that nothing can condition or qualify this relation. It issues from the fact that this relation endures *in spite* of any act on the part of man or the devil designed to reject or break this relationship.

For both Bushnell and the therapeutic analogy, the continuation of this relation in spite of man's resistance to it is accomplished at some cost to God, engenders some suffering and anguish in his life, and, in fact, sets up the cross of Calvary in the Godhead *ab aeterno*. This also seems to be the case with Irenaeus. The suffering of Jesus is held by him to be also the suffering of Christ, and the activity of Christ on the cross is also characteristic of all the activities of God among fallen men.

It follows from this position (and is sometimes made explicit, as in the case of Bushnell and the therapeutic analogy) that God does not at a certain time *decide* to forgive man. Rather, forgiveness is a necessity, a fundamental structure of God. It is a necessity for God, in order to be God, to continue in loving and empathic relation to his creatures. In addition, the continuation of this empathic love is not conditioned by a prior compensation of the law, as is the case with Anselm. The continuation of this relation does in fact fulfill the law (in its primary sense), insofar as law refers to the structure of God's own nature.

It is clear that for the therapeutic analogy, Bushnell, and Irenaeus, forgiveness is not a reality which appears in God with the advent of Jesus Christ. Whatever the unique contribution of the life and death of Jesus Christ, it must not be thought that he effects the forgiveness of God. Rather, his life and death manifests this forgiveness in a way that makes it more available for sinful man.

The Person of Jesus Christ

Two principles arose from the therapeutic analogy relevant to the person of Jesus Christ. First, we found that the therapeutic relationship suggested an epistemo-soteriological necessity for the incarnation. Secondly, we discovered that when the character of the therapeutic agent is used as a model to interpret the person of Jesus Christ, it emerged that Jesus is the Christ by virtue of the conformation of his self-concept with the original vicarious datum that intersects and undergirds all reality and that is the original possibility of creation.

Something like an epistemo-soteriological necessity for the incarnation is found in the thought of Bushnell. But the epistemo-soteriological basis of the position I am proposing does not rest on a metaphysics that makes a distinction between things of the spirit and things carnal or material, as does Bushnell. In our theory, sin is indeed a bondage to things in the created order, especially the social order. But the sinfulness of this stance is not due to the materiality of these orders; it is due to an unhealthy priority which the attitude of sin gives to these orders. The sinner attempts to justify himself and base his worth on these orders rather than upon his original relationship to God. Having clarified this important difference, it seems that otherwise Bushnell and the position I am defending are indeed quite similar. For both, the event of Jesus Christ manifests a reality that is present already. The event of Jesus Christ in no way reconstitutes our relationship to God or changes God himself. The necessity of the incarnation, for both positions, rests in the nature of sin. For both positions, the incarnation is a grand strategy on the part of a uniquely flexible and always relevant God to make a special appeal to man that will become comprehensible among the peculiar distortions which characterize man's sin. In addition, for both, the incarnation is a " manifestation " of God's love and not just an " expression " or " revelation " of it. The noetic or revelatory element expressed is based firmly upon a dynamic and actual manifestation of God's primordial love at the level of man's social interaction, i.e., in the life and death of the man Jesus

Christ. Lastly, the very idea of the incarnation, for both positions, assumes a passible and conditioned God, a God who can manifest himself in the conditions of estrangement and allow a contingent element within his life without ceasing to be God.

At the same time, Bushnell is somewhat deficient, from the standpoint of the history of Christian thought as well as the therapeutic model, in his conceptualization of the human element in the person of Jesus Christ. From the standpoint of the therapeutic analogy, the human element in the person of Jesus Christ refers to the " self-concept " that perfectly and unambiguously conforms to the basic vicarious datum (stimulus hunger or " the image of God ") which intersects adverbial experiencing. From the standpoint of the model of the therapist's character, Jesus Christ would also be the Second Adam. He would have the integrity of original man, but would have a mature self-concept completely organized around the image of God in man. The therapeutic analogy as well as the history of Christian thought would be critical of Bushnell's de-emphasis of the human element in Christ and his inability to show continuity between the goodness of creation in the first Adam and Jesus of Nazareth as the Second Adam.

At this point, the therapeutic model has significant affinities with Irenaeus. In his thought, Jesus Christ performs a twofold recapitulation. He recapitulates the original integrity of the first Adam and, in addition, recapitulates (*sums up* or *goes over the same ground*) the distortions of human existence without succumbing to these distortions. For Irenaeus, the first Adam has the propensity to conform to the image of God in him, but he is inexperienced and immature. The immaturity of the first Adam can be interpreted by the client-centered model of the neonate. The neonate is congruent to his organismic valuations and actualization tendency (stimulus hunger) but is without a self-concept and a mature self-understanding built around these fundamental realities of his life. This can serve as a model for interpreting the integrity, but immaturity, of the first Adam. In a similar manner, the client-centered understanding of the mature therapist can serve as a model for interpreting the mature integrity of the Second Adam. This model gives us an intelligible way in which to appreciate the wisdom of calling Jesus Christ the Second Adam. It also gives us an appreciation for the witness that the concept of the Second Adam gives to the continuity between original creation and the final manifestations of God's healing power in the person of Jesus Christ. According to the therapeutic model, Jesus would be congruent to the basic vicarious datum intersecting adverbial experiencing, but would have assimilated this into a mature self-concept. In this way he is the Second Adam.

On the other hand, Irenaeus does not demonstrate a clear epistemo-soteriological necessity for the incarnation as does both Bushnell and the therapeutic analogy. But the incarnation — the manifestation of God's love in the person of Jesus Christ — does have a noetic function. Irenaeus sees the incarnation as a unique adaptation of God to the peculiar distortions of sinful man. In Chapter II we learned that for Irenaeus, *incarnatus* was almost equal to *passus*. For God to manifest his love in the incarnate Christ is to relativize his love so that it will be comprehensible to man within the midst of man's own sinful distortions. In this way God presents himself as " milk-nourishment " to man. God is born as a child and lives to an old age. In so doing, he participates in the distortions characteristic of every stage of life. And he does this, as Irenaeus puts it, so that man might be " capable of beholding Him." Here, in a rudimentary and unsystematic form, is an epistemo-soteriological necessity for the incarnation.

For Anselm, the incarnation and the person of Jesus Christ are established on a different basis. The problem for the three positions above is to demonstrate how a God already related to mankind in love and forgiveness must make a further manifestation of his love in the form of one man, the man called Jesus. This is not Anselm's problem, since for him, God is never defined in relational terms.

For him, the incarnation is necessary to help man pay a debt that man *must* pay but that only the God-man *can* pay. Anselm maintains the traditional "fully God and fully man" formula with reference to the person of Christ. But Jesus is not fully God with regard to suffering. Only the human Jesus suffers. In this way he removes God from any direct interaction between himself and the resistances and hostility of man.

As a secondary consequence, Christ's suffering even unto death effects no direct change in man. It only effects the condition whereby God can forgive man without compromising his managerial justice. *It is my feeling, though, that Anselm's reluctance to admit the suffering of God overlooks completely what psychotherapy has to tell us about the efficacy of the passive element in any act of healing.* When the "fully God and fully man" formula is built upon an understanding of God based upon the principle of absolute relativity, the traditional God-man formula can be applied with more consistency. For then it can be admitted that Jesus Christ is truly man and truly God in all respects, even in his suffering. Then, the suffering of Jesus Christ even unto death becomes an active interplay between God and man in which, at some cost to God, man actually is changed in a dynamic sense. But this brings us to the next and last subject of our discussion — the work of Jesus Christ and the efficacy of his death.

THE WORK OF JESUS CHRIST

We have already said much that bears on the work of Jesus Christ. Everything related to the *dynamic* operation of unconditioned empathic acceptance is relevant to the work of Jesus Christ, since it has been our contention that these are formally similar structures and processes. But, for the sake of clarity, we will have to summarize all earlier discussions so that their relevance to this issue will be evident.

The Cross and the Acceptance of Negative Feelings

In Chapter VII the cross and the resurrection of Jesus Christ were identified respectively with the passive and unconditioned elements in the structure of absolute relativity. The efficacy of the cross and the resurrection of Jesus Christ, when interpreted by the therapeutic analogy, must be seen in terms of their potency to liberate man from these supra-individual conditions of worth. We have seen how the sinner reacts with hostility when confronted with an experience that contradicts his conditions of worth. The cross of Jesus Christ stands for a massive attempt on the part of these supra-individual conditions of worth to " fend off " God's incarnate unconditioned empathic acceptance. The cross further stands for God's complete empathic acceptance of all of man's feelings, even his most hostile ones. It is in this way that the sinful self's bondage to its conditions of worth is broken. When the sinner learns that God can accept empathically all his feelings, even his most hostile ones, and still endure, the sinner then indeed knows that there are no conditions placed on his worth and acceptability. He now realizes that he can repudiate his own conditions of worth and still be acceptable. The conditions of worth are defeated and rendered impotent. The passive element in God's empathic acceptance is crucial to this dynamic process. It conveys to the sinner that God has a full empathic knowledge of the sinner's hostility, yet still prizes him, cares for him, and accepts him into relationship.

We already have pointed out the similarity between Irenaeus' mythological devil and the conditions of worth of psychotherapy. In addition, the process of change suggested by psychotherapy has been best symbolized in the history of Christian thought under the rubric of "battle and victory." Irenaeus' *Christus Victor* motif captures the essence of this struggle. Here Jesus Christ is understood as a "ransom," a brave fighter who enters into battle with the devil and, through the steadfastness and persistence of his own righteous obedience, defeats the devil, even at great cost to himself. I think that Irenaeus presents this drama with a vigor which deserves our attention. I have pointed out the formal similarity between the concept of recapitulation and unconditioned empathic acceptance. Furthermore, as Irenaeus demonstrates, when God in Jesus Christ recapitulates and "sums up" the distortions of the world he also "summed up in Himself" the world's "enmity" toward him. Just as our therapeutic analogy sees man's hostility toward love as a maneuver on the part of our conditions of worth, so does Irenaeus teach that the devil took it "in hand to render this [workmanship] an enmity with God." As a consequence of this hostility, Jesus Christ was "buffeted" and did "suffer." But it was through the obedience of Jesus Christ and the "long-suffering" of God that the devil learned that there was nothing it could do to make God give up man, i.e., "abandon" him forever. Not even the devil's most hostile attacks could "conquer" God in the work of his "two hands" and in his unambiguous manifestation in Jesus Christ.

In dramatic and mythological terms, Irenaeus captures a significant feature of the process of atonement. But Irenaeus' molar mythological images can be made more specific when interpreted by the therapeutic analogy. Irenaeus does not understand that in Christ's recapitulation of all of man's distortions, God empathically *accepts that about man which man cannot accept about himself.* He understood that Christ restores creation, but he did not understand that Christ does this by accepting repressed and denied creation in sinful man. He understood how the devil seduces man into justifying himself on things external to God, but he did not know how the self becomes organized around conditions of worth that become the self's *own* conditions as well as supra-individual structures into which each person is born. He understood that in the incarnation there is a noetic element, a way in which God makes himself comprehensible to man within the framework of man's own distortions, but he did not demonstrate clearly the relationship between the defeat of the devil and man's own subjective response. He makes the devil real and objective, but does not understand that the power which the devil has over the self is, in part, a power which the self gives to the devil. If the model of incongruence is correct, the power which the devil has, although ultimately from God, is immediately from the deeper growth potentials that should nourish the self but that have been drained off by the conditions of worth which the self has adopted. The point is, within the framework of the psychotherapeutic model of incongruence and the way empathic acceptance overcomes it, the defeat of the supra-individual structures which hold man is not something which happens over man's head, but something which involves some element of participation on the part of the self.

In discussing the work of Jesus Christ in Bushnell, let me reassert a generalization which we discussed in Chapter IV. There we said that Bushnell's so-called Moral Influence theory of the atonement is nothing more than an internal and less mythological view of the same truth which Irenaeus' ransom theory expresses in externalistic, objectified, and highly mythological terms. Central to the action of both is Christ's passive-active subjection to the hostile reaction of sinful man. The major difference between them rests in the way they regard the devil, the supra-individual powers that hold man in bondage. For Bushnell, the devil rises as a consequence of man's misuse of freedom. For Irenaeus, the devil precedes man's fall and is partially responsible for it. As a consequence, Irenaeus sometimes can concentrate Christ's work so directly upon defeating the devil that he neglects giving due attention to man's subjective response. On the other hand, Bushnell sometimes seems to make Christ's work appeal so directly to man that he neglects due regard for the supra-individual power which holds him. In reality, the question whether the devil precedes or is consequent to the fall of man, is a question that cannot be answered satisfactorily. From the standpoint of the model of incongruence, this one fact is evident; any discussion of how God's love in Jesus Christ overcomes sin must give due attention to both the *supra-individual structures* which hold the self and the *self* held by these structures. The psychotherapeutic analogy does just this. For this reason, it can serve as a coordinating analogy that can correct the excesses of both the Moral Influence theory and the mythological ransom theory of Irenaeus.

We have discussed already how guilt is much more important for Anselm than it is for the therapeutic analogy, Irenaeus, or Bushnell. Anselm sees man as totally responsible

for the fall and completely guilty because of it. The therapeutic analogy, Bushnell, and Irenaeus distribute the causal
factors. Guilt is doubly important for Anselm because sin
constitutes an offense to God, and it is this offense, for which
man is responsible, that constitutes the major obstacle to
salvation. On the other hand, for the therapeutic analogy and
Irenaeus, and to some extent Bushnell, guilt is subsumed under bondage; it is an obstacle to salvation not because of what
man's guilt means to God but because of what it means to
man. That man is in bondage to his own false gods — his
own standards of self-justification — which assume demonic
power over his life, is a picture of the human situation
strongly supported by the insights of psychotherapy. Even
though Anselm's Christ, through his obedience even unto
death, compensates for man's guilt, it is not clear how this
compensation overcomes man's *subjective experience of guilt*.
How does this compensation effect any subjective change in
man? Anselm does not answer this question. When children break windows and destroy property, it is not enough
for their fathers to restore, on their behalf, the damage they
have caused. Nor is it enough that the children themselves
repay the damage out of their own efforts. Instead, they must
be freed from the conditions of worth which led them to believe that they were adding to their own justification and
self-worth through the pursuit of these acts. Only when they
are free from these conditions is their guilt really removed.
Only when they approach awareness that there are *no* conditions placed on their worth and acceptability, and thereby
helped to repudiate the conditions they felt compelled to
hold, are they really free from the basic cause of all guilt.
Only a relation of empathic acceptance which is unconditioned and can endure every hostile effort to reject it can help
us to repudiate the conditions of worth which produce our

guilt. It is precisely the work of Jesus Christ, in his cross and his resurrection, to manifest this structure and to overcome this bondage.

The Analogy and the Penal Consequences of Sin

That sin has involved itself in penal consequences has been the universal testimony of the Christian faith. Christian theology has either tended to see God as the direct author of these penal consequences (Anselm, Calvin) or, at least, allows or permits them to occur (Irenaeus, Bushnell) so that it can be said that these consequences still are subject to his sovereign rule. The model of brokenness, which the concept of incongruence provides, clearly illustrates how conditions of worth involve themselves in their own experiences of judgment, contradiction, threat, anxiety, tension, estrangement, and death. As was pointed out earlier, it is not necessary to draw a tight causal line between these consequences and God's active will in order to establish their existence.

The wisdom of the penal-substitutionary theory of the atonement is its insight that the savior of man somehow must involve himself in and suffer the penal consequences of sin. Empathy, at least in some sense, takes these penal consequences upon itself. The therapist, insofar as he has empathic acceptance for the denied and distorted feelings of the other, becomes the curse and the criminal. Calvin saw this with penetrating clarity. What he failed to see was the dynamic significance of this process of identification with the criminal. In his thought, the actual dynamic transaction between Christ and the sinner is obscured. He failed to see that through this empathic identification, the saving agent (Christ) moves the sinner toward wholeness by activating and accepting certain aspects within his life which, by himself, the sinner cannot accept. The savior becomes the criminal, not as a substitute for the wrath that man deserved, but as one who saves man by participating in the distortions that beset his fallenness. Even within the *Christus Victor* motif, which we are suggesting should be the guiding and organizing center of atonement thinking, we can see how we are saved when the savior endures the hostile reaction of the conditions of worth, a hostility which, it must be added, there is no way for the sinner by himself to escape.

The Analogy and the Priestly Motif

By the priestly motif, I am referring to theology's efforts to conceptualize what Christ has accomplished on behalf of man toward God.

There is an important sense in which the therapist helps the client make a confession that the client cannot make by himself. Empathic acceptance helps the client own and symbolize feelings that he formerly denied and distorted. To symbolize these feelings is, in fact, to confess them. In addition, in order to confess them, the client must, to some extent, repent of the conditions of worth that led him to disown this part of his experience. Therapy follows a sequence — empathic acceptance, repentance (of conditions of worth), and confession (of denied and disowned experiencing). Clearly it is the therapist's empathic acceptance that helps the client to revise and eliminate his conditions of worth and begin experiencing himself more completely. To some extent, it can be said that the therapist makes a confession in behalf of the client, slightly prior to the client's. This is to say that the therapist emotionally accepts and owns (confesses) the client's unacceptable feelings slightly prior to the moment when the client begins to accept (confess) them himself. This is what happens when the therapist, according to Gendlin, helps the client symbolize a feeling that the client can refer to consciously but not yet symbolize.

When this is applied as an interpretation to the work of Jesus Christ, it becomes possible to see his priestly function as an act of confession of man's sin which, empathically and sensitively, precedes man's own confession and helps man to make a confession which, by himself, he would be unable to make. In addition, it would be God's righteousness that would demand and itself work for this confession. For God's righteousness is the perfect equality and adequacy of his capacity to feel the feelings of all his creatures, even their most unacceptable ones. Jesus Christ, perfectly manifesting God's righteousness, in the name of righteousness and, in fact, with the power of divine righteousness, leads man in the making of this confession. Christ's empathic acceptance activates the flow of denied experiencings (as it did for Mrs. Oaks) and induces them to conscious symbolization and confession.

But the confession that Christ helps us to make has a deeper element. First there is the confession of important but comparatively superficial feelings of anger, worthlessness, fear, anxiety, and pride. But as these so-called negative feelings are confessed and accepted, therapy invariably moves to a deeper stage. This deeper stage is a new set of self-experiences in which one experiences himself as valid, of worth, a person of dignity and primary value. The therapist also empathically accepts these experiences and helps to symbolize and confess them.

Applying this to the work of Christ, subsequent to his empathic acceptance of sin's negativities, Christ then helps sinful man to accept his own deeper experiences of his created goodness which his conditions of worth have led him to deny and repress. Sin, according to the model of incongruence, is in part a repression of the goodness of creation. The work of Christ as confessor helps the sinner to confess and name this created goodness once again.

Clearly there are vast areas of similarity between the therapeutic analogy and the vision of the priestly functions of Christ as set forth by McLeod Campbell. For him, Christ's work on the cross constituted a perfect participation in and subsequent confession of the sins of man. In addition, the ultimate end of this confession was to confess man's basic created status as a son of God. We should not be surprised to find this similarity between Campbell and the therapeutic analogy since it is clear that Campbell freely uses human analogies, as does Bushnell. What is important is that more controlled studies of interpersonal processes have confirmed his insights as has the excellent Biblical scholarship of men like Vincent Taylor. All in all, a great deal of internal and external coherence is beginning to develop, confirming the essential correctness of his insights.

But the therapeutic analogy makes two additional contributions. First, it demonstrates that Christ's confession of man's sin actually effects a change in man as well as accomplishes something consistent with the righteousness of God. Campbell, whose work tends to stop with Christ's confession before God, does not demonstrate how this confession actually helps man to make his own confession and thereby own that about himself from which he formerly was estranged. Secondly, the therapeutic analogy demonstrates the importance of the supra-individual conditions of worth (structures of evil) and how these must be defeated (or in the process of being defeated) before repentance and confession can occur. Hence, the therapeutic analogy seems to suggest that, even here, bondage to conditions of worth is man's main difficulty and that liberation involves a struggle and a battle between God in Christ and the powers that have subdued the individual and collective self of man. Unless this struggle is entered into and this literal process of unlearning conditions of worth is embarked upon, repentance will be meaningless and confession will be idle prattle and introspective navel watching. Anything more than just superficial confession will arouse defenses, resistances, and negative feelings. Without a clear understanding of confession as taking place in the context of a battle and victory over man's conditions of worth, confession becomes rationalistic, moralistic, and ultimately guilt enhancing. The importance of the *Christus Victor* imagery for protecting the centrality of these truths cannot be emphasized too vigorously.

The close relationship between the confessional and the Latin theory of the atonement has tended to obscure the *Christus Victor* dynamics operating in all instances of meaningful confession (*exomologēsis*). Exorcism seems to be central to the ministry of Jesus Christ, whether he is preaching, teaching, healing, or bringing man to repentance and confession. The first missionary excursions of his disciples were understood as a battle and victory over Satan (Luke 10:17-20). There is evidence that the church's early practices of confession were not put within a rationalistic and moralistic framework, but were associated with a defeat of the temptations of Satan. On the modern scene, the advent of the small group in the church for purposes of sharing, fellowship (*koinōnia*), and study is a recognition that repentance, confession, realization of forgiveness, and healing must be done in an interactional situation, over a period of time, so that an individual can unlearn (defeat) old conditions of worth and learn to accept the justifying love of God to which the group witnesses. For purposes of theological clarity, the relation between the essential action of these groups and the dynamics of exorcism and the *Christus Victor* theory of the atonement should be made clear. But this task cannot be pursued within the limitations of our present study.

The Therapeutic Analogy and Exemplar Views

The question of the position of exemplar motifs in a valid theory of the atonement is parallel, in psychotherapy, to the question of the relationship between unconditioned empathic acceptance and so-called processes of identification. To what extent, in therapy, does the client identify with the counselor? To what extent does this identification prove efficacious?

That the process of identification (the tendency to become like the therapist) occurs in therapy has seldom been acknowledged or discussed in the literature except in a negative sense, i.e., the phenomenon of countertransference as a process whereby the therapist identifies with the neurotic components in the client. The so-called evocative therapies (of which both client-centered counseling and psychoanalysis are considered examples) have tended to think that the therapist must handle himself in such a way that the client will not identify with him; hopefully the client's progress can be in terms of his own rudimentary identity and set of values.

Yet, as Jerome Frank has pointed out, it probably is naïve to think that no identification whatsoever takes place in the long and intimate relationship which sometimes occurs in extended counseling.[12] Let me suggest that as the client begins to experience the justifying and freedom-giving effects of unconditioned empathic acceptance, he tends to identify with this attitude in the therapist and begins taking this same attitude toward himself, his own self-experiences, and the experiences of others. The point is that the experience of unconditioned empathic acceptance precedes the process whereby the client begins to emulate, imitate, or identify with the therapist as one who possesses (is an example of) this attitude.

Corroboration for this point of view comes forth from the field of child development. There is more than one kind of identification process. Psychoanalysis has had much to say about defensive identification — a process whereby a child identifies with the values of the parent in order to defend himself from punishment, rejection, or disapproval (castration).[13] For some time it was thought that moral values were taught only through the process of defensive identification, a theory that O. H. Mowrer seems to be vigorously suggesting. Recent research seems to indicate that the basis for the development of a healthy, autonomous, and ego assimilated moral character may occur through what Lawrence Kohlberg calls "personal identification." Personal identification seems to operate when the child *likes* an adult, i.e., when the adult has been warm and affectionate toward the child. As Kohlberg writes, "a child should more readily accept the values of an adult who is liked or accepted, and an adult should be better liked if he is himself accepting and nurturant."[14] Transferring this to the context of therapy, the prizing, nurturant, and caring relationship the therapist has with the client precedes the process of identification. In turn, the identification that does occur is most likely to be an internalization of the very empathic acceptance with which he was first liberated.

Applying these insights analogically to the meaning of atonement, the work of Christ in liberating man from his conditions of worth through his unconditional positive regard and empathy precedes and provides the foundation upon which identification with the form of Christ can occur. Healthy identification springs from an attitude of gratitude. We want to become like another out of gratitude for what the other has done for us. But from the standpoint of Christian theology, imitating (*memisis*) Christ is also, at the same time, the actualization of man's original possibility as a Son of God. Hence, in imitating Christ we do not become another so much as we become what we originally were supposed to be.

To emphasize the noetic, pedagogical, and exemplar features of Jesus without prefacing this with an understanding of his suffering, through empathic acceptance, the hostility of man's conditions of worth is to present man with a standard of perfection devoid of a dynamic process that can empower man to conform to this norm. Insofar as exemplar theories of the atonement have done this, they have been in error. What is not clear is that they have been as guilty of this mistake as some commentators have suggested. Our earlier comments about Abelard and Schleiermacher pointed out that both, in some sense, put their understanding of Christ as perfect example in the context of a doctrine of grace and power designed to provide for the very element we are proposing. What may have been the shortcoming of both these thinkers, as well as others emphasizing the exemplar motif, was their failure to understand man's condition as captivity to the "principalities and powers" and the consequent importance of *Christus Victor* imagery with the truly dynamic and transactional features it implies.

POSTSCRIPT ON THE DEATH OF GOD

In many ways, in the process of this study, I have entered into the popular modern theological pastime of killing God. But as is the case with most contemporary efforts to wax eloquent on the death of God theme, I have killed some gods but I have not killed God. I have attempted to kill the God of traditional scholastic orthodoxy — the God above time and space, without parts or movements, unrelated to and impenetrable by the world and its suffering. Modern man has become aware of the world, and this awareness has made it no longer possible to identify with a God who maintains his dignity and perfection by standing above and apart from the anguish of the world. Modern man, immersed as he is in the tragedy of life, must find a new model for perfection, a model that will give him the strength to stand in the world without succumbing to the world. The God of Greek metaphysics and Latin scholasticism is dead and should not be resurrected no matter what the disguise, be it some newly developed form of Catholic Thomism or some variation of the Tillichian concept of God as " being itself."

Dead also is the God of religion, the God of our conditions of worth. Man stands on a new threshold of giving up his idolatrous tendency to use God to support his own absolutized provincialities. Dead also is God as *deus ex machina,* the God who miraculously intervenes in history to save us in terms of our own demonic conditions of worth. The God who supports us in our brokenness by succumbing to our neurotic demands must be buried forever. The God who confirms our personal and national idolatries is the God who robs us of our autonomy, who undermines our own creativity and growth by failing to expose our inability to cope with reality in terms of our own parochial perspectives.

But the God of religion who prevents man from " coming of age " is not the God we have been describing in the process of this study. The God who affirms us and who enters into our lives with unconditioned empathic acceptance does not rob us of our autonomy or stifle our growth toward maturity. The God of the atonement, the God of suffering and weakness of the cross, does not take over the executive functions of our lives; he does not frustrate our attempt to master and direct our own future responsibly. Nor does this God infantilize man by doing for man what man should do for himself. Instead, this is the God who constitutes the ground of all advance into responsible autonomy by being an invariant source of affirmation and love. He provides the support and foundation for all growth into maturity by communicating to man that inner sense of validity upon which all development depends. All human relationships that facilitate growth operate in analogy to his atoning love for mankind. It is God's love which gives men the strength to differentiate calmly and trustingly his experience, accept it for what it is, and name it as honestly as possible. It is God's patient and enduring sacrificial relation which enables man to develop symbolic hunches about the world, which gives him the nerve to act on these hunches, and which provides man with the confident poise required to undergo their correction and refinement by subsequent experience.

In contrast to the position of several contemporary theological commentators, I do not believe that God must be forgotten before man can attain a fully mature humanity. In contrast to certain strands of existentialism and Eastern mysticism, man's experience of nothingness is not what frees him for authenticity. It is not necessary to repeat the ancient myth of the killing of the tribal god so that his children can possess their rightful personhood. Anxiety and loneliness are stimulators of growth only when they appear in a larger context of love and mutual respect. Without this more embracing experience of fellowship and support, life's moments of anxiety and nothingness lead to despair, bitterness, and resignation. Those who would like to smash and defeat our contemporary army of idols, who would like to dethrone our modern principalities and powers, our outmoded tribal values and malfunctional parochial hypotheses, will not accomplish this task of cultural exorcism by an act of deicide. If man becomes convinced that he lives in a cosmically cold and indifferent world, he will cling to his conditions of worth all the more tenaciously or slink away from life in cowardly withdrawal. In both instances he will still be idolatrously subservient to worldly standards of value, either in a spirit of frantic desperation or an attitude of placid hopelessness.

It may be that God seems dead to so many because our age is really standing on the boundary between its own death and resurrection — the death of a narrow self-definition based on Western middle-class technological values and the birth of a more universal identity based on a broader sense of continuity between ourselves and the rest of humanity. Possibly our experience of the death of God is really our experience of uncertainty, an uncertainty that would be characteristic of any transition from the old to the new. Insofar

as we are in the midst of expanding our identities, this in itself is evidence that God is not dead in our time. If we experienced God as totally dead, if we considered ourselves sur-
rounded by a sea of cosmic nothingness, I doubt if man
would have the nerve to face this leap. Certainly the experience of uncertainty that appears in the course of our journey
will be experienced as a nothingness, but this nothingness is
an illusion. It is the nothingness of indefiniteness and transition; it is not the nothingness of total nothingness. Even before we submit to change, we experience preveniently the
affirming and supportive love of God. It is this prior experience of God that gives us the courage to face the nothingness
and indefiniteness of the leap from an old to a new self-
understanding.

In killing the God of our conditions of worth, I have attempted to move beyond and above the God of religion but
not beyond and above the God of theism. I do not understand the God of religion and the God of theism as the
same God. The Tillichian God above God is finally an
immovable God whose relatedness to and involvement with
the world of finite men is only symbolic and nonliteral. Regardless of the insistence of thinkers such as Paul van Buren
and Anthony Flew, modern man will continue to make references to God. Granted the many difficulties inherent in
speaking of God, God will not die simply because our language about him sometimes appears faulty and confused. If
man is truly coming of age, he has done so on the basis of a
more deeply appropriated experience of affirmation and self-
trust. It has been my contention that this inner datum of experiencing oneself as an object of primary value cannot be
reducible to the totality of interpersonal sources of positive
regard and empathy. Instead, it is the consistent witness of
life that there is a source of human affirmation which tran-

scends and constitutes the ground of all its specific interpersonal origins. Although this has been asserted, I have urged that we learn to talk about this transcendent source of affirmation on the basis of the interpersonal models that exemplify and witness to it. This necessitates a God of theism, a God who is in some sense a Supreme Individual, a God who can be described by the categories that apply to finite individuals. Such a God need not be considered as a " God out there," a grand old man who dispenses gifts to the obedient and punishment to the rebellious after the pattern of an authoritarian feudal lord or a modern fuzzy-minded Santa Claus. Instead, such a God can emerge as a very human God, a very related God, a God who is strong in his weakness and weak in his strength, who judges us in his affirmation of our humanness and who affirms us in his judgment of our conditions of worth.

And finally, the revolutionary God who is celebrated today by those who have joined the militant church and manned the outposts on the battlefield of social change is the God of the atonement. The God of social revolution is first of all the God who enters into our experiencing with positive regard and empathy, who feels our feelings, suffers our anger and resistance and who thereby provides the foundation for our capacity to affirm and empathize with the sufferings of others. It is the God who relates to us through a justifying and transforming love, without any conditions attached, who prompts man to implement this love in all his social relations, by proclaiming liberation from the principalities and powers and witnessing to a new ground of worth in the " yes " and " no " of the cross.

NOTES

Chapter I The Atonement and Psychotherapeutic Illumination

1. Reuel Howe, *Man's Need and God's Action* (The Seabury Press, Inc., 1953), p. 105.
2. *Ibid.*, pp. 101–119.
3. *Ibid.*, p. 88.
4. *Ibid.*, p. 132.
5. Daniel Day Williams, *The Minister and the Care of Souls* (Harper & Brothers, 1961), p. 87.
6. *Ibid.*, pp. 80–87.
7. *Ibid.*, p. 89.
8. *Ibid.*
9. *Ibid.*, p. 90.
10. *Ibid.*, p. 91.
11. *Ibid.*
12. J. S. Whale, *Victor and Victim* (Cambridge: Cambridge University Press, 1960), p. 69.
13. Gustav Aulén, *Christus Victor* (The Macmillan Company, 1961), p. 19.
14. Robert S. Paul, *The Atonement and the Sacraments* (Abingdon Press, 1960), p. 154.

Chapter II Irenaeus: Atonement as Defeat of the Devil

1. *AH*, II.4.2.
2. *AH*, II.2.2.
3. *AH*, II.2.1.
4. *AH*, II.1.2; *AH*, II.2.4.

5. *AH*, III.8.3; IV.7.4.

6. *AH*, IV.20.1.

7. *Ibid*. See also *AH*, III.16.6; *AH*, IV.20.3.

8. John Lawson, *The Biblical Theology of St. Irenaeus* (London: The Epworth Press, Publishers, 1949), p. 122. See also *AH*, IV.19.2.

9. *AH*, V.27.2. See also IV.20.5.

10. *AH*, IV.6.2. " For if Christ did then [only] begin to have existence when He came [into the world] as man and [if] the Father did remember [only] in the times of Tiberius Caesar to provide for [the wants of] men, and His Word was shown to have not always coexisted with His creatures; . . . the reasons for so great carelessness and neglect on His part should be made the subject of investigation."

11. *Ibid*.

12. *AH*, IV.6.4-5.

13. Lawson communicates his position in a discussion of the distinction that Seeberg makes between Justin's and Irenaeus' use of the concept of the Logos. He writes, " To Justin the Logos is the hypostatized Divine Reason. On the other hand, Irenaeus thinks in the manner of the old Johannine tradition: the Logos is the revealed God. The consequence is drawn from this that for Justin the Logos is part of God, for Irenaeus He is God, God self-revealed. This well describes the position of S. Irenaeus " (Lawson, *op. cit.*, p. 136). Harnack expresses a similar idea when he writes, " In Irenaeus' sense we shall have to say: The Logos is the revelation hypostasis of the Father, ' the self-revelation of the self-conscious God,' and indeed the external self-revelation. For according to him the Son always existed with God, always revealed the Father, and it was always the full Godhead that he revealed in himself. In other words, he is God in his specific nature, truly God, and there is no distinction of essence between Him and God " (Adolf von Harnack, *History of Dogma* [Dover Publications, Inc., 1961], Vol. III, p. 264). Without an elaborate discussion Gustav Wingren simply writes: " There has been a great deal of discussion whether Irenaeus has also the philosophical conception of *logos* or whether by *logos* or *verbum* he always means *spoken word*. . . . There is fairly general unanimity on Irenaeus' ' unphilosophical ' character " (Gustav Wingren, *Man and the Incarnation* [London: Oliver and Boyd, Ltd., 1959], p. 71).

14. *AH*, IV.6.2.

15. *AH*, IV,14.1.

16. *Ibid.*
17. *Ibid.*
18. *AH*, IV.15.1.
19. *AH*, IV.37.1.
20. " Now it was necessary that man should in the first instance be created; and having been created, should receive growth, and having received growth, should be strengthened, and having been strengthened, should abound." (*AH*, IV.38.3.)
21. *AH*, V.27.2.
22. *AH*, IV.12.3.
23. *AH*, IV.28.3.
24. St. Irenaeus, *Proof of the Apostolic Preaching* (The Newman Press, 1952), p. 12. See also *AH*, III.23.3.
25. *AH*, IV.6.5.
26. *AH*, IV.41.1; *AH*, III.8.3; *AH*, IV.23.1.
27. *AH*, III.8.1.
28. *AH*, III.8.2.
29. *AH*, IV.39.4.
30. *Ibid.*
31. *Ibid.*
32. *AH*, IV.39.3.
33. *AH*, III.23.1.
34. Wingren, *op. cit.*, p. 70. See also *AH*, V.1.3.
35. *AH*, IV.39.2.
36. *AH*, IV.13.1.
37. *AH*, IV.15.1-2.
38. *AH*, IV.12.3.
39. *AH*, IV.12.4.
40. *AH*, III, Preface.
41. Irenaeus, *Proof*, p. 37; *AH*, III.18.7; *AH*, III.19.3.
42. Several recent interpreters of Irenaeus have emphasized this point. Aulén writes, " In Irenaeus's thought, the Incarnation is the necessary preliminary to the atoning work, because only God is able to overcome the power which holds man in bondage, and man is helpless " (Aulén, *op. cit.*, p. 20). Wingren makes the same point when he writes, " Christ has come into the world in order to fight a battle. He was born not only to reveal God and show man's nature in its purity, but also was sent as an armed man into enemy-occupied territory. His purpose was battle and His mission was victory, for

only so could man be rescued " (Wingren, *op. cit.*, p. 114). John Lawson agrees with this line of thinking. On one hand he writes, " The whole conception of ' divination by vision of the divine,' with its allied notions, occurs in a far more emphatic and systematic form in the writings of Irenaeus. . . . At the same time this development is amply complemented by the doctrine of Christus Victor " (Lawson, *op. cit.*, p. 163). These testimonies contrast considerably with certain earlier interpretations of Irenaeus, notably that of Adolf von Harnack, who writes, " The work of Christ is contained in the construction of His person as the God–Man " (Harnack, *op. cit.*, Vol. II, p. 274).

43. Lawson, *op. cit.*, p. 238
44. *AH*, IV.34.2; *AH*, V.8.3.
45. Lawson, *op. cit.*, pp. 196–197.
46. Wingren, *op. cit.*, p. 48.
47. L. S. Thornton, *Revelation and the Modern World* (London: The Dacre Press, 1950), p. 147. Even though Thornton offers this as a valid generalization qua generalization, he does say that as all generalizations it is not completely adequate to the concreteness of the Biblical perspective from which Irenaeus writes.
48. *AH*, V.21.1.
49. Lawson, *op. cit.*, p. 143.
50. *AH*, III.22.3.
51. *AH*, III.21.4.
52. *AH*, III.18.2.
53. *AH*, III.18.7.
54. Irenaeus, *Proof*, p. 38.
55. Irenaeus, *Proof*, p. 67.
56. *AH*, IV.38.2
57. *AH*, V.21.2.
58. *Ibid.*
59. *AH*, IV.40.3
60. *AH*, V.14.3.
61. *AH*, IV.40.3; *AH*, III.16.9.
62. *AH*, III.19.3.
63. *AH*, I.9.3 (*Italics mine*). See also *AH*, III.18.3.
64. *AH*, III.18.3; *AH*, III.16.9.
65. *Ibid.*
66. *AH*, III.18.6.
67. *AH*, II.22.4. " Being a Master, therefore, He also possessed the

age of a Master, not despising or evading any condition of humanity, nor setting aside in Himself that law which He had appointed for the human race, but sanctifying every age, by that period corresponding to it which belonged to Himself."

68. *AH*, III.18.6.

69. *AH*, III.18.5-6.

70. *AH*, III.23.1.

71. *AH*, V.3.2. The meaning of the resurrection in Irenaeus in its full sense would have certain implications for the resurrection of man. But at this point we are only discussing what it means for the concept of God undergirding his theory of the atonement.

72. *AH*, V.17.3.

73. *AH*, V.16.3.

74. *AH*, II.13.3.

75. *AH*, II.34.2.

76. J. K. Mozley, *The Impassibility of God* (Cambridge: Cambridge University Press, 1926), p. 24.

77. St. Irenaeus, " Fragments from the Last Writings of Irenaeus," *Writings of the Ante-Nicene Fathers*, Vol. I, p. 572. Evidence for the fact that God's unchangeableness really stood as a guarantee of God's faithfulness, for Irenaeus, can be seen in the following quote: " God is not as a man. He thus shows that all men are indeed guilty of falsehood, inasmuch as they change from one thing to another; but such is not the case with God, for He always continues true, perfecting whatever He wishes."

78. *AH*, IV.6.2.

79. Aulén, *Christus Victor*, p. 67.

80. William A. Clebsch and Charles R. Jaekle, *Pastoral Care in Historical Perspective* (Prentice-Hall, Inc., 1964), p. 35.

81. *Ibid.*, p.38.

82. Harvey Cox, *The Secular City* (The Macmillan Company, 1964), p. 127.

Chapter III   Anselm: Atonement as the Satisfaction of God's Honor

1. *CDH*, I.1.

2. *CDH*, I.2.

3. *CDH*, I.3.

4. *CDH*, I.7.

5. *CDH*, I.5.
6. *CDH*, I.8.
7. *CDH*, I.8.
8. St. Anselm, *Proslogium* in *St. Anselm — Basic Writings*, XII.
9. *CDH*, II.18.
10. St. Anselm, *Monologium* in *St. Anselm — Basic Writings*, XXV.
11. *Ibid.*, XXII.
12. *CDH*, II.18 (*italics mine*).
13. *CDH*, I.25.
14. *CDH*, II.1.
15. *CDH*, I.11.
16. *Ibid.*
17. *CDH*, I.7.
18. *CDH*, II.8.
19. *CDH*, I.15.
20. Harnack, *op. cit.*, Vol. VI, p. 76.
21. John McIntyre, *St. Anselm and His Critics* (Edinburgh: Oliver & Boyd, Ltd., 1954), p. 72. McIntyre quotes James Denny's agreement with this: " When Anselm speaks of sin as robbing God of honour, it is his way of saying that when we sin we wrong a person, and an infinitely great person, not merely a law or principle."
22. *CDH*, I.12.
23. *CDH*, I.13.
24. *CDH*, II.18.
25. *CDH*, I.14.
26. *CDH*, I.18.
27. *Ibid.*
28. *CDH*, I.19.
29. *CDH*, I.24.
30. *CDH*, II.5.
31. *Ibid.*
32. *Ibid.*
33. *CDH*, II.7.
34. *CDH*, II.13; I.8.
35. *CDH*, II.13.
36. *CDH*, II.8.
37. Emil Brunner, *The Mediator*, tr. by Olive Wyon (The Westminster Press, 1947).

38. *CDH*, II.10.
39. *Ibid.*
40. *Ibid.*
41. *CDH*, II.18.
42. *CDH*, II.19.
43. *Ibid.*
44. *Ibid.*
45. *CDH*, II.19.
46. *CDH*, II.20.
47. William Wolfe, *No Cross, No Crown* (Doubleday & Company, Inc., 1957), p. 104.
48. John Calvin, *Institutes of the Christian Religion* (Wm. B. Eerdmans Publishing Company, 1957), II.16.2.
49. *Ibid.*, II.16.6.
50. *Ibid.*, II.16.6; Gal. 3:13-14.
51. Vincent Taylor, *The Atonement in New Testament Teaching* (London: The Epworth Press, Publishers, 1940), pp. 176, 200.
52. John McCleod Campbell, *The Nature of the Atonement* (London: Macmillan and Co., Ltd., 1878), p. 292.
53. *Ibid.*, p. 291.
54. *Ibid.*, p. 248.
55. *Ibid.*, p. 247.
56. *Ibid.*, p. 299.

Chapter IV   Horace Bushnell: A Moral Influence Theory

1. Barbara M. Cross, *Horace Bushnell: Minister to a Changing America* (The University of Chicago Press, 1958). William Alexander Johnson, *Nature and the Supernatural in the Theology of Horace Bushnell* (Lund: C. W. K. Gleerup, Publishers, 1963).
2. *VS*, I, p. 235.
3. *VS*, *I*, p. 237.
4. Bushnell quotes from the *Biblical Repertory* to demonstrate the traditional position on God's ends from which he is differentiating himself. " A being determined by considerations outside Himself (considerations of public effect, for example) cannot be God. It is essential to the very nature of God that he be independent and omniscient; but with these attributes a determination *ab extra* (as where God is conceived, in the death of his son, to be actuated by

considerations of public law and authority, and results of salvation gained, or to be opened, by his sacrifice) is utterly foreign and irreconcilable. . . . God is himself the highest end for which he can act." (*VS*, I, p. 374.)

5. *VS*, I, p. 374.

6. *AH*, IV.14.1.

7. *VS*, I, p. 240; see also p. 306.

8. *VS*, I, p. 307.

9. *VS*, I, pp. 307–308.

10. *FL*, p. 61.

11. *Ibid.*

12. *VS*, I, p. 224.

13. *NS*, p. 253.

14. *GIC*, p. 140.

15. *Ibid.*

16. *GIC*, p. 136.

17. *Ibid.*

18. *VS*, I, p. 422. Bushnell sets forth the meaning of man's original righteousness very clearly in the following passage: " The subject is not conceived to be made righteous personally, by infusion, and started off as an inherently right-going character, but is thought of as being held in everlasting confidence and right-going, because he is vitally connected, by his faith, with the inspirations of God, or of the righteousness of God."

19. *NS*, pp. 84–90.

20. *NS*, p. 86.

21. *NS*, p. 92.

22. *NS*, p. 93.

23. *NS*, p. 86.

24. *Ibid.*

25. See the discussion of the similarity of these psychological concepts in *The Individual Psychology of Alfred Adler*, ed. by Heinz L. and Rowena R. Ansbacher (Basic Books, Inc., Publishers, 1956), p. 114.

26. Pierre Teilhard de Chardin, *The Phenomenon of Man* (Harper & Row, Publishers, Inc., 1959).

27. *NS*, p. 135.

28. *GIC*, p. 189.

29. *VS*, I, pp. 243–244.

30. *VS*, I, p. 269.
31. *VS*, I, p. 282.
32. *VS*, I, pp. 280–382.
33. *VS*, I, p. 385.
34. *Ibid*.
35. *VS*, I, p. 382.
36. *VS*, I, p. 272.
37. *VS*, I, pp. 77, 84, 86.
38. *VS*, I, p. 85.
39. Rudolf Bultmann, *Theology of the New Testament* (Charles Scribner's Sons, 1951), pp. 232–239.
40. *GIC*, p. 142.
41. *Ibid*.
42. *GIC*, p. 156.
43. *GIC*, p. 147.
44. *FL*, p. 150.
45. *FL*, p. 75.
46. *VS*, I, p. 424.
47. *VS*, I, p. 436.
48. *VS*, I, p. 169.
49. *VS*, I, p. 170.
50. *VS*, I, p. 223.
51. *VS*, I, pp. 223–228; *GIC*, pp. 239–243.
52. *FL*, p. 40.
53. *VS*, I, p. 79.
54. *GIC*, p. 241.
55. *Ibid*.
56. *VS*, I, p. 177.
57. *GIC*, p. 161.
58. *GIC*, p. 227.
59. *FL*, p. 62.
60. *FL*, p. 168.
61. *FL*, p. 166.
62. *GIC*, p. 233; *VS*, I, pp. 487–491.
63. *FL*, p. 51.
64. *FL*, p. 41.
65. Taylor, *op cit.*, p. 172.
66. Peter Abailard: "Exposition of the Epistle to the Romans (An Excerpt from the Second Book)," *A Scholastic Miscellany: Anselm to*

Ockham in The Library of Christian Classics, Vol. X, ed. and tr. by Eugene R. Fairweather (The Westminster Press, 1956), pp. 276–287.

67. Paul, *op. cit.*, p. 84; Aulén, *op. cit.*, p. 151.

68. James Ramsay McCallum, *Abelard's Christian Theology* (Oxford: Basil Blackwell & Mott, Ltd., 1949), pp. 7–8.

69. Richard R. Niebuhr, *Schleiermacher on Christ and Religion* (Charles Scribner's Sons, 1964), pp. 218–226.

70. Anselm, *Proslogium*, p. 13.

71. Aulén, *op. cit.*, p. 34.

72. Robert S. Franks, *The Atonement* (London: Oxford University Press, 1934), p. 182.

Chapter V   The Essence of the Psychotherapeutic Relation

1. *CCT*, p. 487.

2. *CCT*, pp. 488–489.

3. *CCT*, p. 488.

4. *CCT*, p. 4.

5. *PASS*, p. 196.

6. John M. Butler and Laura N. Rice, " Self-Actualization, New Experience, and Psychotherapy," Counseling Center Discussion Paper, Vol. VI, No. 12 (University of Chicago Counseling Center, 1960), p. 3.

7. *Ibid.*, pp. 14–15.

8. *Ibid.*, p. 15.

9. *Ibid.*

10. *Ibid.*, p. 13.

11. *Ibid.*, p. 20.

12. *Ibid.*

13. Recently a revised version of the unpublished paper by Rice and Butler has appeared under the title of " Adience, Self-Actualization, and Drive Theory," in *Concepts of Personality*, ed. by Joseph M. Wepman and Ralph W. Heine (Aldine Publishing Company, 1963), pp. 79–110. This second paper represents the same basic point of view as does the one I refer to. The main difference is a stress on the drive reduction character of stimulus hunger and an added use of the experimental work of S. S. Fox. Fox makes a distinction between chronic and acute levels of stimulation. From this, Rice and Butler define stimulus hunger as the need to " match " chronic and acute

levels of stimulation, that is, levels of stimulation which the organism is used to with presently available levels. If the acute level is below the chronic level (what the organism is used to), the organism will attempt to seek out (adience) novel and more complex sources of stimulation in an effort to increase the acute level. Curiosity, exploratory behavior, exteroceptive motivation, in short, all positive motivation that leads to the development of expanded ranges of new experience are explained as the organism's attempt to satisfy stimulus hunger by matching chronic and acute levels.

For theological purposes, this is an important concept. Several theologically oriented thinkers — most notably Lewis J. Sherrill in his *Struggle of the Soul* — have identified the Imago Dei with man's growth and developmental drive as this drive seems to be portrayed by the self-actualization theorists such as Goldstein, Maslow, and Rogers. It might be pointed out also that Rice and Butler's belief that stimulus hunger is the ground of man's symbolic capacities and that man's thought processes constitute a self-administered way of further stimulating himself constitutes a point of contact between psychology and the metaphysical speculations of Teilhard de Chardin, who works out a theory of evolution that sees man as moving from biosphere to noosphere, the sphere of symbol and meaning. Man seems to have a drive to find meaning (something that Viktor Frankl has suggested as well), that is even more important than his maintenance needs as a propelling force behind the pilgrimage of evolution. It is also true that there is an interesting similarity between the concept of stimulus hunger and A. N. Whitehead's belief that man has an innate need to experience ever enlarged circles of novelty organized in patterns of harmony and contrast. Christian theologians have seized on this concept as a concrete referent for the image of God in man — note John B. Cobb's *A Christian Natural Theology* (The Westminster Press, 1965), pp. 125–130. That there seems to be empirical (even experimental) evidence for this basic motivational factor seems to argue well for the continued fruitfulness of the kind of speculation practiced by the Whiteheadians and the use to which they have put their system for the purposes of Christian theology.

14. *PASS*, p. 198.
15. *PASS*, p. 197.
16. *CCT*, p. 524; *PASS*, p. 232.

17. Eugene T. Gendlin, *Experiencing and the Creation of Meaning* (The Free Press of Glencoe, Inc., 1962), p. 255.

18. *CCT*, p. 499.

19. *CCT*, pp. 501, 527–528; *PASS*, p. 205.

20. *CCT*, pp. 501, 529; *PASS*, p. 201.

21. *PASS*, p. 206.

22. *Ibid.*

23. *Ibid.*

24. *PASS*, p. 205.

25. Stanley W. Standal, " The Need for Positive Regard " (unpublished doctoral dissertation, Department of Psychology, University of Chicago, 1954), p. 26; *PASS*, p. 208.

26. *CCT*, p. 497.

27. *PASS*, p. 223.

28. *PASS*, p. 224.

29. *Ibid.*

30. *Ibid.*

31. *Ibid.*

32. Dorothy Baruch, *How to Live with Your Teenager* (McGraw-Hill Book Company, Inc., 1953), p. 55.

33. *PASS*, p. 226.

34. *PASS*, pp. 204, 229; *CCT*, p. 516.

35. *CCT*, p. 506.

36. *PASS*, p. 200.

37. *PASS*, p. 199.

38. *CCT*, p. 516.

39. *PASS*, p. 230.

40. *CCT*, p. 197. That energy systems or motivational systems can begin to work in partially independent senses seems to be suggested when Rogers writes, " If self and experience are incongruent, then the general tendency to actualize the organism may work at cross purposes with the subsystem of that motive, the tendency to actualize the self."

41. *CCT*, p. 148. Here Rogers refers to the work of Thetford who demonstrated that posttherapy clients expended smaller amounts of energy and had higher frustration thresholds according to measures of their autonomic nervous systems than they did before therapy or than did nontherapy groups to which they were compared. An inference from this would suggest that having conditions of worth and

incongruence significantly diffuses and expends energy, since the lowering of incongruence in therapy seems to lessen this energy waste.

42. This brings us to one of the central concepts of the client-centered school — the self-image and the idealized self-image. The self-image or self-concept looked at from the perspective of what that self would like to be most is called the ideal self. The ideal self is what the self feels it should be like according to its conditions of worth. Operational definitions of the self and ideal self can be obtained through the use of the Q-sort. Discussion of this technique can be found in *CCT*, pp. 53, 140; *PASS*, pp. 200–203; and Carl Rogers and Rosalind F. Dymond, *Psychotherapy and Personality Change* (The University of Chicago Press, 1954).

43. Fred E. Fiedler, " A Comparative Investigation of Early Therapeutic Relationships Created by Experts and Nonexperts of the Psychoanalytic, Nondirective, and Adlerian schools." (Unpublished doctoral dissertation, Department of Psychology, University of Chicago, 1949.)

44. *PASS*, p. 213; Rogers, " The Necessary and Sufficient Conditions of Therapeutic Personality Change," *Journal of Consulting Psychology*, Vol. 21 (1957), pp. 95–103.

45. Rogers, " The Necessary and Sufficient Conditions," pp. 95–103.

46. *PASS*, p. 207.

47. *PASS*, p. 208.

48. John Butler, " The Goals of Counseling," Counseling Center Discussion Paper, Vol. II, No. 20 (University of Chicago Counseling Center, 1953), p. 9. (Mimeographed.)

49. Carl Rogers, *On Becoming a Person* (Houghton Mifflin Company, 1961), p. 130.

50. Standal, *op. cit.*, p. 119.

51. *Ibid.*, p. 125.

52. *Ibid.*, pp. 127–128.

53. *Ibid.*, p. 130.

54. *Ibid.*, p. 128.

55. *CCT*, p. 20.

56. *PASS*, p. 210.

57. *Ibid.*

58. *PASS*, p. 213.

59. *PASS*, p. 210.

60. *CCT*, p. 495.

61. Eugene Gendlin, "Experiencing: A Variable in the Process of Therapeutic Change," Counseling Center Discussion Paper, Vol. V, No. 1 (University of Chicago Counseling Center, 1958), p. 15. (Mimeographed.)

62. *CCT*, p. 194.

63. *CCT*, p. 41.

64. Gendlin, "Experiencing: A Variable," p. 15.

65. Robert L. Katz, *Empathy: Its Nature and Uses* (The Free Press of Glencoe, 1963), pp. 134–160.

66. Abraham H. Maslow, *Toward a Psychology of Being* (D. Van Nostrand Company, Inc., 1962), pp. 67–96.

67. *PASS*, p. 214.

68. Carl Rogers, *Counseling and Psychotherapy* (Houghton Mifflin Company, 1942), p. 133.

69. *CCT*, p. 158.

70. Carl Rogers, "The Essence of Psychotherapy: A Client-centered View," *Annals of Psychotherapy*, Vol I (1959), pp. 51–57.

71. Eugene Gendlin, "A Process View of Relationships," Counseling Center Discussion Paper (University of Chicago Counseling Center, 1957), p. 3.

72. *Ibid.*, p. 6.

73. *PASS*, p. 216.

74. *CCT*, p. 205.

75. *CCT*, p. 201.

76. *CCT*, p. 199.

77. John Butler, "Interaction of Client and Therapist," *Journal of Abnormal and Social Psychology*, Vol. XLII (1952), pp. 366–378.

78. *CCT*, pp. 168–171.

79. *Psychotherapy and Personality Change.*

80. Sidney M. Jourard, *The Transparent Self* (D. Van Nostrand Company, Inc., 1964), p. 64.

81. Rogers and Dymond, *Psychotherapy and Personality Change*, p. 311. Rogers gives the following key to his presentation of this case material. "Certain conventions will be utilized in this section. 'C.' refers to the client; 'T.' to the therapist. Three-dot ellipses (. . .) indicate a hesitation or very brief pause, while longer pauses are indicated in parentheses (pause). Five-dot ellipses (. . . . .) mean that some material, irrelevant to the main point being illustrated, has been omitted." In presenting this material, I will follow those conventions.

Since there will be occasions where I will be illustrating points different from those of Rogers, I will omit sections that he has included. In doing this, I will use the five dots as he has used them in his omissions.

82. Sigmund Freud, "Recommendations for Physicians on the Psychoanalytic Method of Treatment," *Collected Papers,* ed. by Philip Rieff, Vol. 3, *Therapy and Technique* (Collier Books, 1963), p. 118.

83. Medard Boss, *Psychoanalysis and Daseinsanalysis* (Basic Books, Inc., Publishers, 1963), pp. 61–74.

84. Heinz L. and Rowena R. Ansbacher (eds.), *op. cit.,* pp. 326–329.

85. *Ibid.,* p. 340.

86. *Ibid.,* p. 341.

87. *Ibid.*

88. Karl Menninger, *Theory of Psychoanalytic Technique* (Basic Books, Inc., Publishers, 1958), p. 71.

89. *Ibid.,* p. 93.

90. Boss, *op. cit.,* p. 72.

91. *Ibid.,* p. 62.

92. *Ibid.,* p. 69.

93. *Ibid.,* p. 71.

94. Carl Whitaker and Thomas Malone, *The Roots of Psychotherapy* (The Blakiston Co., 1953), p. 89.

95. *Ibid.,* p. 205.

96. *Ibid.,* p. 91.

97. *Ibid.,* p. 90.

98. *Ibid.,* p. 151.

99. *Ibid.,* p. 152.

100. *Ibid.,* p. 192.

101. *Ibid.,* p. 150.

Chapter VI   Some Methodological Considerations

1. Thomas C. Oden, "Revelation and Psychotherapy," *Continuum,* Vol. II, No. 2 (Summer, 1964), pp. 239–263; Paul Tillich, *The Courage to Be* (Yale University Press, 1952), pp. 165–166; Don Browning, "Psychotherapy and the Atonement" (unpublished dissertation, Divinity School, University of Chicago, 1964), pp. 272–282.

278   ATONEMENT AND PSYCHOTHERAPY

2. Jerome Frank, *Persuasion and Healing* (Schocken Books, Inc., 1963), p. 34.

3. *Ibid*. "In many settings he is representative of the larger culture, so that his acceptance of the patient implies acceptance by the larger group."

4. *CCT*, p. 20.

5. William, *op. cit.*, p. 67.

6. Wayne Oates, *Protestant Pastoral Counseling* (The Westminster Press, 1962), pp. 57–74.

7. William E. Hulme, *Counseling and Theology* (Muhlenberg Press, 1956), p. 108.

8. Oden, *loc. cit.*, pp. 272–282.

9. Karl Barth, *Church Dogmatics,* tr. by T. H. L. Parker *et al.* (Edinburgh: T. & T. Clark, 1957), Vol. II, Part 1; pp. 47–48.

10. Charles Hartshorne, "Tillich's Doctrine of God," *The Theology of Paul Tillich* (The Library of Living Theology), ed. by C. W. Kegley and R. W. Bretall (The Macmillan Company, 1961), p. 179.

11. The culmination of these efforts can be seen in Hartshorne's *The Logic of Perfection* (The Open Court Publishing Company, 1962).

12. Karl Barth, *Anselm: Fides quaerens intellectum,* tr. by Ian W. Robertson (A Meridian Book, The World Publishing Company, 1962).

13. Barth, *Dogmatics,* Vol. II, Part 1, pp. 257–272.

14. *Ibid.,* Vol. I, Part 1, pp. 17–25.

15. *Ibid.,* Vol. II, Part 1, pp. 82–84.

16. Oden, *loc. cit.,* pp. 239–263.

17. Charles Hartshorne, *Man's Vision of God* (Willet, Clark & Company, 1941), p. 317.

18. Hartshorne, "Tillich's Doctrine," in Kegley and Bretall, eds., *The Theology of Paul Tillich,* p. 179.

19. Charles Hartshorne, *Reality as a Social Process* (The Free Press of Glencoe, 1953), pp. 163–176.

20. Barth, *Dogmatics,* Vol. I, Part 1, p. 3.

21. Hartshorne, *Man's Vision of God,* pp. 60–79, 174–203.

22. John Baillie, *The Sense of the Presence of God* (Charles Scribner's Sons, 1962), p. 187.

23. *Ibid*.

24. *Ibid.,* p. 121.

25. Seward Hiltner, *Preface to Pastoral Theology* (Abingdon Press, 1958), pp. 219–223.

26. Dorothy M. Emmet, *The Nature of Metaphysical Thinking* (London: Macmillan & Co., Ltd., 1945), p. 42.

27. *Ibid.*, p. 43.

28. *Ibid.*, p. 64.

29. *Ibid.*, p. 61.

30. *Ibid.*, p. 86.

31. *Ibid.*, p. 90.

32. *Ibid.*

33. Daniel Day Williams, "Truth in a Theological Perspective," *Journal of Religion*, Vol. XXVIII, No. 4 (October, 1948).

34. Schubert Ogden, *Christ Without Myth* (Harper & Brothers, 1961); John B. Cobb, Jr., *A Christian Natural Theology;* see also Daniel Jenkins' plea for a natural theology within a theology of revelation in his article "Whither the Doctrine of God Now," *New Theology, No. 2*, ed. by Martin E. Marty and Dean G. Peerman (The Macmillan Company, 1965); and James W. Woelfel's plea for Dorothy Emmet's method of analogy as an answer to the positivistic and linguistic analytic attacks on the meaningfulness of theological language — to be found in *New Theology, No. 2* under the title " 'Non-metaphysical ' Christian Philosophy and Linguistic Philosophy."

35. Thomas C. Oden, *Kerygma and Counseling* (The Westminster Press, 1966).

36. Harry S. Sullivan recognized the existence of interpersonal rapport but failed to stress that it conveyed elements other than anxiety. For an analysis of the communication by rapport between mother and infant, see his *The Interpersonal Theory of Psychiatry* (W. W. Norton & Company, Inc., 1953), pp. 64–70. For an analysis of interpersonal anxiety between patient and therapist, see his *The Psychiatric Interview* (W. W. Norton & Company, Inc., 1954), pp. 100–106. For an explicit use of the concept of rapport as we have developed it with some acknowledgment to the Whiteheadian school of process philosophy, see Edward S. Tauber and Maurice R. Green, *Prelogical Experience* (Basic Books, Inc., Publishers, 1959), p. 24.

37. *CCT*, p. 497.

38. *Ibid.*, p. 164.

39. For a discussion of the difference between literal and nonliteral

predicates common to God and man, see Charles Hartshorne, " Tillich's Doctrine of God," in Kegley and Bretall (eds.), *The Theology of Paul Tillich*, pp. 164–197.

40. *CCT*, p. 262. What is the stated rationale for these limits? Elaine Dorfman's chapter on play therapy in *CCT* states the following reason: " There is now far more concern with the problem of determining just what activity restrictions are required in order to permit the therapist to *remain emotionally accepting of the child* [*italics mine*]. Indeed, some therapists believe that this is the only reason for having limits."

41. *CCT*, p. 258. " In the second place, hurting the therapist may arouse the child's deep guilt and anxiety in relation to the only person who can help him. Fear of retaliation, especially of withdrawal of this unique kind of permission to be oneself, may destroy the possibility of therapy." For an example of the therapeutic efficacy of controls in residential milieu therapy, see Bruno Bettelheim, " Harry, a Delinquent," in *Truants from Life* (The Free Press of Glencoe, 1955), pp. 394, 405.

Chapter VII   Empathic Acceptance and the Doctrine
of the Atonement

1. Igor A. Caruso, *Existential Psychology* (Herder & Herder, Inc., 1964), pp. 28–56.

2. Rudolf Bultmann, *Theology of the New Testament*, p. 240.

3. Paul Tillich, *Systematic Theology* (The University of Chicago Press, 1951), Vol. I, p. 46.

4. Charles Hartshorne, *Beyond Humanism* (Willett, Clark & Company, 1937), pp. 125–130.

5. Erich Fromm, *Man for Himself* (Rinehart & Co., Inc., 1947), p. 61.

6. *CDH*, p. 231.

7. O. Hobart Mowrer, *The Crisis in Psychiatry and Religion* (D. Van Nostrand Company, Inc., 1961) and *The New Group Therapy* (D. Van Nostrand Company, Inc., 1964).

8. An understanding of God as the final object of all change and the final recipient of all feeling is suggested by Charles Hartshorne in his book entitled *Man's Vision of God*, pp. 255–296. But Hartshorne does not place his doctrine of God in a context of a theory of

sin. I differ from Hartshorne in just this sense. I am trying to place God, understood according to the principle of absolute relativity, in a context of sin interpreted by the model of incongruence. For Hartshorne, since God is the object of every change, he is also the element of self-identity in all change. God is the factor that finally gives all change some unity (*Man's Vision of God,* p. 274). From the perspective of this study, since God is the " open end " that receives every feeling, he also performs this function of giving identity and unity to the world process. The therapist in a group situation performs the same function in quite limited ways. He may constitute the unifying factor in the process by the extent to which he is able to receive and accept all other feelings into his experiencing. But the position that I am defending goes a step farther. Not only would God be the element of identity in every change; his receptiveness to all change also would constitute a distinctively *regenerative* function as well. Since brokenness is precisely the denial and distortion of experiencing and since brokenness tends to be overcome when some other agent besides ourselves seems capable of accepting and receiving into his experiencing some feeling that we cannot accept ourselves, God's open receptiveness performs a regenerative as well as a unifying process. In fact, from our perspective, God's unifying function rests precisely in the regenerative capacity. He unifies the world precisely because he is always in the process of bringing brokenness to wholeness by accepting that about the world which the world cannot accept itself.

9. We saw examples of this hostile resistance in our case studies. One client said that she " fought vigorously " against the care and sensitivity of the therapist. She thought that his care, his love, meant " selling my soul," i.e., giving up her own conditions of worth, according to our categories. She admits that she " tried hating and attacking " her therapist. Since unconditioned empathic acceptance receives and cares for all feelings, even those that the client would prefer not be received, cared for, and appreciated, this also provokes hostility in the client. Once again, the therapist accepts what the client rejects. The " no conditions " of the therapeutic relation contradicts and outreaches the conditions of worth and acceptability of the client. Mrs. Oaks refers to this intractable concern of the therapist which forces her to face feelings that she preferred to avoid by saying, " Well, it certainly refuses to stay forgotten, that's for sure. . . . You're not being very helpful." Later she says that she is " resent-

ful " that the therapist's persistent reception of her feelings forces her to take responsibility for her feelings.

10. An example of how the therapist's durable acceptance proves efficacious was seen in Chapter V. Here the client refers to the therapist's empathic acceptance as a " firm rock which I beat upon to no avail and which merely said clearly that your love did not control me and I could not control it." The intractable nature of the therapist's relation finally rendered all of the client's resistance impotent.

Chapter VIII   The Psychotherapeutic Analogy and
the Historic Options

1. Maslow, *op. cit.,* pp. 31, 39, 78, 81.

2. Martin Jarrett-Kerr, *Atonement for Our Time* (Morehouse-Gorham Co., Inc., 1953), pp. 65–70.

3. Paul Tillich, *Systematic Theology,* Vol. I, pp. 239–244.

4. Bishop John A. T. Robinson, *Honest to God* (The Westminster Press, 1963), pp. 29–44.

5. Thomas Hywel Hughes, *The Atonement* (London: George Allen & Unwin, Ltd., 1949), p. 106.

6. Aulén, *op. cit.,* p. 53.

7. *AH,* V.1.1.

8. *AH,* V.1.2.

9. Frieda Fromm-Reichmann gives an intelligent discussion of the destructive consequences of the therapist's security operations in an article entitled " Notes on Personal and Professional Requirements of a Psychotherapist," *Psychoanalysis and Psychotherapy,* ed. by D. Bullard (The University of Chicago Press, 1959), pp. 70–72.

10. Dorothy Baruch, *New Ways in Discipline* (McGraw-Hill Book Company, Inc., 1949), p. 11.

11. Fromm-Reichman, *op. cit.,* pp. 76–87.

12. Jerome Frank, *op. cit.,* pp. 166–169.

13. Anna Freud, *Ego and the Mechanisms of Defense* (London: Hogarth Press, 1937); see also Mowrer's discussion of defensive identification in *Learning Theory and Personality Dynamics* (The Ronald Press Company, 1952).

14. " Development of Moral Character," in *Review of Child Development Research,* ed. by M. L. and L. W. Hoffman (Russell Sage Foundation, 1965), p. 414.

INDEX